GLOBAL HEALTH SECURITY IN CHINA, JAPAN, AND INDIA

The Asia Pacific Legal Culture and Globalization series explores intersecting themes that revolve around the impact of globalization in countries on the Asia Pacific Rim and examines the significance of legal culture as a mediator of that impact. The emphasis is on a broad understanding of legal culture that extends beyond traditional legal institutions and actors to normative frameworks and the legal consciousness of ordinary people. Books in the series reflect international scholarship from a wide variety of disciplines, including law, political science, economics, sociology, and history.

Other volumes in the series are:

Richard Barichello, Arianto A. Patunru, and Richard Schwindt, eds., *Globalization, Poverty, and Income Inequality: Insights from Indonesia*

Pitman B. Potter, *Exporting Virtue? China's International Human Rights Activism in the Age of Xi Jinping*

Sarah Biddulph and Ljiljana Biuković, eds., *Good Governance in Economic Development: International Norms and Chinese Perspectives*

Moshe Hirsch, Ashok Kotwal, and Bharat Ramaswami, eds., *A Human Rights Based Approach to Development in India*

Daniel Drache and Lesley A. Jacobs, eds., *Grey Zones in International Economic Law and Global Governance*

Sarah Biddulph, *The Stability Imperative: Human Rights and Law in China*

Pitman B. Potter, *Assessing Treaty Performance in China: Trade and Human Rights*

Pitman B. Potter and Ljiljana Biuković, eds., *Globalization and Local Adaptation in International Trade Law*

GLOBAL HEALTH SECURITY IN CHINA, JAPAN, AND INDIA

Assessing Sustainable Development Goals

Edited by Lesley A. Jacobs,
Yoshitaka Wada, and Ilan Vertinsky

UBCPress · Vancouver · Toronto

32 31 30 29 28 27 26 25 24 23   5 4 3 2 1

Printed in Canada on FSC-certified ancient-forest-free paper (100% post-consumer recycled) that is processed chlorine- and acid-free.

Library and Archives Canada Cataloguing in Publication

Title: Global health security in China, Japan, and India : assessing Sustainable
 Development Goals / edited by Lesley A. Jacobs, Yoshitaka Wada, and
 Ilan Vertinsky.
Names: Jacobs, Lesley A., editor. | Wada, Yoshitaka, editor. | Vertinsky, Ilan, editor.
Series: Asia Pacific legal culture and globalization (Series)
Description: Series statement: Asia Pacific legal culture and globalization | Includes
 bibliographical references and index.
Identifiers: Canadiana (print) 20220415188 | Canadiana (ebook) 20220415242 |
 ISBN 9780774867702 (hardcover) | ISBN 9780774867719 (paperback) |
 ISBN 9780774867726 (PDF) | ISBN 9780774867733 (EPUB)
Subjects: LCSH: Public health — China. | LCSH: Public health — Japan. | LCSH:
 Public health — India. | LCSH: Medical care — China. | LCSH: Medical care —
 Japan. | LCSH: Medical care — India. | LCSH: Sustainable Development Goals.
Classification: LCC RA418 .G56 2023 | DDC 362.1 — dc23

UBC Press gratefully acknowledges the financial support for our publishing program of the Government of Canada (through the Canada Book Fund), the Canada Council for the Arts, and the British Columbia Arts Council.

Printed and bound in Canada by Friesens
Set in Futura and Warnock by Artegraphica Design Co.
Copy editor: Frank Chow
Proofreader: Sophie Pouyanne
Indexer: Noeline Bridge
Cover designer: Alexa Love

UBC Press
The University of British Columbia
2029 West Mall
Vancouver, BC V6T 1Z2
www.ubcpress.ca

Contents

Foreword / vii
PITMAN B. POTTER

Acknowledgments / x

Introduction: Framing Global Health Security
in China, Japan, and India Using the Sustainable
Development Goals / 3
LESLEY A. JACOBS, YOSHITAKA WADA, and ILAN VERTINSKY

Part 1: Strengthening Access to Health Care Services

1   Providing Access to Affordable Medicines and Health
    Care for All in China / 19
    WENQIN LIANG and ILAN VERTINSKY

2   Mixed Billing and New Medicine in Japan:
    Will Lifting the Ban on Mixed Billing Improve Access
    to Health Care or Crash the System? / 46
    YOSHITAKA WADA

3   Health for All: Can India Meet Its International Human
    Rights Obligations? / 74
    TIFFANY CHUA, MARC McCRUM, and ILAN VERTINSKY

Part 2: Protecting and Promoting Public Health

4 Linking Public Health Targets of the Sustainable
   Development Goals to Human Rights Performance
   in China / 103
   LESLEY A. JACOBS

5 Moving Japan toward the Global Standard for
   Vaccines / 124
   TOSHIMI NAKANASHI

6 Global Health Standards and Food Security: Exploring
   the Double Science Standard of Review under the SPS
   Agreement after India – Agricultural Products / 154
   MARIELA de AMSTALDEN

Part 3: Engaging Global Markets in Primary Health Care and Public Health

7 Does the China National Tobacco Corporation
   Threaten Global Public Health? / 169
   JENNIFER FANG, KELLEY LEE, and NIDHI SEJPAL POURANIK

8 Exit and Voice Strategies by Patients in Dealing
   with Incentive Structures in the Chinese Health
   Care System / 188
   NEIL MUNRO and ZIYING HE

9 Global Markets in Medicine: Japan's Health Care
   Service Exports to Singapore and India / 229
   HIROYUKI KOJIN

References / 243

List of Contributors / 269

Index / 274

Foreword

PITMAN B. POTTER

This volume examines the challenge of coordinating local performance of international trade and human rights standards in the Asia-Pacific region, with particular attention to questions about public health policy. The book is part of a group of edited volumes examining different aspects of trade and human rights performance presented by the Asia Pacific Dispute Resolution (APDR) project and published in the UBC Press series, Asia Pacific Legal Culture and Globalization. The APDR program began in 2001 with a SSHRC/MCRI–supported project on normative and operational conditions for local compliance with international trade and human rights standards in Canada, China, and Japan. Since 2009, the APDR project has focused on "Understanding Integrated Compliance with International Trade and Human Rights Standards from a Comparative Perspective." This has involved building conceptual understanding and generating policy analysis on coordinating performance of international standards on trade and human rights in the Asia-Pacific region, with particular attention to Canada, China, India, Indonesia, and Japan. The APDR project is based at the Peter A. Allard School of Law and the Institute of Asian Research of the University of British Columbia, and involves a collaborative network of colleagues from UBC and from partner institutions in North America, Asia, and Australia.

The challenge of coordinating local compliance with international trade and human rights standards is a critical issue for the globalized world. International, regional, and subnational disputes over issues of trade and human rights present increasingly serious obstacles to international cooperation. Resolving and, where possible, preventing such disputes will benefit the course of international cooperation in areas of trade and human rights. Such efforts will also help reduce transactional, operational, and opportunity costs resulting from international disputes that make existing relationships more complex and costly, entail significant management costs, and distract public and private sector leaders from more productive pursuits.

Coordinating local compliance with international trade and human rights standards has been difficult in part because of conceptual differences and assumed trade-offs between these two regimes. All too often, human rights standards around the right to health, for example, are seen as inconsistent with trade goals of efficiency, economic growth, and private property rights. Conversely, trade policy on cross-border transit of labour and technology is often seen as an obstacle to human rights goals in local access to health care. As well, coordinated compliance with international trade and human rights standards has been elusive because the officials and specialists who manage local interpretation and implementation of these regimes often have few opportunities for institutional collaboration.

Mindful of these conceptual and organizational challenges, this project works to build knowledge and policy support for coordinating local compliance with international trade and human rights standards in ways that are mutually sustaining rather than conflicted. The project has generated policy proposals for building treaty compliance programs, processes, and institutions that are more responsive to cross-cultural differences and aim to resolve and, where possible, prevent disputes over trade and human rights. The results of the research are enabling interdisciplinary scholars and policy makers to better understand the requirements for coordinated compliance and have potential to reduce and prevent disputes over trade and human rights, thus benefiting international cooperation.

This UBC Press series will publish new volumes edited by leading international scholars in their respective fields on the interaction of trade policy with human rights issues such as the right to development; labor relations; health policy; poverty and inequality; and government accountability. The books are grounded in original empirical research as well as qualitative and quantitative analysis relating to international trade and human rights. The work is characterized by a high degree of interdisciplinarity and focuses on questions of legal culture, international law, and globalization in the countries that compose the Asia-Pacific region.

Research for this volume and the APDR project of which it is a part has been supported by the Social Sciences and Humanities Research Council (SSHRC) of Canada under its Major Collaborative Research Initiatives (MCRI) program, for which my colleagues and I are deeply thankful. The APDR project has also benefited immensely from input and advice from an International Advisory Board comprising the following:

- The Honourable Jack Austin (former Government Leader in the Senate, former President of the Canada China Business Council)
- Joseph Caron (former Canadian High Commissioner to India, Ambassador to China, and Ambassador to Japan)
- The Honourable Irwin Cotler (former Member of Parliament, former Minister of Justice)
- Professor Thomas Cottier (former Managing Director, World Trade Institute, Berne, Switzerland)
- Jonathan Fried (Senior Associate, Center for International and Strategic Studies; former Coordinator for International Economic Relations, Global Affairs Canada; former Ambassador and Permanent Representative of Canada to the World Trade Organization, Geneva, Switzerland)
- Professor John Hogarth (Professor Emeritus, Peter A. Allard School of Law, University of British Columbia), and
- Professor Hans-Ulrich Petersmann (European University, Florence, Italy).

This project has included a wide range of graduate students contributing as researchers, analysts, and writers. Graduate students contributing to the work presented in this volume include Iryna Ponomarenko, Keshav Kelkar, and Brandon Allison.

I have been privileged to serve as Principal Investigator for the APDR project. I am grateful to the many colleagues from across our research network who have contributed of their time and expertise to strengthen the work we have done together. Particular thanks go to Project Manager Rozalia Mate, for her stellar contributions to the operational details of the project.

Acknowledgments

The commitment and vision for this volume is something that Ilan Vertinsky, Yoshi Wada, and myself established many years ago. The value of that vision has been cemented by the COVID-19 pandemic. Our core vision was for a book-length multi-disciplinary comparative study of health and human rights in three major Asian countries that brought together legal scholars and social scientists with an eye to better understand global health security by examining what happens locally within counties. The contributors to this volume have realized that vision, while at the same time making visible the need for much more work to be done. I want to thank them and my co-editors for their patience and resilience as this book has taken form, along with the ever-professional staff at UBC Press.

This book is part of a much bigger project, the Asia Pacific Dispute Resolution (APDR) Project, housed at the University of British Columbia (UBC) Law School. That project received more than fifteen years of continuous, generous funding from the Social Sciences and Humanities Research Council of Canada, beginning in 2003 – this reflects an immense investment by the Canadian Government in socio-legal research in Asia. The APDR Project was initiated and lead by Professor Pitman Potter. As editors, we owe an immense amount to Pitman for his unwavering support for this volume. And on a personal note, I owe so much to Pitman for introducing me to an incredible array of scholars from around the world who have been my friends and collaborators for almost two decades. I would like to single out in particular Sarah Biddulph at the University of Melbourne Law School; Ljiljana Biuković at the UBC Law School; and Daniel Drache in the Department of Politics at York University; along with, of course, Ilan, Yoshi, and Pitman. Any scholar could only dream to have such friends and colleagues.

– Les Jacobs

GLOBAL HEALTH SECURITY IN CHINA, JAPAN, AND INDIA

Introduction
Framing Global Health Security in China, Japan, and India Using the Sustainable Development Goals

LESLEY A. JACOBS, YOSHITAKA WADA,
and ILAN VERTINSKY

National health security focuses on the ability of individual countries to prevent, detect, and rapidly respond to public health emergencies such as pandemics, as well as to meet the primary health care needs of their citizens. These challenges have increasingly become multinational as fewer public health emergencies are contained by national borders and important segments of primary health care delivery, especially pertaining to pharmaceuticals, have become integrated into the global economy. The corresponding feeling is that when it comes to health security, we are all in this together: an undeniable lesson during the COVID-19 pandemic. The concept of global health security is at its core the idea that national health security today requires countries to coordinate and cooperate with one another to address pressing public health threats such as COVID-19 and to meet many domestic health care needs.[1] State membership in and engagement with United Nations (UN) organizations such as the World Health Organization (WHO), International Health Regulations (IHR), and Codex Alimentarius Commission (CAC) have recently increased in part because these organizations can facilitate such coordination and cooperation. The expanding reach of these organizations reflects a broad consensus among nations that the key to achieving global health security is the establishment of a set of international health standards and norms that can engage and guide domestic governments in the design and use of their systems for public health and primary health care delivery.[2]

This book focuses on how global health security is evolving in three major Asian countries – China, India, and Japan – that have committed to complying with international health standards and norms established by the United Nations Sustainable Development Goals (SDG). The citizens of these three countries constitute almost 40 percent of the world's total population. If challenges to global health security are genuinely something that we all must face together, a better understanding of health security in these major Asian countries is fundamental.

Rights-Based Global Health Standards

Over the past three decades, the United Nations has gradually established a set of global health standards based on the right to health in international human rights law, culminating in the Sustainable Development Goals adopted by 193 UN member states in 2015. The 1946 constitution of the World Health Organization (WHO) states: "The enjoyment of the highest attainable standard of health is one of the fundamental rights of every human being without distinction of race, religion, political belief, economic or social condition" (WHO 1946). Twenty years later, the UN International Covenant on Economic, Social and Cultural Rights (ICESCR)[3] similarly recognized the right to the highest attainable standard of physical and mental health (UNGA 1966).

The UN Committee on Economic, Social and Cultural Rights, which is responsible for monitoring the ICESCR, observed in 2000 that "the right to health must be understood as a right to the enjoyment of a variety of facilities, goods, services and conditions necessary for the realization of the highest attainable standard of health" (UNCESCR 2000a, para. 9). The committee's framing of the right to health, which is today dominant in international human rights circles, includes not only medical services but also public health and safety measures that address issues such as vaccinations, maternal health, safe drinking water and food, workplace safety, obesity, tobacco control, and alcohol consumption. In other words, the principal focus of the right to health is on health security, understood in terms of concerns about public health emergencies and primary health care services. International human rights instruments pertaining to health have long been accepted in Asia. Both China and India became founding member states of the WHO in 1948. (Japan was not invited to join the United Nations until 1956.) India and Japan ratified the ICESCR in 1979; China ratified it in 2001. All three were among the first countries in the world to adopt the UN Sustainable Development Goals.

The SDGs establish a robust set of global health standards and norms to measure progress toward global health security that underlie the discussion of health security in China, India, and Japan throughout this book. There are seventeen SDGs and 169 targets (United Nations 2015). The SDGs are broad objectives, whereas the targets are specific and in some cases numerical. Many of the targets set global health standards in areas of medical services or public health and safety. For example, SDG 3 sets the goal: "Ensure healthy lives and promote well-being for all at all ages," whereas its thirteen associated targets include, for example, doing the following by 2030: "reduce the global maternal mortality ratio to less than 70 per 100,000 live births"; "reduce by one third premature mortality from non-communicable diseases through prevention and treatment and promote mental health and well-being"; and "support the research and development of vaccines and medicines for the communicable and non-communicable diseases that primarily affect developing countries" (ibid.). SDG targets are used to identify specific global health standards in each of the chapters below.

Although the SDG agenda is in part an exercise in setting standards applicable to global health security, that agenda provides each country with immense flexibility in the selection and realization of specific targets. The SDGs are designed to be global in nature and universally applicable, but nonetheless allow for different national realities, capacities, levels of development, institutions, and policy-making. Likewise, the associated targets are defined as aspirational and global, with each government setting its own national targets guided by the global level of ambition but taking into account national circumstances. Each government also decides how these aspirational and global targets should be incorporated in national planning processes, policies, and strategies (United Nations 2015, para. 55).

In this book, we explore three challenging areas embedded in the UN Sustainable Development Goals – strengthening access to primary health care, protecting and promoting public health, and integrating global economic markets into health care provision – that have contemporary relevance for global health security. As noted above, the right to health is today framed around the importance of medical services and public health, which mirror the first two areas we have selected for the focus of this book. The theme of global economic markets for health care provision reflects perhaps the most important emerging issue in Asia for health security. As China, India, and Japan have all committed in the past twenty-five years to trade liberalization through multilateral trade agreements – ranging from the World Trade Organization (WTO) to the Comprehensive and Progressive

Agreement for Trans-Pacific Partnership (CPTPP)[4] to separate trade agreements with the European Union – global economic markets have increased their reach into all three countries, with significant effects on medical services, supplies of pharmaceuticals, and public health. The SDG agenda shares this commitment to engaging, and to a certain extent embracing, trade liberalization and the global economy.

Three chapters are devoted to each of these three areas. The individual chapters are designed to show the different ways in which China, Japan, and India have each contributed to global health security in light of the global health standards set by the SDG agenda. The common framework for these discussions is that in all three countries, domestic decisions about how to best meet global health standards balance considerations of health care programs, delivery, and infrastructure against issues of cost and affordability; the demands of stakeholders that deliver health care, such as hospitals and physicians; political ideology; and the pressures of global economic markets. The chapters highlight the barriers as well as the success factors of the various approaches taken by governments in the provision of public health and primary care as well as by for-profit firms engaged in the health care sector.

Part 1: Strengthening Access to Health Care Services

The three chapters in Part 1 focus on the first of the three areas of concern outlined above: strengthening access to primary health care services in China, Japan, and India, respectively. The 2015 SDGs can provide a good sense of the global health standards and norms concerning access to health care services. Targets set for all countries under SDG 3 include "ensur[ing] universal access to sexual and reproductive health-care services, including for family planning, information and education, and the integration of reproductive health into national strategies and programmes" (SDG 3.7), and "achiev[ing] universal health coverage, including financial risk protection, access to quality essential health-care services and access to safe, effective, quality and affordable essential medicines and vaccines for all" (SDG 3.8).[5]

In China, as Wenqin Liang and Ilan Vertinsky explore in Chapter 1, the challenge remains to fulfill the basic SDG 3 obligation to create a health care system that provides sustainable, high-quality essential medical services. China has invested heavily in its public health care system and there is clearly progress on improving access to essential services. Liang and Vertinsky observe, however, that despite the impressive strides China has made in the past decade toward increasing health care coverage for its population, public insurance covers only a fraction of the cost of medicines and services. Focusing on measures taken by the Chinese government in the past decade, they identify the barriers to realizing universal access and strengthening its primary health care provision, many of them a direct reflection of China's transition to a market economy. They draw out how price controls on generic drugs, designed to maintain affordability for patients, are in tension with basic principles of market pricing mechanisms and have, in a market economy, created drug shortages in many parts of the country. At the same time, in order to encourage direct foreign investment in its pharmaceutical industry, China has facilitated an increase in the cost of non-generic drugs and the prescribing of non-generic drugs, drugs that are affordable only for wealthier patients and their families. Moreover, the salary structure for physicians has created perverse incentives for those physicians to prescribe treatment – often pharmaceuticals – that is neither effective nor high-quality to achieve national health care goals, especially with respect to the provision of essential medicines. The authors conclude with some recommendations for measures that the Chinese government can take to overcome these barriers to realizing access to health care for all in China.

In Chapter 2, Yoshitaka Wada examines how Japan is struggling with the issue of who pays for new or experimental services and drugs not yet covered by the Japanese universal health insurance scheme. At present, patients in Japan bear the full costs of these new services and drugs, with no contribution from the public insurer. This contrasts with most other countries with a universal health care system, including Canada, which allow for a mixed billing process where the patient pays a portion and the public insurer pays the rest. The upshot is that many Japanese patients do not have access to the latest, most innovative health care, raising the question of how well Japan is fulfilling its international rights-based obligations to provide universal health care for all, as required by SDG 3.8. Wada provides a careful, nuanced account of Japan's twenty-year journey toward adopting some sort of mixed billing process – it now has a limited scope of mixed billing for some new and innovative health care services and products. His chapter illustrates how even in advanced industrial countries with established health care systems providing universal access, there are ongoing challenges in extending and improving the system to meet evolving global health standards.

India's health care system is far less developed than either China's or Japan's, although it has made very significant improvements in the past decade on some important measures, such as infant mortality and the incidences of certain infectious diseases. Tiffany Chua, Marc McCrum, and Ilan Vertinsky illustrate in Chapter 3 how India's health care system has been built in the context of an immense, diverse country with a complex form of constitutional federalism where responsibilities for health care are shared between the central and the state governments. Like China's, India's health care system suffers in part from very significant underfunding by the central government. Major access initiatives appear inadequately funded. Unlike in China, however, where many of the barriers to access to health care are directly linked to the transition to a market society, the difficulties for health care measures initiated by the central government in India are often traceable to design flaws, tensions with market pricing mechanisms, or corruption. These barriers for the central government in India are so immense that it is hard to see a policy pathway for it to lead efforts to fulfill the obligation to provide universal access to affordable, high-quality medical services for all, which is the global health standard set by the target of SDG 3.8. In contrast to both China and Japan, where the central government is the leader in innovative health care policy, in India very promising innovation is occurring selectively at the state level as the country's federal system of government facilitates immense diversification and experimentation in health policy among state governments. Ultimately, the authors conclude that a commitment by the central and state governments in India to radical innovation in the delivery of health promotion and care, including the adoption of non-traditional methods of delivery and the deployment of new types (less expensive) of health and allied professional services, is required for significant progress to be made toward the universal access to essential health care services required by SDG 3.

Part 2: Protecting and Promoting Public Health

The three chapters in Part 2 focus on specific measures to safeguard public health in China, Japan, and India, respectively. The US Centers for Disease Control and Prevention (CDC) explains that "public health is the science of protecting and improving the health of people and their communities. This work is achieved by promoting healthy lifestyles, researching disease and injury prevention, and detecting, preventing and responding to infectious diseases. Overall, public health is concerned with protecting the health of entire populations. These populations can be as small as a local neighbor-hood, or as big as an entire country or region of the world."[6] The point is that public health refers to the measures, such as hygiene, vaccinations, food and drug safety, and maternal health, that are designed to benefit everyone, as opposed to the medical procedures, such as surgery, that benefit princi-pally individual patients. Since public health includes the prevention and detection of and response to health emergencies such as COVID-19, it is an integral part of global health security. Apart from global pandemics, coun-tries differ on what are the most pressing public health issues for their na-tional health security. China is especially challenged by emerging infectious diseases, tobacco control, and drug addiction. Food and water safety is an especially important issue in India. Japan is struggling with vaccination pro-grams and institutional long-term care for an aging population. These coun-try-specific public health issues are the subject of Chapters 4 to 6.

Many of the global health standards for public health pertaining to these different issues are expressed as targets for SDG 2 and SDG 3.[7] The relevant targets for 2030 include "achiev[ing] ... access to quality essential health-care services and access to safe, effective, quality and affordable essential medicines and vaccines for all" (SDG 3.8); "end[ing] the epidemics of AIDS, tuberculosis, malaria and neglected tropical diseases and combat[ting] hepa-titis, water-borne diseases and other communicable diseases" (SDG 3.3); "strengthen[ing] the implementation of the World Health Organization Framework Convention on Tobacco Control in all countries, as appropri-ate" (3.a); "strengthen[ing] the prevention and treatment of substance abuse, including narcotic drug abuse and harmful use of alcohol" (SDG 3.5); and "ensur[ing] access by all people, in particular the poor and people in vulner-able situations, including infants, to safe, nutritious and sufficient food all year round" (SDG 2.1).

In Chapter 4, Lesley Jacobs focuses on linking SDG targets on infectious diseases, tobacco control, and drug addiction to China's broader human rights performance. China has been a model in the Global South for devel-oping a responsive public health system that has progressively realized the right to health by improving the health status of its people, without embra-cing other human rights centred on individual freedoms and liberties. Jacobs puts pressure on the idea that China can successfully realize pro-gressively the right to public health without attending in tandem to issues of freedom. The right to health in international human rights law is now formulated as having two components – entitlements and freedoms – and respecting, protecting, and fulfilling the right to health requires attention to both of these components. China's decades-old position that right to health performance requires attention only to entitlements and guarantees of health services and a public health infrastructure is simply inconsistent with the SDG approach to global health standards that now also encompasses freedoms. Jacobs shows that on measures to deal with tobacco control and emerging infectious diseases, including SARS and COVID-19, China has been effective at securing public health entitlements, but in areas such as the administrative detention of drug users it has disregarded the protections that must be afforded to basic freedoms. The upshot is that for compliance with health standards set by SDG 3.3 and 3.5 targets, the performance record in China is clearly stronger on entitlements but weaker on freedoms.

In Chapter 5, Toshimi Nakanishi shifts the focus to public health measures in Japan. Vaccinations and immunizations for disease prevention have long been among the most important public health measures a particular country can undertake to advance health security. The global health standard for vaccines in SDG 3.9 is for access to affordable, quality vaccines for everyone. In the wake of the COVID-19 pandemic, the importance of access to vaccines for all to deal with emerging infectious diseases is readily visible. Nakanishi examines the surprising vaccination gap that exists in Japan, where many vaccinations widely used in other countries are either not available or are underutilized. The vaccination gap in Japan refers to the vaccine strains that are recommended by the WHO but are not being implemented. In this sense, Japan is not meeting global health standards and is under pressure to fulfill its obligations in accordance with international health and human rights law. Nakanishi traces the gap to two factors that operate in tandem: 1) a drug approval system that is especially sensitive to Japanese societal norms and concerns about product safety, and 2) a preoccupation with medical malpractice avoidance. The second factor is a reflection of how lawsuits in Japan over harm caused to individuals by compulsory vaccinations have transformed much of the country's vaccination regime into one predicated on patient choice, insulating physicians, the government, and pharmaceutical companies from financial liability. Nakanishi builds his analysis with an eye ultimately to map out how vaccination policy in Japan can move toward the global health standard expressed in SDG 3.9, something that is especially relevant in helping the country deal with COVID-19.

Food security in India is the focus of Mariela de Amstalden's discussion in Chapter 6. SDG 2.1 identifies food security as a fundamental public health issue. India has been a pioneer in the innovative use of international trade law provisions to advance its domestic health security. The government has, for example, successfully invoked provisions of the Agreement on Trade-Related Aspects of Intellectual Property Rights (TRIPS Agreement)[8] in the World Trade Organization to defend the unlicensed manufacture of patented pharmaceuticals by its generic drug companies from claims that they have violated international intellectual property law (Drache and Jacobs 2014). Amstalden focuses on India's import prohibition, beginning in 2007, against certain agricultural products, including poultry meats, eggs, and feathers from countries reporting avian influenza based on the WTO Agreement on the Application of Sanitary and Phytosanitary Measures (SPS Agreement).[9] The SPS Agreement was designed to create domestic policy space for countries like India to limit trade in certain circumstances out of a concern for public health, in this case food safety. The global health standard of food security expressed in SDG 2.1 supports this policy decision by the Indian government. Since ultimately India's position rested on a risk assessment about public health, and not prescribed scientific evidence, Amstalden draws out how well these health security assessments fit with India's other international obligations.

Part 3: Engaging Global Markets in Primary Health Care and Public Health

The expanding scope of international trade and the global economy over the past thirty years, including the adoption of global business strategies by local profit-oriented firms, has resulted in the introduction of market pricing mechanisms and for-profit provision into the delivery of primary health care and public health in China, Japan, and India. This pertains especially to the provision of medicines and other pharmaceuticals. All three countries are major players in the global economy and prominent voices in international economic law venues such as the World Trade Organization, which was founded in 1995. International trade and economic law is, at its core, about a complex body of law that sets out the legal rights and obligations of non-state actors (individuals, multinational firms, international organizations) and state actors (governments, state agencies, and so on) in the context of the global economy to support trade liberalization and enable private markets in goods and services, including in health care, to thrive. Trade and investment agreements are the most familiar legal instruments of this body of law. Becoming members of major international trade law bodies such as the World Trade Organization also requires a commitment for those countries to become market societies (Drache and Jacobs 2018). In market societies, the state and for-profit market function in a complementary fashion (Polanyi [1994] 2001). The state has certain spheres in which it can operate through law and regulations and other spheres in which it has no role, and provision of goods and services is instead provided in large part through private markets. The economy in these societies is a configuration of the overlap of these different spheres. Japan and India have a long history of commitment to being market societies dating to the post–Second World War period. In China, that commitment emerged in the 1980s.

Although the SDGs are often associated with priorities of the Global South, such as poverty reduction and gender-sensitive economic development, the SDG agenda is distinctive because it also includes the integration of trade liberalization, market pricing mechanisms, private for-profit provision, and other levers of the global economy as instruments for the realization of the SDGs and correlated targets. The SDG agenda seeks to "respect each country's policy space and leadership ... domestic public resources, domestic and international private business and finance, international development cooperation, international trade as an engine for development, debt and debt sustainability" (United Nations 2015). The implementation of the 2015 SDGs "will facilitate an intensive global engagement ... bringing together Governments, civil society, the private sector, the United Nations system and other actors and mobilizing all available resources" (ibid.).

Underlying the SDG agenda is the embrace of the belief that global private markets and trade liberalization can advance global health security. This is reflected in the targets of SDG 8, 9, and 10. SDG 8, which aspires to "promote sustained, inclusive and sustainable economic growth, full and productive employment and decent work for all," includes targets such as "achiev[ing] higher levels of economic productivity through diversification, technological upgrading and innovation" (SDG 8.2); "promot[ing] development-oriented policies that support productive activities, decent job creation, entrepreneurship, creativity and innovation, and encourage the formalization and growth of micro-, small- and medium-sized enterprises" (SDG 8.3); and "increase[ing] Aid for Trade support for developing countries" (SDG 8.a).[10] SDG 9 includes the target of "develop[ing] quality, reliable, sustainable and resilient infrastructure, including regional and transborder infrastructure, to support economic development and human well-being" (SDG 9.1).[11] SDG 10 includes the targets of "improv[ing] the regulation and monitoring of global financial markets and institutions" (SDG 10.5) and "implement[ing] the principle of special and differential treatment for developing countries ... in accordance with World Trade

Organization agreements" (SDG 10.a).[12] The three chapters in Part 3 draw out tensions between strengthening health security in China, Japan, and India and their engagement with international trade law and the global economy.

In Chapter 7, Jennifer Fang, Kelley Lee, and Nidhi Sejpal Pouranik explore whether the China National Tobacco Corporation (CNTC), a state-owned Chinese monopoly, poses a threat to global public health. CNTC is the dominant supplier of cigarettes in China and an important source of tax revenue for the national government and many provincial governments. However, tobacco use globally as well as within China is the single biggest cause of chronic disease, particularly cancer, heart disease, and stroke. The tobacco epidemic causes more than 8 million deaths annually across the world, and those numbers are continuing to rise.[13] The tobacco industry has flourished in the global economy, with cigarette manufacturing and sales concentrated in six giant for-profit transnational companies that have operations around the world – so-called Big Tobacco (Jacobs 2014). The World Health Organization adopted the Framework Convention on Tobacco Control (FCTC) in 2005 as a response to the tobacco epidemic, with the stated purpose of curtailing the global spread of the tobacco industry. An important target of SDG 3 is to "strengthen the implementation of the World Health Organization Framework Convention on Tobacco Control in all countries, as appropriate" (SDG 3.a).[14] CNTC is the largest tobacco company in the world, producing one-third of the world's cigarettes. Over the past sixty years, it has focused on supplying a huge domestic market in China. However, as the domestic Chinese market has become increasingly saturated and potential foreign competition looms, the company has turned to expansion abroad. This is entirely consistent with the support for global economic liberalization in the SDGs but clearly contrary to the goal of tobacco control. The chapter discussion focuses on the global business strategy of the CNTC as a global public health threat. Using Chinese- and English-language sources, Fang, Lee, and Pouranik describe the globalization ambitions of the CNTC, and its global business strategy focused on internal restructuring, brand development, and expansion of overseas operations in selected markets. They conclude that the company has undergone substantial change over the past two decades and is consequently poised to become a new global player among Big Tobacco, one that has the potential to weaken the FCTC, not strengthen it as required by SDG 3.

In Chapter 8, Neil Munro and Ziying He turn the discussion to hospital services in China. For-profit, competitive markets for medical services among hospitals in urban settings are now widespread in that country. Focusing on the economic incentive structures for Chinese physicians and hospitals to mis-prescribe some treatments, especially involving pharmaceuticals, Munro and He ask how in this competitive market patients can act strategically to deal with this incentive structure. This focus aligns with SDG target 16.6, which requires countries to "develop effective, accountable and transparent institutions at all levels."[15] Using Albert Hirschmann's well-known framework of exit, voice, and loyalty to identify types of responses to failing firms by employees and customers, Munro and He distinguish between "voice," where the patient speaks up in an effort to improve the behaviour of the physician or hospital, and "exit," where the patient moves to a different hospital. Using results from a survey of 3,680 Chinese citizens about their strategies and responses to hospital or physician behaviours, Munro and He found that patients in urban areas are in fact much more likely to exercise their voice or exit when they faced mis-prescribed treatments, suggesting that their choices are impacted by the existence of a competitive market in cities that is far rarer in rural China. This chapter provides guidance in how the SDG agenda and global health security can be advanced with private markets in primary health care provision in China.

In Chapter 9, Hiroyuki Kojin reports on his study of two Japanese companies that are now successfully selling Japanese medical services and technology to other Asian countries, including India, at prices set in the global marketplace. In Japan, an important part of the government's strategy to strengthen the economy is to support companies exporting Japanese-style health care services and medical instruments overseas for profit. This is entirely consistent with UN framing of the SDGs, which acknowledges "the role of the diverse private sector, ranging from micro-enterprises to cooperatives to multinationals, and that of civil society organizations and philanthropic organizations in the implementation of the new Agenda" (United Nations 2015). One of the targets for SDG 3 is to "substantially increase health financing and the recruitment, development, training and retention of the health workforce in developing countries (SDG 3.c)."[16] The two Japanese companies are expanding their international service delivery in the context of trade liberalization in the Asia-Pacific region, where the export of health care has become much easier for Japan. One of these firms, based in Singapore, employs Japanese physicians and nurses and sells services to Japanese citizens living there. The other firm is based in India, and all the physicians and nurses are Indian; moreover, the patients are mainly poor, local residents. Kojin emphasizes that both of these medical companies face significant obstacles and challenges because there are restrictions or prohibitions on employing Japanese physicians and nurses, reflecting limitations on the licensing of health care professionals with foreign credentials. The underlying point is that although there is growing liberalization of the for-profit market for health care services in Asia, there is not yet a corresponding liberalization of professional health care licences and similar forms of collaboration among different countries, which are also required for global health security.

This book is designed to sharpen discussion of three key areas of health security – primary health care, public health, and market provision – in major Asian countries by linking those areas to targets embedded in the UN Sustainable Development Goals. Those targets can be viewed as setting global health standards for China, Japan, and India. The underlying point is that since global health security requires countries to coordinate and cooperate with one another to address pressing public health threats such as COVID-19 and meet many domestic health care needs, the SDGs provide a framework for assessing global health security in these three Asian countries. Each chapter in this book offers an assessment of global health security within this framework. Ultimately, however, since using the SDGs to assess global health security is still in its infancy, especially in Asia, these assessments are intended to ignite a conversation that will continue long into the future.

NOTES

1 See, for example, the Global Health Security Index: https://www.ghsindex.org/.
2 https://www.cdc.gov/globalhealth/strategy/default.htm.
3 https://www.ohchr.org/en/professionalinterest/pages/cescr.aspx.
4 https://www.mfat.govt.nz/vn/trade/free-trade-agreements/free-trade-agreements-in-force/comprehensive-and-progressive-agreement-for-trans-pacific-partnership-cptpp/comprehensive-and-progressive-agreement-for-trans-pacific-partnership-text-and-resources/.
5 https://sdgs.un.org/goals/goal3.
6 https://www.cdcfoundation.org/what-public-health.
7 https://sdgs.un.org/goals/goal2; https://sdgs.un.org/goals/goal3.
8 https://www.wto.org/english/docs_e/legal_e/27-trips_01_e.htm.
9 https://www.wto.org/english/tratop_e/sps_e/spsagr_e.htm.
10 https://sdgs.un.org/goals/goal8.

11 https://sdgs.un.org/goals/goal9.
12 https://sdgs.un.org/goals/goal10.
13 https://www.who.int/news-room/fact-sheets/detail/tobacco.
14 https://sdgs.un.org/goals/goal3.
15 https://sdgs.un.org/goals/goal16.
16 https://sdgs.un.org/goals/goal3.

PART 1

STRENGTHENING ACCESS TO HEALTH CARE SERVICES

1

Providing Access to Affordable Medicines and Health Care for All in China

WENQIN LIANG and ILAN VERTINSKY

Access and affordability have become major challenges for China's health care system. Among the sources of social discontent with regard to health care, affordability of medicines causes high levels of public concern. In a survey of 10,000 households carried out in January 2013, 46 percent of respondents thought that the greatest problem with health care in China was that "getting healthcare was difficult and medicines were expensive" (Fang 2013). In recent years, a lament among Chinese patients, "*kan bing nan, kan bing gui*" (getting medical care is difficult and expensive), appears in the introductory remarks of most academic research and media commentaries on China's health care system (see, e.g., *Xinhua wang* 2011). The topic of affordable medicine (*chi yao gui*) is raised frequently by deputies at the National People's Congress (NPC) and committee members of the Chinese People's Political Consultative Conference (CPPCC).

These concerns about access to affordable and accessible medicines and health care for all align with the 2015 United Nations Sustainable Development Goals (SDG). The Introduction to this book framed the SDGs as providing standards for global health security. A target set for China under SDG 3 is to "achieve universal health coverage, including financial risk protection, access to quality essential health-care services and access to safe, effective, quality and affordable essential medicines and vaccines for all" (SDG 3.8).[1] How can China be assessed on this target?

A key factor to such an assessment concerns the direct outlays of cash that patients or families pay to health care providers (i.e., the "out-of-pocket payments"). When these become the principal source of individuals' health care expenses, it is likely that the threat of financial catastrophe, or deepening poverty, will prevent them from seeking necessary health services and essential medicines (Gotsadze et al. 2005).

From 2007 to 2016, China's expenditures on health care quadrupled, increasing from $144 billion (CNY 1,096.6 billion) to $698 billion (CNY 4,634 billion), and though the growth of government expenditures on health was "much higher than that of the total fiscal expenditure and public expenditure on education" (Zhu 2019, 110), expenditures in China on health as a proportion of the country's gross domestic product still remained low.[2] Moreover, the share of out-of-pocket payments by individuals of total health expenditures was initially comparatively large, growing from 20% in 1980 to 49% in 2006, with a peak of 59% in 2000 (Hu et al. 2008). This was considerably higher than the average shares of less than 20% in high-income countries and 35% in upper-middle-income countries (Gottret and Schieber 2006). Since then, the share of out-of-pocket spending on health care has fallen to 28.8%, though it is noteworthy that around 35% of the out-of-pocket expenditure on health care was on medicines, one of the highest proportions in the world (Fu et al. 2018).

Paying for health care, including medicines, has thus become a notable cause of impoverishment for households that lack adequate health insurance. In 2008, over 35% of urban households and 43% of rural households had difficulty affording needed health care and were left without health care, or became impoverished by the costs they bore (Hu et al. 2008). Recent reports indicate, however, some improvement in the situation as a result of the government-run New Rural Cooperative Medical Scheme (NRCMS). For example, in Yanbian, as a result of this scheme, the number of "medically impoverished" households dropped by 24.6% in 2016 (Sun et al. 2016). Not surprisingly, low-income groups have a higher probability of not seeking health care when ill, and also of incurring catastrophic medical spending when seeking medical care (Liu et al. 2008). Even in Zhejiang, a relatively wealthy province, the average annual medical expenditures of low-income rural households in 2014 was CNY 1,026, 8.7% higher than the provincial average of rural residents (Zhejiang Provincial Bureau of Statistics 2014). The proportion of total living expenses accounted for by medical expenditures was 18.8%, 10.8% higher than the provincial average of rural residents. Persistent complaints from the public about access to, and affordability of, health care in general and medicines in particular, as well as data on impoverishment due to expenses on health care indicated that simply increasing expenditures was an inadequate response to these problems. Arguably, this may explain the increasing and persistent efforts by the government to seek ways to reform the health care system.

In this chapter, we focus on describing and assessing the various attempts by the Chinese government over the years to resolve the problem of affordability of medicines. These efforts included increased funding, institutional development, and reform. We begin by examining the key factors that tend to reduce access to affordable medicines. We then investigate policies and programs that have been designed to deal with some of these factors and promote access to affordable essential medicines and examine revisions to the Patent Law of China that were specifically designed to reduce the deleterious impact of patents on affordability. We also explore China's policies and programs designed to strengthen primary care that were intimately linked to enhancing the system of affordable essential medicines. Lastly we examine the unintended consequences of some reform measures and implementation challenges that they faced.

Factors Contributing to the Lack of Access to Affordable Medicines

High Cost of Medical Products
The high cost of medical products, in particular that of medicines, is a major obstacle to access to medicine in China (Sun et al. 2008; Zhang 2010). There are several key drivers of the costs of drugs.

Prescription of Expensive Branded Drugs
In China, generic medicines are typically sold at substantial discounts from the price of branded medicines. Recognizing that promoting generic drugs has the potential to reduce consumers' annual spending on prescriptions, China's national policy is to promote the production and prescription of generic medicines (Zeng 2014). As a result, generic drugs are the mainstay of China's pharmaceutical industry (Li Hui 2014).

Prescription of expensive patented drugs is increasing, however. One reason for the preference for branded medicines is the unsatisfactory quality control of generic drugs (*Jiating yisheng zaixian* 2013). Although a generic drug is supposed to be bioequivalent to its branded counterparts, its safety, strength, quality, purity, and stability are not always as good. This is especially so in the case of specialty drugs for treating various types of cancers, multiple sclerosis, HIV, and other diseases (*Xinhua ribao* 2014;

Nanfang ribao 2014; Yan 2013; Wang Jianmin 2014). Concern over therapeutic effectiveness makes branded drugs more trusted than generic ones,
by both doctors and patients (Wang Jiamin 2014).

The high confidence of Chinese consumers in branded drugs, which are
produced by reputable foreign companies, is increasing further due to advertising directed at the public and marketing campaigns directed at physicians by multinational pharmaceutical giants that are moving in, seeking to
tap latent demand and take advantage of lower costs of drug production in
China (Deloitte 2011). Branded medicines are expected to continue winning
customers away from domestic generic drug manufacturers, causing their
proportional market shares to shift accordingly. From 2007 to 2010, sales of
branded patented drugs had a compound annual growth rate average of
35.7% and were forecast to continue growing at just over 25% until 2015.

Demographic and Epidemiological Transition
China has undergone rapid demographic and epidemiological changes in
the past few decades (Yang et al. 2013). A steady improvement in life expectancy is leading to increases in the number of seniors (over sixty-five years).
The share of seniors in the population grew from 8.4% in 2011 to 13.5% in
2020 (National Bureau of Statistics of China 2021).

The aging population has generated higher demand for health care services, since elderly people have weaker immune systems, resulting in a
higher incidence of illness (IMA Pharma 2013). Aging also leads to a shift
from acute disease to chronic disability, stroke, and obstructive pulmon-
ary and other chronic diseases that require longer care and more expensive
medicines. The effect of population aging on drug and other health care
expenditures is likely to persist for the foreseeable future (Morgan and
Cunningham 2011).

Low Income Levels
Without sufficient insurance coverage, the link between price and affordability depends on income level.[3] China's extraordinary economic growth
in the past few decades has made it the second-largest economy in the
world, yet it remains a developing country with a per capita income that is
still a fraction of that in advanced economies. Official data show that about
5.5 million people still lived on incomes below the national poverty line of
CNY 3,747 per year at the end of 2019 (World Bank 2021). This means that
low wage earners in China face spending multiple daily wages on even generic medicines.

Take the northwestern province of Shaanxi, for example. According to a field study of the treatment of common conditions undertaken in Shaanxi in 2012, the lowest-paid unskilled government worker had to spend between 0.1 and 4.7 days' wages to purchase the lowest-priced generic medicine from the private sector (Fang 2013). If brand name medicines had been prescribed, the costs would have escalated to between 0.7 and 11.5 days' wages. High medicine prices increase the cost of treatment. Some treatments become clearly unaffordable; for example, the treatment of an ulcer with the branded drug Prilosec (omeprazole) would have cost 11.5 days' wages.

Perverse Incentives for Hospitals and Doctors

Hospitals in China today remain the dominant sales channel for pharmaceuticals, accounting for 70% of all drugs sold and distributed. Retail pharmacies comprise the remainder (AT Kearney 2012). The public system, in particular, provides 80.8% of in-patient services (National Health Commission of the People's Republic of China 2021).

Public hospitals in China receive limited funding from the government, however; government subsidies made up only 10% of their revenues in 2018 (*Xinhua* 2019). With few other sources of income, hospitals had to maximize their profits from drug sales in order to fund medical services (Ibid). In addition, much of doctors' incomes depended on how many drugs they prescribed (*Economist* 2014a). The distorted incentives embedded in the medical service system increase costs for patients.[4]

Under the former planned-economy regime, medical services were provided free to everyone in China (Zi 1998). Public health facilities heavily relied on government subsidies, and the government set prices for pharmaceuticals that were far below real costs. From the mid-1950s to the present, the government has officially permitted a 15% markup for hospitals. Government financial support to public hospitals declined during the economic reform process. At the beginning of the 1980s, state financing constituted about 60% of hospital revenues, falling to 8.2% by 2003. Thus, drug sales had become one of the main sources of revenue of hospitals (Ministry of Health 2006). However, government policy reforms (discussed later in this chapter), signaled a potential shift from past patterns. In 2011, Beijing was the first pilot-project city in China to remove the markups on medicines. More pilots were chosen in the following years, and as of September 2017, all public hospitals in China had removed medicine markups (Li 2017). The elimination of markups on medicines directly reduced their costs to patients. Moreover, the removal of the incentives for prescribing and dispensing more expensive branded drugs instead of cheaper generic ones resulted in an overall a shift to cheaper drugs, further reducing patients' expenditures on medicines.

Complex Pharmaceutical Distribution Chains

Findings of a study on the affordability of medicines in Shaanxi province in 2012 showed that patients spent 1.69 times more for the lowest-priced generic medicines in the public sector than their international references, and 11.83 times more for branded medicines (Fang 2013). Although generic medicines in the public sector were 24.2% cheaper than in the private sector, many patients had to purchase medicines in the private sector because of the lower availability of both originator-brand and generic medicines in the public sector (ibid.). A similar phenomenon was found in other provinces (Kanavos, Schurer, and Vogler 2011). The price differences between public and private sectors and the shortages of originator-brand and generic medicines raise questions about the efficiency of China's drug distribution system.

Public health care institutions in China above the county level must procure almost all drugs through centralized bidding procurement. China's pharmaceutical distribution network is extremely fragmented, with more than 13,000 distributors, most of whom provide access to only one local market or even just one or two hospitals (AT Kearney 2012). The three largest distributors – Sinopharm, Shanghai Pharmaceuticals, and China Resources – claim only about a 20% share of the market. This statistic contrasts sharply with the United States, where the top three players have a share of over 95% of a market almost triple the size of China's in 2010 (ibid.). Fragmentation leads to high distribution costs, as intermediaries at each distribution layer collect fees that cover their costs and profit margins before the medicines reach hospitals or pharmacies. Ninety-five percent of China's prescription and over-the-counter drugs flow through distributors. Typically, the supply of drugs passes from a national distributor to multiple distributors in each province, city, and town before reaching hospitals or pharmacies.

Distributors in China often require markups as high as 8% from pharmaceutical companies, but most margins hover between 1% and 2% (AT Kearney 2012). It is estimated that the price of a drug in China comprises 80% in distribution costs and 20% in manufacturing costs (Ding and Huang 2010). The complex system also means that there is a greater possibility of corruption. Key risk areas include inappropriate benefits given, and payments made, to practitioners by distributors through kickback payments, sponsorships, and excessive gifts (Deloitte 2013).

Inadequate and Unequal Access to Health Care Insurance

To mitigate the rise in out-of-pocket payments, the government has established insurance schemes. There are two major components of China's public health insurance system: the Urban Employee Basic Medical Insurance (UEBMI) and the Urban and Rural Residents' Basic Medical Insurance Scheme (URRBMS). The latter is a system initiated in 2016 through the merger of the Urban Resident Basic Medical Insurance (URBMI) and the New Rural Cooperative Medical Scheme (NRCMS). Other supplementary schemes include Enterprise Supplementary Medical Insurance, Commercial Health Insurance, Civil Servants Medical Subsidy, and Medical Security for specific groups (Ngorsuraches et al. 2012). The coverage provided through these programs, however, is still very small in terms of both the service benefits package and the financial protection provided (Hu et al. 2008).

Outpatient services are very inadequately insured in many parts of China. In-patient services, where covered, leave patients with significant costs (copayments, deductibles, or additional fees) to bear (Ministry of Human Resources and Social Security 2013). The basic medical insurance for urban and rural residents in Beijing, for instance, reimburses only around half of in-patient expenditure. The medical assistance program for poor people simply helps its participants enroll in the rural scheme in many instances, rather than covering more of their costs. As a result, access to primary care for poor people has not really improved, and protection against high health care expenses remains very restricted (ibid.).

Before their merger, the urban and rural health systems in China were independent of one another and had distinct funding and benefit schedules. Under the UEBMI, the per-person financial contributions from government and beneficiaries were equivalent to 14% of annual salary in Shanghai but only 8% in most of the western provinces (Hu et al. 2008). Relevant government sectors have made a great effort to narrow the urban-rural reimbursement difference. However, because the urban-rural income gap is also widening, it is not sufficient to mitigate the urban-rural inequalities in healthcare by generally levelling reimbursement ratios between urban and rural residents (Chao Ma et al. 2021). Moreover, with China's rapid progress of urbanization, an increasing number of rural residents migrated from rural to urban areas to seek better employment opportunities. But compared to original urban residents, these rural migrant workers in the cities have limited access to a range of social services, including healthcare services, due to China's unique household registration system (*hukou* system) (Dian Luo et al. 2021).

TABLE 1.1

Coverage of basic medical insurance for urban and rural residents in six cities

Classification of hospital	Deductible line (CNY) Children and students	Other	Reimbursement rate (%) Children and students	19–59 years old	60 and older/ disabled	Ceiling (CNY)
BEIJING						
Primary	650	1,300	75			20,000/ year
Secondary	400	800	78			
Tertiary	150	300	80			
SHANGHAI						
Primary	300		60	70	70	n/a
Secondary	100		75	80	80	
Tertiary	50		80	90	90	
CHANGSHA, HUNAN						
Primary	1,100		60			15,000/ year
Secondary	500		65			
Tertiary	300		70			
Community	200		85			
WUHAN, HUBEI						
Primary	800		60			15,000/ year
Secondary	400		70			
Tertiary	200		90			
LANZHOU, GANSU						
Primary	2,400 (Level A) 1,000 (Level B)		60 (Level A) 70 (Level B)			40,000/ year
Secondary	400		80			
Tertiary	200		85			
ZHENGZHOU, HENAN						
Primary	1,500		Below CNY 8,000: 55; over CNY 8,000: 65			
Secondary	1,000		Below CNY 5,000: 60; over CNY 5,000 70			150,000/ year
Tertiary	600		Below CNY 3,000: 65; over CNY 3,000 75			
Community	300		Below CNY 1,000: 80; over CNY 1,000: 90			

Sources: Municipal Government Records, accessed October 2017.

Local governments have been asked by the central government to design regulations on funding, reimbursement, and other details that are tailored to local economic conditions and residents' demands for health care services. Some local governments have abundant funds for basic medical insurance and use part of the funds to cover serious illnesses, while poorer governments with only limited funding for basic medical insurance must find new ways to raise money for serious-illness coverage.[5]

In general, richer locations have higher reimbursement rates and ceilings. The higher the classification of the hospital, the lower the deductible and the copayment rates (see Table 1.1).

Policy Interventions to Increase Access to Health Care

There are basically two approaches (that can be combined) to increase affordability, apart from increasing incomes: 1) controlling prices and costs and eliminating perverse incentives and inefficiencies that lead to price increases, and 2) increasing third-party payments (i.e., expanding insurance coverage and enhancing benefits) (Freeman and Boynton 2011).

Controlling Prices and Costs and Eliminating Perverse Incentives and Inefficiencies

The National Essential Medicines List and Price Setting

China launched the first action plan to offer its population affordable essential medicines in 1979. The central guidance for what this plan and future action plans covered was the National Essential Medicine List (NEML). Theoretically, the selection of medicines for this list is based on the health needs of the majority of the population; the drugs chosen must be safe, clinically effective, affordable, and available (Wang 2005). Provinces can supplement the national list to form their own drug selection according to their economic situation and specific needs. These needs have been amended from time to time to reflect, in addition to perceived changes in the needs of the population, changes in the state of art in medicine, financial conditions, and the increasingly ambitious objectives set for the system by the Chinese Communist Party (CCP) and its leaders. The initial list published in 1981 included only Western medicines. In 1996, a list that included both Western and Chinese traditional medicines was published for the first time.[6] Later lists increased the number and scope of medicines included. The number of Chinese herbal and patent medicines grew proportionately over the years, as government policies required that both Chinese and Western medicines be considered equally important and spurred the development of Chinese medicines industry. The 2018 NEML includes 417 chemical and biological products and 268 Chinese patent medicines and herbal medicines (He et al. 2018).

In April 2009, China unveiled its health care reform plan with the goal of providing affordable and equitable basic health care for all by 2020. This reform included a series of initiatives to improve access to affordable medicines. On August 18, 2009, China issued its "Opinion on Implementing the National Essential Medicines," containing a list of 307 essential medicines. The objectives of the essential medicines system were to reduce irrational drug use (e.g., counterfeit drugs, over-prescription of antibiotics, and intravenous injections) and to improve access to safe and effective essential drugs to satisfy the health care needs of the majority of the population. The program focused on public primary health care institutions, with the intention of eventually extending to private providers and hospitals (Yip et al. 2010). Essential medicines are heavily subsidized. The National Development and Reform Commission (NDRC), which tracks the price and supply of essential medicines in the market, sets price ceilings for drugs on the essential list.

Reducing the Costs of Medicines
To reduce the costs of medicines, the government reformed the way medicines are procured. In the past decade, drug procurement has been primarily carried out at provincial levels. Drugs on the provincial drug list are purchased for the whole province in bulk at the agreed bid prices and supplied to facilities for further distribution to public hospitals.

In January 2019, the State Council announced the National Centralized Drug Procurement Pilot Program (General Office of the State Council of the People's Republic of China 2019). Four municipalities and seven sub-provincial cities were designated as pilot cities. Under the program, the participating cities submit the agreed procurement volume of each drug to the National Health Security Administration (NHSA)'s procurement list. Based on the total annual agreed procurement volume of the eleven pilot cities, the NHSA organizes the bidding and price negotiation. The drug manufacturer with the lowest bid price wins the bid. Study shows that under the pilot program, the daily cost of bid-winning original and generic drugs, as well as non-winning original drugs, were all significantly decreased (Wang et al. 2021). The pilot program was expanded in September the same year (National Health Security Administration 2019). In 2021, the central government decided to make this centralized drug bulk-buying "a regular and institutionalized practice to lower medical costs for the general public" and cover essential drugs and consumables as the mainstay of the procurement (*Xinhua* 2021). By the end of 2021, six rounds of centralized bulk-buying were carried out, and drugs under the program saw an average price cut of 53 percent (National Health Security Administration 2022).

Another way to lower prices is to eliminate built-in perverse incentives that lead to inefficient prescribing by doctors (i.e., over-prescribing and the tendency to opt for more expensive drugs) as a result of the sale of drugs being used as a source of hospital financing. China is undergoing comprehensive public hospital reforms aimed at improving the quality of medical services and lowering drug costs. Reforms attempting to separate health care from drug sales are designed to change China's long-standing system of monetary incentives for doctors and hospitals, which leads to irrational prescribing of drugs from a public welfare perspective.

In recognition of the complexity of the public hospital reform, the government initially designated sixteen cities to test different governance models (Yip et al. 2010). More pilot programs were added in the following years. In 2014, the sixth year of China's health care reform, Premier Li Keqiang called for a full effort to be made in overcoming difficulties in implementing the reform, focusing on public hospitals at the county level (*Global Times* 2014). On April 1 that year, the National Health and Family Planning Commission (NHFPC) announced the addition of another 700 counties and cities for piloting public hospital reform experiments, on top of the 311 counties and cities designated in June 2013.

A key policy element of the reform was a "zero markup" policy under which essential medicines are sold to patients for the procurement price plus a fixed distribution cost, with no profit to the health facility for the sale. Following Beijing's reform in 2011, provinces such as Anhui, Zhejiang, Shaanxi, and Qinghai also started to implement the policy as pilots. Anhui, for example, started the pilot experiments with twenty-one designated county-level public hospitals, with the aim of expanding the reforms to all the other counties and cities in the province (Chen and Zhao 2014). The hospitals' 25% revenue loss as a result of the reform was compensated mainly by the health insurance fund, partly by the provincial government, and partly by charging for medical consultations (ibid.).

As the reform expanded, the share of drug sales in hospitals' total revenues dropped – from 46.3% in 2010 to 38.1% in 2016 (Xu 2017) – reflecting both the declining prices to patients as a result of the elimination or reduction in markups and probably a shift from expensive branded medicines to cheaper generic ones as a result of the removal of financial incentives to prescribe the former. By September 2017, all public hospitals in China had joined the reform program, ending the long-established practice of medicine price markups that helped fund hospitals (ibid.).

The increases in medical consultation fees to cover losses to hospital revenues from removal of the markup on medicines were quite substantial. For example, during the pilot trial period at Beijing Friendship Hospital, consultation costs rose from CNY 42 to CNY 100. Patients covered by the capital's public health care insurance were reimbursed CNY 40 for each medical consultation, so the out-of-pocket cost of seeing a top specialist was CNY 20–60 (Shan and Wang 2012).

Expanding Health Insurance Coverage: Striving for Universal Coverage
China unveiled its ambitious health care reform plan in April 2009, committing to spending an additional CNY 850 billion (about US$125 billion) in the next three years, with the goal of providing affordable and equitable basic health care for all by 2020. One of the targets was to expand health insurance coverage to over 90% of the population.

Government spending and Chinese citizen's incentives for participation have been gradually expanding the basic medical insurance coverage,[7] from an estimated low point of 40% of urban residents and only 4% of rural dwellers in 2009 (Meng and Tang 2010) to 96.6% by 2012, with the UEBMI scheme insuring 17.7% (237 million), the URBMI scheme insuring 14.5% (194 million), and the NRCMS insuring 62.4% (836 million) of the residents. By the end of 2021, China's basic medical insurance covered 1.36 billion people, accounting for over 95 percent of the entire population (National Healthcare Security Administration 2022).

The government plan for implementation identified a sequence of steps for increasing coverage. The first wave of NRCMS and URBMI, initiated in 2003 and 2007, respectively, covered only in-patient services (NCMC household-based savings accounts paid for outpatient visits but barely covered one annual outpatient visit per person). Since the end of 2010, coverage for outpatient services has gradually been expanded. Since 2011, policies have identified priority diseases for further reduction of copayment, including chronic and major disorders (e.g., hypertension, diabetes, cirrhosis, nephritis, arthritis, asthma, cancer, and cardiovascular disease) (Yip et al. 2010).

Reimbursement of Catastrophic Illness Expenditures

Chinese health policy makers have long been concerned with protecting people from the possibility that illness would lead to catastrophic financial payments and subsequent impoverishment. In 2012, China announced a decision to expand the coverage of the country's health care insurance system to include the treatment of catastrophic illnesses, in order to prevent patients from slipping into poverty as a result of payment for necessary health care costs.

On August 30, 2012, the National Development and Reform and six other ministries jointly issued the "Opinion on the Supplementary Insurance of Major Diseases for Urban and Rural Residents." This document indicates that twenty major diseases, such as childhood leukemia and lung cancer, should be covered as a priority (National Health and Family Planning Commission 2012). The reimbursement rate for the identified major diseases was constrained to be at least 50% of the excess amount remaining after the basic health insurance reimbursement (National Development and Reform Commission 2012).

On January 1, 2014, cities such as Beijing and Chengdu released their reimbursement policy on catastrophic diseases for urban and rural residents. These policies increased reimbursement rates for treating severe diseases for unemployed urban and rural residents. Moreover, these cities did not set a ceiling for catastrophic disease reimbursement. According to the reimbursement policy in Beijing, unemployed residents can get additional reimbursement if their out-of-pocket medical expenses exceed a certain level after they are reimbursed by the city's health insurance programs for urban and rural unemployed residents. The city takes 5% of the funding from the programs to set up a fund for this additional reimbursement (Li Yahong 2014).

Unemployed urban residents can be reimbursed for 50% of their out-of-pocket medical payments if the amount of such payments in the previous year was more than the city's urban disposable per capita income that year. Rural residents can get reimbursed if their out-of-pocket medical payments in the previous year exceeded the average net income for the city's rural residents that year (Wang Qingyun 2014).

Promoting Equal Treatment of Farmers in Rural Areas and Urban Residents

Recent reforms have been aiming to reduce inequality in medical insurance benefits between farmers in rural areas and urban residents. During the Third Plenary Session of the 18th Central Committee of the Chinese

Communist Party, the "Decision on Major Issues Concerning Comprehensively Deepening Reform" proposed to coordinate the basic medical insurance system for urban and rural residents. It stipulated that farmers in rural areas should be treated equally to urban residents; at the same time, authorities should speed up the integration of medical insurance funds nationwide, and create a national medical insurance network encompassing workers and urban and rural residents, enabling the free flow of medical insurance funds nationwide (Wilkinson 2013). In January 2016, the government released the document titled "Opinions of the State Council on the Integration of Basic Medical Insurance System for Urban and Rural Residents," which required local governments to provide concrete implementation plans by the end of that year. By January 2018, most cities in China had combined the urban and rural basic health care insurance programs.

Revised Intellectual Property (IP) Laws

Patent protection provides patentees with market power, which permits them to increase prices above those that would prevail in a freely competitive market. Thus, patenting of new essential medicines for which there are no effective substitutes is likely to reduce the affordability of such medicines and restrict access to them until the patent expires, their costs are fully reimbursed by insurance, or their prices are reduced by government action (e.g., price controls). Changes in the patent law that make it more difficult to patent medicines reduce the ability of pharmaceutical companies to raise their prices or protect existing monopoly prices. For example, raising patentability standards reduces the ability of pharmaceutical companies to patent minor changes in their patented products and extend the life of patents about to expire. The World Trade Organization's Agreement on Trade-Related Aspects of Intellectual Property Rights (TRIPS Agreement) normally ensured that governments maintained the high level of protection prescribed by the agreement through their legislation.[8] This created a conflict between countries' international obligations to provide affordable medicines for their citizens and the preservation of the rights of patent holders of essential medicines. The Doha Declaration on the TRIPS Agreement and Public Health, adopted by the WTO Ministerial Conference of 2001, resolved the conflict by reaffirming that TRIPS member states had the flexibility to circumvent patent rights to ensure the provision of affordable medicines. China has used its so-called TRIPS flexibilities to introduce legislation that supported its policies of constraining patenting and allowing the production of much less expensive generic medicines before their patents expired.

A Raised Patentability Standard – Adoption of Absolute Novelty

The Third Amendment of the Patent Law of the People's Republic of China was adopted on December 27, 2008, and became effective on October 1, 2009. A notable change was the adoption of an absolute novelty standard in assessing the novelty of all three categories of patents: invention patents, utility model patents, and design patents. The amendment replaced the old blended novelty standard with an absolute one, thus raising the bar of patentability for pharmaceutical products. Under the absolute novelty standard, it is required that any patent should not belong to any prior art or prior design, which means any technology or any design known to the public, in China or abroad, before the date of filing. This stringent novelty requirement holds regardless of who is responsible for the prior art activities. Under the amended Article 22, an identical invention or utility model disclosed in an earlier application by the same applicant prior to the filing date of a later application can be used as a novelty bar against any later application.

This new patentability standard may have a significant impact on the way in which patent validity is challenged in China. Under the new standard, public use or knowledge outside China destroys novelty and is therefore relevant in patent invalidation proceedings.

A Broader Standard for Issuing Compulsory Licensing

Compulsory licensing provides governments with the power to force companies to issue licences to other companies to produce the patented products under certain circumstances. While the patentee is supposed to be compensated for granting the licence, such compensation is typically significantly lower than the monopoly profits that would accrue from the sales of the patented product by the patentee. The use of compulsory licences or often the threat of imposing a compulsory licence offer important means for governments to achieve a reduction in the costs of medicines.

The amended Patent Law provides a more definitive statutory basis for compelling compulsory licences, incorporating the Doha Declaration principles into the Patent Law, and contains new rules that restrict the general scope of compulsory licensing while making it more feasible and likely for compulsory licences to be granted in the area of pharmaceuticals (new Article 50).

The option of compulsory licensing provided under the amendment is no longer limited to just "for the treatment of contagious diseases" as under the Pharmaceutical Compulsory Licensing Measures. In theory, this opens up a broad range of pharmaceutical therapies to compulsory licensing.

Moreover, China's State Intellectual Property Office (SIPO) promulgated the "Measures for the Compulsory Licensing for Patent Implementation" in 2012. The Measures waive the charges for applying for compulsory licensing, which reduces the cost of a compulsory licensing application.

The Bolar Exemption

To obtain marketing authorization, a generic company will usually require the use of patent-protected medicinal products in tests and trials. Such production and use of the products by generic manufacturers for testing may be considered a patent infringement. In order to facilitate the market entry of generic products, many countries have introduced legal exemptions from patent infringement for tests and trials involving patented medicines for purposes of obtaining marketing authorization. These provisions are called "Bolar exemption."

The 2008 amended Patent Law of China specifies that it is not an act of infringement if a patented drug or medical apparatus is manufactured, used, or imported solely for the purposes of obtaining and providing information for administrative approval. This regulation gives producers of generic medicines a "free pass" to conduct pre-marketing research and take other actions associated with the approval process, thus hastening the introduction of the cheaper generic versions of the drug very soon after expiration of the patent.

According to the Drug Registration Regulation, which was approved by the China Food and Drug Administration (CFDA) on June 18, 2007, a company may, within two years prior to the expiration of a patent held by another firm, apply for registration to use the patented product for research and other pre-marketing approval operations. The CFDA must "review the application according to the Regulation and, after expiration of the patent, approve production or import for an application that meets the requirements" (Article 19). On February 20, 2014, the CFDA released a second proposed draft of revisions to the Drug Registration Regulation (second draft DRR). The second draft DRR modifies Article 19 by deleting its limitation on the submission of generic drug applications to no earlier than two years prior to the expiry of originator patent terms, thus allowing generic applications to be filed at any time. Under the second draft DRR, the CFDA may issue a licence for a generic drug while a patent exists, but the licence will not become effective until the originator manufacturer patent has expired. The CFDA was replaced in 2018 by the National Medical Products Administration (NMPA).

Despite all these constraints on patenting by foreign firms and the provision of the option for domestic manufacturers to produce generic substitutes for expensive patented medicines, successful branding has enabled the multinational corporations to compete successfully with generic substitutes. Arguably, the Chinese government's inclination to restrict foreign firms' promotional strategies was constrained by the desire to attract them to invest in and move some of their research and development activities to China.

Strengthening Primary Health Care

China's long-term strategy to improve the efficiency of resource allocation involves building a strong delivery system based on primary health care, anchored in community health centres in cities and village clinics in rural areas (Waldmeir 2013). Providers of primary health care are eventually supposed to serve as so-called health gatekeepers, managing referrals to specialist care and hospitals (e.g., Xu and Lu 2014). This planned expansion of their role will have an impact on the costs of medicines since medicines prescribed at community health centres are usually cheaper than those at large hospitals. Furthermore, the strengthening of primary care and health promotion is likely to reduce the incidence of illnesses and thus contribute to cost reduction in the long run.

The Thirteenth Five-Year Plan for Health Sector Development, promulgated and implemented by the State Council on December 27, 2016, proposes to "improve the community-level medical service model, [and] make headway in improving the capacity of general practitioners (family practitioners)." It sets the goal to develop a more logical system for obtaining medical care, where "a patient's initial diagnosis takes place at a community-level institution" and more medical health care service can be provided within the county (State Council Information Office of the People's Republic of China 2017).

Unintended Consequences and Implementation Problems

Despite the government's renewed emphasis on health care in general and access to affordable medicine in particular, expressed in the Healthy China 2030 Outline (October 25, 2016) (The State Council Information Office of the People's Republic of China 2017) and the various programs and reforms initiated as a result, a variety of unintended consequences and implementation problems slowed progress toward the goal of providing access to affordable essential medicines to the population.

Drug Shortages and Quality Problems Associated with Price Control

Medicines on the central and provincial essential drug lists and reimbursement lists are subject to price controls: the NDRC establishes maximum retail price ceilings used for procurement and dispensing. As a result, the average price of essential drugs at primary medical facilities has been reduced by 30 percent (*China News* 2013). However, while China's leaders want medicines to be more accessible and affordable, their attempts to ensure the lowest prices for drugs have had some unintended consequences (Wen 2014).

The first unintended consequences were drug shortages. Government statistics show more than 2,000 incidents of drug shortages in 2018 (Zhu 2019). In more recent years, the number of such incidents has been rising (Huang et al. 2021). Most of these shortages involve critical care drugs and common clinical drugs. One thing common to these classes of drugs is that they are usually the so-called cheap drugs (*lianjia yao*) (Ibid). For instance, two of three pharmaceutical companies registered to produce Pyridostigmine Bromide Tablets (Pyridostigmine is used to treat the symptoms of myasthenia gravis) have halted production in recent years after restrictions squeezed out profits (Yu 2016). In September 2016, the state-owned Shanghai Zhongxi Sunve Pharmaceutical Co. Ltd, the only company still making Pyridostigmine Bromide, found problems in its production process and issued a nationwide recall of the Pyridostigmine Bromide produced between October 2015 and April 2016. At the time, Chinese patients suffering from myasthenia gravis symptoms found themselves running out of the life-saving tablets (Li 2016).

Drug shortages adversely affect the efficacy of drug therapy and compromise or delay medical procedures. In some cases, patients have to turn to foreign branded drugs or other substitutes.[9] While cheap versions of the drugs are disappearing from the market, "new drugs" with the same element name hit shelves across the country, in new dosage forms or with different packaging. For example, a bottle of vitamin C tablets that used to be sold at CNY 2 is priced at about CNY 100 when provided as a vitamin capsule (Liao Haijin 2014).

A second unintended consequence of price control is that it raises the probability that drug quality and safety will be compromised as manufacturers seek to cut costs to maintain profit margins. For example, in 2012, some drug-capsule manufacturers were found to be using industrial gelatin to cut production costs (Sina 2012), even though industrial gelatin contained chromium, which can be carcinogenic with frequent exposure (Burkitt 2014).

To deal with drug shortages and safety problems and give the public better access to commonly used medications at relatively low prices, the government has decided to scrap caps on retail prices for low-cost medicine and has been moving toward free-market pricing for pharmaceuticals. In April 2014, eight government departments, including the National Health and Family Planning Commission, the National Development and Reform Commission, the China Food and Drug Administration, and the Ministry of Finance, issued an "Opinion on Securing the Supply of Commonly Used Low-Price Drugs," "allowing pharmaceutical companies to set prices as long as the daily cost of taking the drug "remains in a certain range." In May 2016, China's NDRC and three other government agencies announced that from June 1st, price control of the majority of medicines would be removed to allow the market to play a larger role in setting drug prices (National Development and Reform Commission 2016).

Corruption in the Drug Procurement Process
In China, public hospitals, clinics, and other medical institutions obtain most of their drugs through a centralized bidding and procurement process at the provincial level.[10] The central government has instructed provincial governments to organize public bidding for essential medicines to achieve the lowest possible procurement prices.

The complex and multi-step process presents many opportunities for corruption at each step, including selection for a provincial procurement list, procurement by a specific hospital, and prescriptions by an individual doctor (Covington and Burling LLP 2014). In 2013, the Ministry of Public Security of the People's Republic of China announced a graft investigation into the Chinese operations of GlaxoSmithKline (now GSK plc), a British conglomerate, in what appears to be part of a broader effort to crack down on bribery in the pharmaceutical and medical service sector. The investigation showed that GSK had used bribery to promote sales of prescription drugs and vaccines in the Chinese market. In an interview with the state media, Liang Hong, a detained GSK executive, estimated that without this sort of spending, GSK's prices could be reduced by 20 to 30 percent (*Economist* 2014a).

Inefficient Management of Health Insurance Funds
Historically, the financial structure underlying China's key insurance schemes was flawed. Public health insurance is normally designed as a pay-as-you-go system (Wasem, Greß, and Okma 2004). There is no need to keep large

reserves, except for a certain percentage for contingencies. Moreover, the huge amount of idle funds raises concerns over risk of embezzlement and misappropriation. Since 1999, the surplus rate has exceeded 20% every year except 2010, which is much higher than the surplus rate of developed countries (with an average of below 10%). Despite the huge amount of idle health insurance funds, not much was done to ease the complaints about low reimbursement rates (Meng et al. 2012). Copayments and deductibles remained high.[11]

The government has begun taking multiple measures to mobilize the idle health insurance funds, such as raising the insurance coverage and health benefits provided under the UEBMI by eliminating the reimbursement limit and raising the proportion of health care expenditures eligible for insurance claims (Wang Jie 2013). Meanwhile, the NDRC and other relevant departments are doing research regarding the equivalent reimbursement system for foreign name brand and domestic generic drugs. Under this system, medical insurance pays the same proportion of the cost for foreign name brand drugs as for domestic generic drugs. Moreover, some effective medicines for treatment of catastrophic disease that were not included in the medical insurance drug list are now eligible for reimbursement. In Nanjing, for example, three expensive anti-cancer drugs – Herceptin, Glivec, and Tasigna – were added to the city's reimbursement formulary on January 1, 2014. By the end of 2017, the surplus had been reduced significantly (Ministry of Finance 2018).

Inadequate Hospital Financing after the Public Hospital Financing Reform

As previously indicated, all public hospitals in China can no longer rely on profits derived from the sale of pharmaceuticals, and they face the dilemma of how funds and revenues previously derived from drug sales will be replaced.

Medical services accounted for just over 50% of public hospital revenue in 2011, according to Ministry of Health data. About 40% came from drug prescriptions, while the rest was from other income as well as government subsidies, which have fallen steadily since the 1980s. Hospital administrators can set fees for in-patient care, nursing, and laboratory tests, but the state fixes the cost of operations to make surgery affordable to ordinary Chinese. It effectively caps the cost of many prescribed medicines by setting a suggested price. This leaves hospitals little room to top up wages required to retain staff (Takada 2013).

Civil service rules set by the Ministry of Personnel give job guarantees to physicians and other personnel, irrespective of productivity. While inadequate

salaries and low social status cause many of the more talented and productive health professionals to leave their positions, and often their professions,
to seek other professional opportunities, those who remain have few incentives to work harder to fill the gaps that are created (Wee 2018). By 2014, the
central and local governments had invested CNY 3 trillion in the health care
system, but the salary of health care practitioners still remained very low
(Bai 2014). In 2016, doctors in China were paid, on average, only CNY 7,144
(US$1,070) a month (Sohu 2017).

As the need for doctors to augment their salaries remains strong, formal
changes to the long-standing practices surrounding the prescription of
drugs in public hospitals face resistance and subversion.

Weak Primary Health Care
Since 2006, the Ministry of Health has been promoting the idea of "minor
illnesses (treated) in the community, serious illness to the hospital" (Wu 2006),
and the Twelfth Five-Year Plan for Health Sector Development set the goal of
improving the service capacity and quality of county hospitals (State Council
of the People's Republic of China 2011). In practice, however, people still prefer to seek medical treatment at prestigious hospitals instead of local health
care centres, even for minor complaints such as colds and flu, leading to over-
crowding and overworked doctors in county hospitals (Wu and Li 2013).

There are several reasons for the preference for hospital care and the
pressure on county hospitals. First, Chinese patients generally have more
faith in hospitals than in clinics and community health centres. Doctors
in hospitals are regarded as more professional and experienced, which is
usually the case. Second, demand for primary health care services is increasing every year due to the aging population, expanded insurance coverage, and rising patients' expectations, but the supply of primary care
physicians continues to decline. From 2008 to 2012, eighty-six county hospitals lost 9,392 doctors, most of whom were clinicians. Among these doctors, over 70 percent left for upper-level hospitals, where their salary would
be more than doubled.

Third, some patients are not able to get the medicines they need from
clinics and community health centres. Under the essential drugs program,
primary-level medical institutions are required to prescribe only essential
drugs in the essential drug lists. Patients with chronic conditions have to go
to hospitals because the drugs they rely on are usually in the health insurance reimbursement drug list but not in the essential drug lists (Wu and Li
2013). The shortage of some essential medicines exacerbates the situation.

Improvement in the efficiency of resource allocation will therefore depend on whether the government can reform the hospital sector to improve the quality and efficiency of service provided at primary-level medical institutions.

Weak Implementation of IP Laws

The publication of new measures and the amendments to existing laws may signify a growing willingness on the part of the Chinese government to use compulsory licensing and other legal tools either to compel licensing or perhaps to use threats of compulsory licensing as a bargaining chip to extract concessions from pharmaceutical companies and other patent holders in limited, strategically important cases. In practice, however, as of June 2020, no single compulsory licence had been issued by SIPO in the preceding decade, even while the basic underlying mechanisms are already in the PRC statute books (Li 2020).

Although high pharmaceutical costs coupled with a vast population are seen as a major hurdle in achieving the goals of China's health care reform as elaborated in its 13th Five-Year Plan (2016–20), competing priorities, such as the desire to foster a favourable intellectual property rights environment either for its own nascent biotech industry or to attract foreign investment, would also temper the government's willingness to exercise these powers.[12]

Generic Medicines Face Longer Wait for Approval

The 2007 amended Regulation on the Administration of Drug Registration governs the approval and registration processes applicable to drugs in China. The amended regulation uses the concepts of "new" drugs and "generic" drugs. A new drug is one that has not been previously marketed in China, whereas a generic drug is one that has an existing national drug standard and was previously approved to be marketed by the CFDA.

A generic drug application is also called an "Abbreviated New Drug Application (ANDA)," as the process may omit pre-clinical and clinical test data on the basis that the drug is already on the market and its effectiveness and safety are understood. In China, the examination and approval process for a generic drug application used to take an average of one year, which was much longer than the average of two months in countries such as the United States and India, according to industry analysts (Miao and Wu 2014). The delays, caused by a growing backlog of applications at the CFDA, are costing consumers and the government money as they continue in some cases to pay for branded drugs even after the drugs' patents expire.

The situation is gradually getting better but is not satisfactory. In January 2020, the State Administration for Market Regulation issued the new Measures for the Administration of Drug Registration to replace the old 2007 version. The new measures provide that the approval process of generic drugs should not exceed 200 days (State Administration for Market Regulation 2020).

Other Challenges

Going forward, access to affordable high-quality medicines in China faces two other important challenges (IMA Pharma 2013): 1) lack of innovation in the domestic pharmaceutical industry and 2) lack of knowledge and entrenched patient beliefs about medicines.

Lack of First-in-Class Innovation in the Domestic Pharmaceutical Industry

A first-in-class medication is a pharmaceutical that uses a "new and unique mechanism of action" to treat a particular medical condition (Lanthier et al. 2013). The "me-too" (or follow-on) model of drug development, on the other hand, is based on the success of a first-in-class medication, by developing drugs that have identical primary mechanisms of action to those of the initial first-in-class drugs but are chemically distinct.

China's pharmaceutical industry has focused on drug targets that have already been validated (Huang 2021). Highly validated targets such a PD-1, PD-(L)1, BTK, CD47, etc., have been extremely popular among Chinese pharmaceutical companies in recent years (Ibid.).

Why is "me-too" drug development so popular in China? Lack of funding is one major reason. The pursuit of First-in-Class drug innovation requires a large investment in research and is time-consuming. There is also the clinical risk that even after early validation, there is no guarantee that the products will result in an effective treatment in humans. Companies that have limited financial resources and are unable or unwilling to take the financial risk usually sell new potential drug candidates to big foreign companies at very early stages of drug development. Local pharmaceutical companies typically cannot afford to compete with foreign multinationals.

Attempting to transform its pharmaceutical sector into an innovation hub, the Chinese government has been providing strong incentive programs to support and foster R&D in the domestic pharmaceutical and biotechnology industry. These incentives include direct funding opportunities (Lux Research 2013) and tax relief (PricewaterhouseCoopers 2009).

Lack of Knowledge and Entrenched Patient Beliefs about Medicines
The degree of prescription and dispensing of generic medicines in a country is largely a function of three characteristics:

- the national and/or private insurance companies' pharmaceutical "out-of-pocket" pricing
- the system of patent protection
- the cultural aspects of pharmaceuticals use, particularly the attitudes of both doctors and patients and the information available to them about the availability and efficacy of generic substitutes for branded and patented medicines. (Dukes et al. 2003)

The first two characteristics can be altered directly as part of the formal regulatory and policy reform of the health care system. The third characteristic is more problematic as it involves a change in patients' entrenched beliefs and practices. Doctors in China often hear patients requesting the most expensive brand medicine (Li 2013). Patients influenced by advertising often insist that certain branded drugs be prescribed. Such insistence has a major impact on prescribing, according to a recent study, reducing its efficacy and increasing costs (McKinlay et al. 2014).

An important pillar of the right to health articulated in the International Covenant on Economic, Social and Cultural Rights (2000) seeks to guarantee every person has access to affordable essential medicines.[13] SDG 3 sets a target for China to achieve universal health coverage, including affordable medicines and vaccines for all. China has accepted this obligation to provide affordable essential medicines to all its citizens as well as more generally accessible affordable health care. The challenges are enormous, and China's achievements are impressive, yet the goal of affordable health care remains elusive. Governments can promote access to affordable health care by setting policies that increase incomes of individuals and families; by reducing the prices of medicines and health care services and/or by reducing the share that individuals pay for them; and by ensuring the availability of supplies of effective, high-quality medicines and services. In recent times, China has pursued a multi-pronged approach emphasizing economic growth, expansion of health care insurance coverage, price controls of essential medicines, and an attempt to rationalize its health care system, all of which strengthen and increase the role of primary care.

China's policies have resulted in impressive economic growth and increases in per capita incomes. While its phenomenal economic growth has propelled its economy to that of the second-largest behind the United States, a significant percentage of the population remains below the national poverty line and cannot afford to pay for essential medicines or access affordable health services. Despite the impressive strides that China has made in the past decade toward increasing health care coverage for its population, public insurance covers only a fraction of the cost of medicines and services. China needs to invest more in financing the expansion of health insurance coverage and use its resources more efficiently. Increasing financial resources without developing an effective governance system that will increase accountability and direct resources to the most vulnerable segments of the population will fail to achieve the goals of providing access to health care to all the people.

In the past, controlling prices of medicines in an attempt to make them more affordable has produced unintended consequences, including shortages and low-quality medicines. Other measures that were introduced to reduce the costs of medicines, such as the elimination of price markups that served to finance hospitals, had unintended consequences for other segments of the health care system, making them less affordable. An infusion of funds into the health care system (to replace the gap that the elimination of markups in the sales of medicines by hospitals created) is needed to adequately finance hospital operations as well as subsidize inadequately financed physicians' salaries. Though the elimination of markups was effective in reducing the prices of medicines, and it eliminated perverse incentives to prescribe expensive branded ones, the resulting financial gap meant increases in the price of health care services that were not regulated, and an aggravation of the shortage of physicians and complementary resources in the health care system.

Another challenge to the reform stems from people's lack of knowledge and unfounded beliefs about health and health care issues. For example, there is evidence that large numbers of patients believe that branded medicines are necessarily more effective than generic ones, which encourages them to demand expensive branded medicines even when generic, functionally equivalent but cheaper medicines are available. China must invest in public health education and impose regulatory controls on pharmaceutical companies that market misleading advertising campaigns directly to patients if it is to change the consumption patterns of medicine and create "smart" consumers.

Competition between suppliers of medicines may help push prices down, but monopolies created by the patent system stifle competition and lead to high prices. The government has in place the legal and regulatory tools to reduce the impact of patents on the availability and prices of medicines. Unfortunately, these tools are often not used because of other government policy concerns, such as the desire to foster innovative domestic R&D activity in the pharmaceutical sector and to attract leading multinational corporations to invest in R&D in China.

The tension between economic and social objectives underlies the debate over the extent and nature of the reform of the health care system. There is, however, an emerging consensus about the need to reform the health care system to remove perverse incentives that are costly both in terms of health and economics, as well as to seek innovative solutions to growing demand. This, however, will require a political resolve to overcome the resistance of entrenched interest groups.

NOTES

1 https://sdgs.un.org/goals/goal3.
2 China's proportion at the end of the period was just below 6.2% of GNP and is considered to be low compared with low-income countries (6.2%) and industrialized countries (8.1%). The proportion of Canada's GDP spent on health care was 11.5% in 2017, and 11.1% in 2016.
3 Catastrophic health spending is defined as out-of-pocket health spending exceeding 10% or 25% of total household consumption of income, according to the Global Monitoring Report on Financial Protection in Health 2021 by the World Health Organization and the World Bank (World Health Organization & World Bank 2021).
4 Patient strategies for responding to the unethical professional practices of physicians and hospitals encouraged by these incentives are discussed in detail in Chapter 8.
5 Some rural residents used to complain about rising insurance fees and having to pay two premiums, one for basic medical expenses and one for serious illnesses.
6 Though the complementary roles of the western and traditional Chinese health care systems and the need to treat them equally were recognized with the foundation of the People's Republic of China, the formal recognition in law giving them equal emphasis and maximizing their roles in health care was introduced only in the 2016 Law of the People's Republic of China on Traditional Chinese Medicine (http://www.lawinfochina.com/display.aspx?id=22978&lib=law).

7 Seeking to build on its success at expanding basic coverage, in 2012 the Ministry of Health announced a special fund of CNY 125 billion (US$20 billion) in new health care spending alongside a proposal to expand insurance plans by offering catastrophic disease coverage nationwide by 2020.

8 https://www.wto.org/english/docs_e/legal_e/27-trips_01_e.htm.

9 For example, in 2013, the cheap and effective drugs such as Tapazole (5 mg, 100 tablets, CNY 1.9–4.9) started to disappear from the market. Patients have to buy Thyrozol, produced by a German company. At present, even Thyrozol is in short supply and doctors have to prescribe propylthiouracil as a substitute.

10 Over 80% of drugs sold through hospitals are purchased through the bidding process (KPMG Advisory [China] Limited 2011).

11 With comprehensive coverage, people pay 40% of all health care costs themselves, as either premiums or out-of-pocket payments (Süssmuth-Dyckerhoff and Wang 2010).

12 The 13th Five-Year Plan (2016–20) released by the Chinese government emphasizes its goal to establish an innovation-oriented economy and to promote IP protections.

13 https://www.ohchr.org/en/professionalinterest/pages/cescr.aspx.

Mixed Billing and New Medicine in Japan
Will Lifting the Ban on Mixed Billing Improve Access to Health Care or Crash the System?

YOSHITAKA WADA

Most developed nations have universally accessible health care systems that aspire to provide quality essential services and access to affordable medicines in alignment with the target of Sustainable Development Goal (SDG) 3.8: "Achieve access to safe, effective, quality and affordable essential medicines and vaccines for all."[1] However, although the treatments covered, the range of medicines available, and the percentage of health care costs covered vary from country to country, there is one issue faced by every country that strives to meet SDG 3.8: how to handle new medicines and new forms of medical treatment not yet covered by health insurance. Of course, once the safety and efficacy of new drugs or devices have been acknowledged, the obvious avenue for the state is to include the new treatment within the scope of the health care insurance plan. However, it is not entirely clear how to treat – and bill – new health services, some of which are at the cutting edge of technology, at the stage when they are not yet officially approved and are therefore still uninsured.

Different countries have taken different approaches to the billing of new or innovative health services in their public health care system. In Canada, for example, if the patient receives medical treatment that exceeds the scope of health insurance coverage, the portion of costs within the scope of health insurance is paid for at an official price, while the portion exceeding this scope is subject to free price setting. Billing can be mixed, meaning that it can be done for both the insured and uninsured portion of care together (Kawaguchi 2012). The same method has been adopted in a number of countries.

In Britain, conversely, availing of both public (recognized) and private (unrecognized) medical care to treat the same illness is not permitted. However, if a difficult-to-treat case falls outside the scope of the National Health Service (NHS), combined medical care is permitted on a self-paying basis for patients with urgent life-threatening conditions. The Compassionate Use (CU) system allows patients to receive unrecognized medical care at their own request and at their own expense, thereby treating it as an emergency escape.

In Japan, if *even one portion* of the treatment or medicines delivered is not covered by health insurance, the entire cost is considered a health care service not covered by health insurance. As such, no health insurance (health plan) is applied, even to the treatment or medicines that would normally be expected to lie within the scope of coverage. In this case, the patient, who would normally pay 30 percent of the costs of medical treatment within the scope of health insurance, will have to either pay the cost in full or abandon treatment or medicines outside the scope of health insurance coverage. With a view to preventing the proliferation of unsafe, unrecognized treatment, combining health care provided by universal health insurance and health care services not covered by health insurance is not permitted. Of course, certain exceptions are recognized, such as coverage of expenses for high-level advanced forms of treatment under the specialized treatment expenses scheme, as well as for clinical trials. In these cases, patients must pay only the portion of costs outside the scope of health insurance coverage, with health insurance covering the rest. However, in Japan, because most forms of treatment and medicines are within the scope of coverage of the health insurance system (universal health care), this approach is taken only in truly exceptional cases.

It bears noting that the problem of the medical expenses burden is not simply a question of patients' access to medical care – it is connected with the trend toward deploying internationally produced medicines and medical equipment. New medicines and medical equipment go on the market only after clinical trials and inspections in their countries of origin. Initially, they are normally seen as lying outside the scope of health insurance. The question of how such newly developed medicines and medical equipment should be included in health insurance, and to what extent, is then naturally of crucial concern to the manufacturers of these products. Furthermore, whether or not mixed billing for medical treatment is allowed is a pressing issue for global companies.

A whole host of interrelated and sometimes conflicting needs and interests converge in this area. They include but are not confined to: patients' needs for cheap and comprehensive access to medical care; patients' needs for advanced special treatment; medical professionals' needs for ongoing improvements in advanced techniques; the needs of companies to make profits in the global arena; and the needs of government and industry to support them. By investigating this interwoven yet tangled web of interests and needs, this chapter will discuss the complexities of the movement to secure domestic access to medical care against the backdrop of international business trends, taking the discussion on mixed billing in Japan as our overarching theme.

Universal Health Care in Japan

Under Japanese law, people, including Japanese and foreign nationals who have been approved for more than three months, are required to be covered by health care insurance. Moreover, Japanese doctors are obliged by the Doctor Act to treat even foreign nationals who are not covered by universal health care insurance, and the uncollectible medical costs in some cases are causing hospital deficits.

If you are an employee, you are covered by Employees' Health Insurance, with employers and employees share the costs equally. In this scheme, the premium is paid on a per-family basis, scaled to the annual income level. This means that as long as an employee joins the health insurance system, the whole family, which includes an unemployed spouse and children, is covered without additional costs. If one is not enrolled in Employees' Health Insurance (for example, if the person is a student or a self-employed individual), one has to join the National Health Insurance, which is run directly by local governments. In short, all Japanese citizens are covered by one of these insurance systems.

When it comes to benefits, there is no difference between the two health insurance schemes. Notwithstanding highly advanced care or medicines that are not acknowledged by the Ministry of Health, Labour and Welfare, a wide range of medical care is covered and the price for care services is strictly regulated by the government to ensure affordability. All prescribed medicines sold at drugstores, rehabilitation costs, and even costs for acupuncture and massage are covered. No matter which health insurance one chooses, each patient pays 30% for the regulated medical care and prescribed drug cost, while the insurance pays the remaining 70%. The patient's premium becomes lower depending on age. Those aged seventy years and older pay only 20% or 10%. Moreover, if a person's monthly payment for health care exceeds approximately US$900, the excess is reimbursed from health insurance.

This means that Japanese citizens can receive a wide range of medical care at the same modest cost no matter what health insurance they have, and the monthly payment for health care seldom exceeds $900. Thus, the universal health care schemes in Japan have tackled one of the most challenging aspects of ensuring access to health care: *affordability*. However, a rare exception is not yet acknowledged – advanced medicine or treatment technology that some patients with serious illnesses are eager to use.

Litigation Calling for Lifting of the Ban on Mixed Billing

In 2001, patient N.K. was diagnosed with kidney cancer and extirpative surgery was performed on the left kidney. Interferon therapy and LAK (Lymphokine-Activated Killer) cell treatment were then commenced because the patient required bone transplants to the back of the head and neck. While LAK cell treatment was not a form of health care provided by universal health insurance at the time, it was covered under the Ministry of Health, Labour and Welfare's specialized treatment expenses scheme. Thus, the go-ahead was given for both types of treatment without any particular difficulty, and all expenses were covered by health insurance.

In 2005, however, an expert panel at the Ministry of Health, Labour and Welfare reported that LAK cell treatment had failed to demonstrate adequate therapeutic effect. Consequently, this type of treatment was excluded from the specialized treatment expenses scheme and, as such, was completely removed from the scope of health insurance coverage. The hospital nonetheless continued the treatment and the mass media quickly got wind of this. One weekly magazine ran a story titled "Combining Medical Treatment Covered and Not Covered by Health Insurance – This Hospital Is Breaking the Law by Flouting the Rules on Mixed Billing." The hospital subsequently ceased the LAK cell treatment. In order to continue therapy with LAK cells, N.K. was forced to pay out of pocket for both insured and uninsured treatment, including interferon therapy.

In 2006, N.K. brought a suit in the Tokyo District Court, arguing that the ban on mixed billing – which had not only denied a patient the opportunity of treatment but even led to penalties such as the revocation of the medical institution's status as health insurance doctors –was unconstitutional. The case was so complex that numerous lawyers declined to take it, and N.K took the stand in his first trial without legal representation.

The arguments in the case revolved around the fact that there were no clearly stated regulations or legislation underpinning the ban on mixed billing. Article 63 of the Health Insurance Act outlines general provision of medical treatment covered by health insurance. Furthermore, Article 86 lays out the provisions for benefits for uninsured treatment, stipulating that certain treatments not covered by health insurance but designated by the Ministry of Health, Labour and Welfare "shall be paid for from health insurance." While not expressly supporting a ban on mixed billing, the government took the opposite interpretation of the letter of the law, arguing that the method of treatment in question was not one of those outside the scope of coverage of health insurance but designated by the Ministry of Health, Labour and Welfare to be paid for from health insurance.[2] The logic of its position on why this combined therapy was inadmissible was that medical treatment forms an indivisible whole, and if any form of treatment whatsoever that is not included under health insurance coverage were to be included, it would have a decisive effect on the character of medical treatment as a whole. On the practical level, the basis of the government's argument was that if the treatment were to be recognized, there was a risk that unsafe forms of medical therapy, of dubious effect, could proliferate.

N.K., arguing against the logic behind this interpretation of the law, stressed the dubious constitutionality of the process leading up to the proceedings. In 2007, the Tokyo District Court found in N.K.'s favour, stating that "examination of the Health Insurance Law, etc. does not find a basis that if medical treatment outside of insurance is used together, insurance medical treatment will not be able to receive benefits," and that interpretations and practices by the state were incorrect.

In 2009, however, the Tokyo High Court reversed that decision, stating that there were logical reasons behind the ban on mixed billing, and so the government's suppression of mixed billing was not unconstitutional. The following issues were raised in this case:

1 In the case where the patient receives both insured and uninsured treatment performed in the same series of medical treatments, was such medical treatment to be seen as an indivisible whole? Does section 1 of Article 63 of the Health Insurance Act on "the provision of medical treatment" apply, and if so, should it be relaxed?

2 Can Article 86, which covers the system of payment for combined therapies not covered under health insurance, be interpreted in such a manner that mixed billing, which was not included in this system, could fall within the purview of section 1 of Article 63 of the Health Insurance Act on "the provision of medical treatment," as health care provided by universal health insurance?

3 Could it be deemed unconstitutional that, even though the same health insurance premiums are paid, in the case of mixed billing, the health insurance benefit of that portion undertaken as health care provided by universal health insurance cannot be received?

With regard to these questions, the Tokyo High Court in 2009 rendered decisions along the following lines:

1 Mixed billing is clearly forbidden under the law.
2 Because mixed billing is forbidden, the application of health insurance is inadmissible, even if there are no clear stipulations.
3 Because health insurance does not apply to medical expenses for the specialized treatment expenses scheme and combined therapies not included in health insurance, health insurance by analogy also does not apply to mixed billing.
4 If health insurance were supposed to apply to mixed billing too, the specialized treatment expenses scheme, which provides exemptions whereby combined therapies involving treatments both covered and not covered by health insurance are recognized, would lose its reason for existing.
5 The Constitution does not forbid distinctions made on logical grounds; since there are certain logical grounds for banning mixed billing, this measure lies within the discretionary power of the law and does not constitute a breach of the Constitution even in cases where health insurance cannot be provided.
6 The Constitution is not breached, because the right to life is not compromised in cases where a certain method of medical treatment is removed from the provisions of the specialized treatment expenses scheme on the grounds that its effectiveness is unclear.
7 The Constitution is not breached, because there is scope for other forms of activated lymph therapy than LAK cell treatment.

In 2011, the Supreme Court rejected N.K's final appeal, confirming the appellate court's earlier decisions. Thus, the legal system also approved the

TABLE 2.1

History of litigation on mixed billing in Japan

Date	Policy	Litigation
2001	Beginning of relaxation of government regulation.	
2004	*Council for Regulatory Reform and Privatization*'s interim report for the medical field proposes to allow mixed billing at hospitals satisfying some conditions on medical care and quality, evoking strong opposition.	
2006	*Non-insurance combined medical expenses scheme* allows mixed billing for medicine and methods of medical treatment still being tested in clinical trials – the result of compromise.	*Litigation at Tokyo District Court* alleges that the ban on mixed billing – which had denied a patient the opportunity of treatment – was unconstitutional.
2007		*Tokyo District Court* decides in favour of the plaintiff.
2009		*Tokyo High Court* overturns Tokyo District Court decision, stating that there were logical reasons behind the ban on mixed billing.
2011		*Supreme Court* rejects the plaintiff's final appeal.
2014	*Council for Regulatory Reform and Privatization* proposes choice-based medical system – patients who wish to avail of advanced medical treatment not covered by health insurance could still have their expenses covered – evoking strong opposition.	
2016	*Medical treatment system that is supposed to be responsive to patients' requests* is nothing more than a framework for listing coverage provided by health insurance and the ban on mixed billing has not been fully lifted.	

policy of banning mixed billing. However, the period around the court case certainly saw heated debate on this policy, with a wide range of viewpoints being put forward. We turn now to how this process unfolded. Table 2.1 summarizes the history of policies and litigation regarding mixed billing. Next, let's consider the development of policies regarding mixed billing.

The Unfolding Debate over the Policy on Mixed Billing

Beginning in 2001, the government headed by Prime Minister Junichiro Koizumi moved forward on the relaxation of government regulation on a range of fronts, perhaps best exemplified by the move to privatize the Post Office – and the resultant furor. Koizumi was the minister of health, labour, and welfare twice, and the medical field was an important issue for him. Even before that, some had called for a lifting of the ban on medical facilities entering the market as publicly traded stock companies, as well as a lifting of the ban on mixed billing. As prime minister, Koizumi demonstrated strong leadership in the relaxation of government regulation in the medical field, and initiatives along these lines made concrete progress. In March 2004, the Council for Regulatory Reform and Privatization recommended that mixed billing be allowed at hospitals that satisfied some conditions on medical care quality and technology. An interim report issued by the council that same year called for a lifting of the ban on mixed billing at medical facilities at or above a certain level, in order to provide patients with freedom of choice. The report identified several adverse effects of the ban on mixed billing:

- Japanese health insurance does not cover medical techniques that have been approved overseas. This lack of coverage obstructs the efforts of medical professionals in Japan and restricts patients' freedom of choice.
- If mixed billing becomes possible, patients will be able to access advanced medical techniques while continuing to have health insurance for general treatment. People will therefore enjoy enhanced access to medical care. The ban on mixed billing is the fundamental obstacle to this.
- Under the specialized treatment expenses scheme, the government allows mixed billing on a limited and partial basis; this limits competition and innovation in the field of medical technology.

In addition, the council recommended that the lifting of mixed billing at the discretion of the individual medical institution be comprehensively allowed at hospitals of a certain standard and over in terms of the use of medicines and methods of treatment not covered by health insurance. Prime

Minister Koizumi also favoured these proposals, and the proceedings wrapped up with the conclusion that the ban should be lifted within the year.

Opposition to this move took a wide variety of forms. The Ministry of Health, Labour and Welfare was clear in its opinion that, given the disparity in knowledge between doctor and patient, there was a risk that the most appropriate experimental medical techniques and medicines might not always be employed. The Japan Medical Association also came out strongly against the proposals. One reason was the risk that the scope of health care provided by universal health insurance could not be further broadened. Another concern was that Yoshihiko Miyauchi, the head of the Council for Regulatory Reform and Privatization, who was also chairperson and CEO of ORIX Corporation, ran a group of companies that included private health insurance firms; this seemed indicative of a shift away from public medical health insurance toward private health insurance, constituting a conflict of interest. On the other hand, during the debate, the heads of the three influential university hospitals of the University of Tokyo and Kyoto and Osaka Universities – all major players in the ongoing development of Japanese medicine – forwarded a joint written statement to the council in support of lifting the ban, on the grounds that doing so would broaden patient choice.

In December 2004, Prime Minister Koizumi and Minister of State for Regulatory Reform Murakami Seiichiro released a document titled "Basic Agreement on the Issue of Mixed Billing." Given the strong opposition from the Ministry of Health, Labour and Welfare, the Japan Medical Association, and other important players, it was decided that the ban on mixed billing would not be completely lifted. Instead, the decision was made to allow the combined use of insured and uninsured treatment under certain fixed rules, and to clarify the procedure for listing non-covered forms of medical treatment for health insurance. Under this system, medicine and methods of medical treatment that were still being tested in clinical trials for the purpose of listing them in the scope of health insurance in the future yet at the same time met set criteria for effectiveness and safety could be used in medical institutions that met certain standards. One might call this approach a provisional evaluation procedure with an eye toward the application of health insurance. In a sense, mixed billing received limited recognition, but the basic rule that medical treatment should be carried out on the basis of public health insurance remained intact. On the other hand, the range of combined therapies not covered by health insurance was broadened, substantially increasing their accessibility for patients who requested them.

Over the next decade, there was no major move in mixed-care issues and the situation was relatively calm. The matter did not stop there, however. The government's initiative to structurally reform the Japanese economy and to relax regulation was still ongoing, and the drive to lift the ban on mixed billing gained momentum in this context. In 2014, the Regulatory Reform Council, working under the government of Prime Minister Shinzo Abe, proposed a "choice-based medical treatment system." Under this system, patients who wished to avail of advanced medical treatment not covered by health insurance could still have their expenses covered. Ignoring previous debates and legal precedents, this proposal amounted to a de facto lifting of the ban on mixed billing in one clean sweep. The Ministry of Health, Labour and Welfare put up ferocious opposition, insisting that the safety and effectiveness of medical treatment could not be guaranteed under this framework, and it was joined in this stance by the Japan Medical Association and patients' groups such as the Japan Patients' Association.[3] Taking this into account, neither Prime Minister Abe nor the government as a whole expressed wholehearted agreement of this proposal, nor were there any major expressions of agreement from patients.

In 2015, on the prime minister's instructions, proposals for a "choice-based medical treatment system" were replaced by a proposal for a "medical treatment system responsive to patients' requests," a form which added in terms of safety and effectiveness to the previously proposed system. This proposal led to a revision of the Health Insurance Act, and went into effect in April 2016. Under the new framework, consideration for safety and efficiency would be demonstrated by setting a number of conditions, such as: 1) establishing the safety and efficiency of new treatments at specialist conferences; 2) restriction of untried forms of advanced medical treatment to specially designated medical institutions; and 3) obligation to present a written plan for listing the treatment for health insurance and to report adverse outcomes. The government has stressed the convenience for patients that will result from the increase in the number of choices available to them and in enhanced access to advanced medical care. However, the Ministry of Health, Labour and Welfare – which was tasked with turning this legislation into concrete reality and with planning out the new system – has maintained its original stance, insisting on treating the new system as nothing more than a framework for listing for health insurance. The system as it stands, from the ministry's point of view, is that while mixed billing may have become more widely practised than in the past, the ban has not been fully lifted. One can point to a certain oppositionist trend within the ministry, which had long been at loggerheads with the government over the question of lifting the ban on mixed billing. One can also point to it as an example of how the process of policy implementation works in a Japan where government agencies are exceptionally powerful.

Not only the Japan Medical Association but also patients' groups show strong opposition, however. Japan's foremost patients' groups – such as the Japan Patients' Association and the Federation of Cancer Patient Associations – also clearly expressed their opposition. A good deal of movement and debate is also predicted in the future with regard to the operation of this system. Specialist evaluation of safety and efficiency has become a necessary condition; the more conservative the approach taken by the specialists, the more the intentions underlying this system will be stymied. On the other hand, the more smoothly such evaluations go, the broader the scope of mixed billing's becoming "unbanned" will become. Further developments must be closely monitored on this score.

Underlying Interest of Each Actor's Position

Behind all the unfolding drama, one must ask, then: What were the various parties' interests underlying their positions? Figure 2.1 illustrates the distribution of the views of each actor. One would expect that patients suffering from incurable diseases such as cancer would welcome mixed billing, which would make available to them advanced medical treatment not covered by health insurance, along with combined therapies. Why did these, of all people, exhibit such strong opposition? Even as the medical profession as a whole was adamantly opposed, why did the heads of the country's three most prestigious and powerful medical schools come out in favour? And what did government and business have to gain? We now examine each of these groups in turn.

The Government and the Ministry of Finance

Why did Liberal Democratic Party governments from Koizumi to Abe persist in attempting to lift the ban on mixed billing in the face of such widespread opposition? Without a doubt, one reason was the need to get the ever-expanding medical budget under some sort of control. In Japan, the government exerts an iron grip on policy and policy-making, but of all the ministries, it is the Ministry of Finance that has the authority to wield general influence through its power over budget allocations. The stance that the government takes is in fact a reflection of the Finance Ministry's stance,

FIGURE 2.1

Conflicting positions on mixed billing

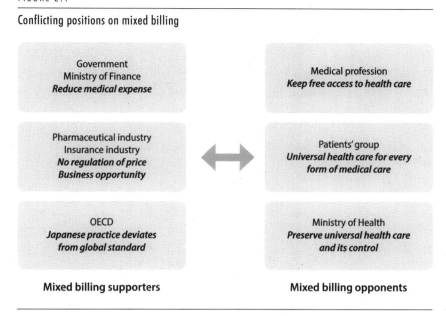

Government
Ministry of Finance
Reduce medical expense

Medical profession
Keep free access to health care

Pharmaceutical industry
Insurance industry
No regulation of price
Business opportunity

Patients' group
Universal health care for every
form of medical care

OECD
Japanese practice deviates
from global standard

Ministry of Health
Preserve universal health care
and its control

Mixed billing supporters   **Mixed billing opponents**

and the government's determination to shrink the medical budget gives us a glimpse into the ministry's thinking.

The greying of society is a problem common to all developed countries, but nowhere is it more acute than in Japan. Figure 2.2 (HIB 2011) gives an overview of medical expenditure per age group in 2011, broken down by age cohort (treatment as carried out by health insurance doctors).

Spending is overwhelmingly directed at the elderly, and the trend is predicted to only grow stronger over time. With the proportion of costs to be paid out of pocket set to only one-tenth for the elderly, the issue of *excessive* access to medical care is coming to be seen as a problem. There are even cases of people resorting to ambulances as a kind of free taxi since patients in Japan are not charged for ambulance services. The declining number of younger people in the population means a precipitous decline in the number of people paying into public health insurance, which puts the health insurance system in a dire financial state. Of course, the shortfall will have to be made up through taxes, but there are limits to how far this can go. Thus, establishing some kind of control over the ever-ballooning cost of health care is an issue of the greatest urgency, to be tackled with the utmost priority by

FIGURE 2.2

Medical expenses per age group, 2011

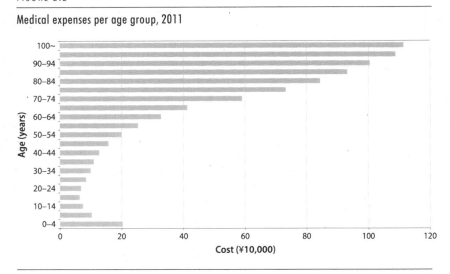

the Ministry of Finance and the government under their policy of cutting back the budget.

It is precisely against this backdrop that mixed billing is getting attention as an effective means of cutting medical costs. The point is that if patients are required to pay out of pocket for treatment that is not covered by health insurance, there will be no need for expensive treatment to be carried out within the health insurance system. If advanced medical treatments and newly developed medicines are left outside the scope of health insurance coverage – as opposed to everything being listed – the financial burden on the health insurance end will remain modest. We have already mentioned that the Ministry of Health, Labour and Welfare has demonstrated its opposition by treating patient-requested medical treatments as "forms of medical treatment being tested in clinical trials for listing for health insurance." However, the government and the Ministry of Finance have been doing what they can to put the brakes on the listing of advanced medical treatments for health insurance, and to limit the expansion of the scope of health insurance. In other words, the Health Ministry's approach is an attempt to throw a spanner in the works when it comes to shrinking the finances allocated to health insurance and slashing the budget available. It is undeniable that the government's ulterior motive in attempting to lift the ban on mixed billing is in fact to rein in medical spending and to cut medical expenses – all of this expressed by the flowery phrasing of "giving patients with incurable illnesses access to advanced techniques of medical care." Mixed billing thus presents itself, in one aspect, as a cost-cutting exercise.

The Pharmaceutical Industry, Medical Equipment Manufacturers, and the Insurance Industry

Turning now to industries that supported the lifting of the ban on mixed billing, particularly the pharmaceutical industry and medical equipment manufacturers, the question arises as to where these players see their profit. It goes without saying that for them, expedited recognition and use of new drugs and medical equipment would lead directly to greater profits. Under Japan's health insurance system (universal health care), however, once products are recognized and listed for use, their prices would be subject to publicly regulated caps, and thus profit margins would suffer. All prices are controlled by the Ministry of Health, Labour and Welfare, and excessive profits are not a feature of the system. Outside the health insurance system, however, these players can fix whatever price the market will support. Handsome profits could be made by offering these items at a favourable price to patients requiring them, if the ban on mixed billing were lifted but advanced medicines and equipment were not listed for health insurance.

Thus, for the pharmaceutical industry and medical equipment manufacturers, an ideal situation would be one where mixed billing *was* put in place but the scope of health insurance listing was *not* enlarged. Although the motives of the business world were different from those of the government, the industry players had more than enough reason to actively lobby for this change in policy.

Negotiations for the Trans-Pacific Partnership (TPP), and now the Comprehensive and Progressive Agreement for Trans-Pacific Partnership (CPTPP),[4] were ongoing when introduction of mixed billing was discussed in Japan (Drache and Jacobs 2018). There were strong apprehensions in Japan that, in the medical field, Japan's ban on mixed billing would become a major bone of contention and a source of further pressure on Japan in the negotiations. But with strong opposition being led by Japan's medical community, the United States agreed not to make an issue of it and to let the matter drop. For industry, however, Japan's ban on mixed billing and its penchant for including all kinds of items in its universal health insurance system comprised in effect a policy of price regulation, restricting free price setting and acting as a barrier to free trade.

The insurance industry also shares the same interests. The public would face relatively low costs if all kinds of treatment were covered by public health insurance, leaving little scope for private medical health insurance to carve out a business niche. On the other hand, the wider the scope of advanced medical treatment not covered by public health insurance, the greater the demand for private health insurance. Thus, for private health insurance companies, an end to the ban on mixed billing would be an absolute boon for business – provided that advanced medical treatment was not included under public health insurance. Private health insurance companies thus joined the ranks of the players calling for an end to the ban on mixed billing.

Thus, several parties – the government, which was trying to cut spending on public health as much as it could, and the pharmaceutical, medical equipment, and insurance industries, which were aiming to invest in a market with free price setting for their wares – found themselves in a position where they could all achieve mutual gains through an end to the ban on mixed billing.

The Medical Profession

The general current of opinion within the medical profession is that universal health insurance should be retained to protect the general public's access to medical care. Even if the patient must pay 30 percent of a ceiling or fixed price (set on a sliding scale on an individual basis), the charges incurred in one month do not exceed predetermined limits. The limit is US$200 per month for low-income patients, and $120 a month for low-income seniors. Even high-income earners pay no more than $1,200 a month, $700 in the case of high-income seniors. Furthermore, medicine and rehabilitation costs are all covered. This means that, no matter what treatment patients receive under the Japanese system, and whether or not they have to stay in the hospital, they will incur no charges for medical services over a certain set limit. Almost all doctors in Japan (with the exception of cosmetic surgeons) work within the system as health insurance doctors. The result of all this is that the numbers of hospital beds and outpatient visits are unparalleled elsewhere in the world – with a commensurate frenetic pace of work for the doctors. Nevertheless, Japan's doctors take the greatest pride in the health insurance system, and see its continued existence as a guarantee of the general population's well-being.

Another point to note is that almost all hospital doctors in Japan are employees of the hospitals they work at, and they are paid on a salary basis.

Differences in pay scale between individual doctors based on the quantity or quality of medical care they provide are basically unheard of. Fees for medical services are fixed by regulation, and doctors are not free to set fees based on the individual patient. Working within this system, doctors can do their jobs free of any consideration of how their work might affect their income; referring only to their specialized medical knowledge, they can concentrate on the task of providing their patients with the most appropriate care they require. Patients in turn, rich or poor, can access this care without distinction.

Another feature of this system is that doctors are free from the influence of private health insurance companies and medical equipment manufacturers. Working under an ethic of being strictly providers of medical care, doctors can maintain their sense of identity as experts in saving lives.

Outside the hospital system are doctors in general practice, running individual clinics. These too work under the umbrella of the health insurance system, and had normally spent part of their career employed at a hospital, acquiring their technical skills and experience. This means that they share the same basic medical culture and attitude toward the health insurance system as hospital doctors. In fact, the core membership of the Japan Medical Association is composed of such doctors in general practice rather than hospital doctors, and it has consistently opposed lifting the ban on mixed billing.

In contrast, we have seen how the heads of Japan's three most influential university hospitals showed a certain degree of support for lifting the ban.[5] They called for: 1) the establishment of a system combining health care paid for by health insurance coverage and out-of-pocket payment (effectively lifting the ban on mixed billing); 2) a changeover to an ex post facto notification procedure when applying for approval for the use of highly advanced medical technology; 3) the free use of drugs and medical equipment approved overseas; 4) the free use of drugs that have completed clinical trials but have not yet been approved; and 5) new medical legislation to modify the health insurance system. Here we can see an attempt to break the iron grip of the Health Ministry on the approval procedure for highly advanced medical technology and for listing medicines and treatments for health insurance – a procedure so slow that it has given birth to the infamous "drug lag" issue. This was, in other words, a challenge to Health Ministry control of the system. The fifth point basically called for legislation that would allow mixed billing and more leeway for doctors engaged in advanced medical care to provide and choose highly advanced medical technologies.

The reason why the heads of Japan's three most prestigious university hospitals bucked the general trend in the medical community is quite clear. University hospitals also function as centres of research; they have had serious concerns about falling behind other countries in this regard, and they want as much free access as possible to highly advanced medical technology. These preoccupations can be glimpsed in their statement.

While these concerns can be considered perfectly legitimate, it cannot be denied that the university hospitals were acting under the influence of the pharmaceutical and medical equipment industries, especially given the never-ending recurrence of scandals in recent years of books being cooked and money being passed under the table. For example, a scandal occurred again in 2015 following a data falsification incident at the Kitasato Institute Hospital Biomedical Research Center, where the sodium level of healthy volunteers was rewritten. Such scandals surrounding the drug clinical trial are endless.

Thus, surrounded by a chorus of strident opposition to the implementation of mixed billing on the part of the medical profession, research doctors involved with highly advanced medical technology have found themselves, in effect, standing shoulder to shoulder with the pharmaceutical industry and medical equipment manufacturers in seeking to free up the provision of advanced medical treatment.

Patients' Groups

What about the underlying interests behind the patients' positions? For example, if patients receive still-unapproved anti-cancer drugs and therapies, they have to pay the full costs for treatment covered by health insurance as well, and so there were patients who opted not to avail of advanced medical treatment. Was it true, as the government said, that for these patients mixed billing would result in exceptionally improved access to these therapies? As we saw in the court case brought by the patient known as N.K., there certainly were people who wanted to combine advanced medical treatment with conventional therapies under health care provided by universal health insurance.[6]

However, most patients and patients' groups view the authorization of mixed billing as an existential threat to the health insurance system and have been vocal in their opposition to the move. This opposition does not come only from patients who have no need of advanced medical treatment; even incurable patients who have such a need – the very people, one would expect, with the most to benefit from easier access to advanced medical treatment – are equally strident. Contrary to the government's reading of the situation, they see the lifting of the ban on mixed billing as a move that would cause their access to medical care to collapse.

In 2007, while debate was ongoing over the Koizumi government's efforts to relax regulation, the Japan Patients' Association passed an emergency resolution expressing its strongly oppositional stance. The resolution read in part:

> At present, treatments not covered by health insurance are permitted on an exceptional basis. If the ban on mixed billing is lifted entirely, [the practice of health care using] these forms of treatment may expand uncontrollably, leading to the instant collapse of the health insurance system (universal health care) which forms the very basis of the public health care system in Japan ... Safe and effective medicines and treatment should come under health insurance coverage promptly.

When the Supreme Court issued a ruling recognizing a de facto lifting of the ban on mixed billing, it might have seemed as though patients and patients' groups were in agreement. This was not the case, however. Having none of it, they issued statement after statement against the move.

In 2013, as the government's economic reform plan was underway, the government announced an expansion of the partial lifting of the ban on mixed billing, calling it a "policy for combined therapy healthcare under the health insurance system." In response, the Japan Patients' Association issued the statement "Against the Destructive Lifting of the Ban on Mixed Billing: Health Insurance Should Apply to Required Medical Treatments as a Rule" (Japan Patients' Association 2013). This strongly worded brief voiced concern that 1) only better-off patients would have access to advanced medical treatment, creating an income disparity in health care and 2) dangerous methods of treatment lacking sufficient evidence would proliferate, compromising safe practice.

The head of a cancer patients' association also stated that "a total lifting of the ban would not be desirable. Disparities in health care based on differences in income would result, and we think that it would be wrong for any unsafe drugs to end up in use. We have a fantastic health insurance system (universal health care), and we want to get world-class cancer therapy under this system."[7]

Thus, we can say that with a few exceptions, the great majority of patients' groups, like the medical profession, lined up in very strong opposition toward lifting the ban.

The Ministry of Health, Labour and Welfare

The government, the Ministry of Finance, and business have all wielded their authority in support of ending the ban on mixed billing, while the medical profession and patients' groups generally opposed it. The Ministry of Health, Labour and Welfare occupies a rather delicate position in the narrow ground between these two opposing coalitions.

Policy in Japan is formed in three different arenas: the legislative, the administrative, and the judicial. It is the administrative branch – the bureaucracy – that wields by far the greatest power. Even if the legislature decides on a major change in policy, it is the bureaucratic elite who exercise their authority in carrying it out. The foundation of their influence is above all their power in issuing authorizations and subsidies, and through these means they exercise informal control on the ground. On the question of mixed billing, the Ministry of Health, Labour and Welfare has the power to safety-check and issue authorizations for new medicines and therapies, and can use its power to list therapies and the like for the health insurance system, as a resource to control both the medical field and the medical supplies sector on the ground. The basic position of the ministry is that Japan's health insurance system, as established, realizes world-beating levels of accessibility and performance, and thus should be protected as a rule. In the absence of any clear legislation to point to as the letter of the law in the first place, it is the Ministry of Health, Labour and Welfare that has sustained a policy opposing an end to the ban on mixed billing.

Basic policy is of course decided by the government and legislature, so the bureaucracy cannot oppose it in toto. In light of this, the strategy that the Ministry of Health, Labour and Welfare has adopted is to pay lip service to the government's approach. Caught between the power of the government and business and the appeals of the medical profession and patients' groups, the ministry has up to now played a mediating role. Until 2006, under a policy titled the "highly advanced medical technology system," the minister permitted – to the extent that it did permit – the combined provision of conventional and highly advanced medical technologies under the health insurance system (health care provided by universal health insurance) at specially designated medical institutions, such as university hospitals.

Mixed billing was not otherwise permitted under this system, with rare exceptions, rigorously examined by target group and institution.

Under the regulatory reforms undertaken by the Koizumi government, a system called the "insurance outside combination recuperation system" was set up. This system partially recognized the combination of insured medical care and uninsured medical care under such rubrics as "advanced but not necessarily high-level technologies" and "medicines not yet authorized domestically"; it expanded the scope of the previous "highly advanced medical technology policy" to the extent that one can say it relaxed the ban on mixed billing all the more. Under this policy, even though patients paid for the approved highly advanced medical technology in full and out of pocket if it was not covered, health insurance coverage applied unchanged to the portion that was.

Then, in 2014, the Regulatory Reform and Privatization Council under Prime Minister Abe proposed a de facto lifting of the ban under the title of a "choice-based medical treatment system." At this juncture, the Health Ministry put up strong opposition and expressed its stance clearly. Subsequently, a new and improved version of the council's proposals was enacted into law as the "medical treatment system [responsive to] patients' requests," and came into effect in 2016. This took the ban on mixed billing even further toward being lifted. Even so, the Health Ministry still sees the health insurance system as the basic premise of the system, and there is no change in its objective of approving advanced medical treatments and new medicines listed for combined use with conventional therapies.

One can certainly say that the dynamism of the conflict between the government and business on the one hand and the medical profession and patients' groups on the other is reflected in the Ministry of Health, Labour and Welfare's course of action. The ministry's interests as a body lie in being the protector of the health insurance system (universal health care) and pushing back against the influence of government and business. In the background lies its self-esteem in defending a health insurance system unlike any other in the world.

Organisation for Economic Co-operation and Development (OECD) Recommendations

An OECD report (OECD 2009, 120–26) discussed Japan's policy on banning mixed billing as an approach unique to the country, and stated that, due to patients' diversifying needs and advances in medical techniques, there was a need to enlarge the scope of mixed billing. This would make access to progressive medical treatments and medicine possible, and enhance the quality of medical care. This, in turn, the report continued, would encourage competition between medical institutions. The report further pointed out that it took an average of 1,417 days for drugs approved as safe abroad to receive approval in Japan, and that this period should be shortened to be like that of other countries. This was in reference to what is commonly known as the "drug lag" issue.

This kind of departure from international standards is certainly visible on a surface level. However, Japan's many distinctive idiosyncrasies are at work behind them. One is that Japan's universal system of health insurance, whereby prescription drugs and rehabilitation expenses are fully covered, is a system that endeavours to achieve universal coverage in the genuine sense of the term.[8] If everything was listed for health insurance, the expenses would of course be colossal. Even so, the scope of coverage is being expanded every year, to the point that any patient suffering from however incurable an illness can expect to receive medical treatment at a reasonable cost under public health insurance. Faced with this dilemma, it is only natural that medicines and medical equipment are rigorously scrutinized, to make sure that only the truly safe and effective ones are listed. Another distinctive point is that the Japanese public is exceptionally safety-conscious and exceptionally demanding when it comes to safety concerns. In recent years, there was a scandal involving side effects from inoculations for uterine cancer, and the Ministry of Health, Labour and Welfare came under mounting criticism. No matter how broad-ranging the consequences, if even just one case of harm had come to light, it would have been no more than natural for the ministry to have been held responsible; thus the ministry's standards may be seen as erring too much on the side of safety.

Although it is undesirable to allow gaps to open up between Japanese practice and international standards, there are certain systemic and cultural factors at play here. The OECD report was on point insofar as it went; however, it only scratched the surface.

Will Lifting the Ban on Mixed Billing Improve Access to Health Care or Crash the System?

Will lifting the ban on mixed billing improve or impede access to medical care? Will disparities and gaps in access to care widen or shrink?

In attempting to answer these questions, it may be useful to refer to particular case studies. The *Asahi Shimbun*'s Masahiko Idegawa (2013,

FIGURE 2.3

Cost of treatment that includes Cetuximab

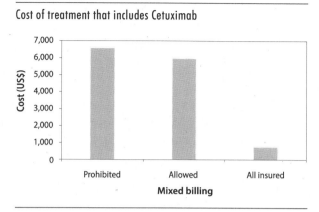

Source: Idegawa 2013.

199–200) provides an example of treatment with the intestinal-cancer drug Cetuximab.[9] Working in collaboration with doctors, he has divided the treatment options involving this drug, along with the corresponding expenses, into three categories: 1) with mixed billing banned; 2) with mixed billing permitted; and 3) with the drug listed for health insurance (health care provided by universal health insurance). Although one course of Cetuximab lasts four months, the figures below calculate one month's expenses (see Figure 2.3).

With mixed billing banned, the patient pays the entire cost of treatment, including the portion normally covered by health insurance. In this case, total medical care costs come to US$6,553. By contrast, if the drug were covered by the health insurance plan, the patient would pay one-third of the expenses, which would amount to approximately US$2,000. Moreover, once subsidies provided under the system covering high-cost medical treatments kick in, the actual upper limit to be paid would drop to about US$743. From this, we can surmise that the two payment options differ by a factor of nearly ten, which serves as a great illustration of the virtues of Japan's health insurance system, along with the negative ramifications of the ban on mixed billing.

Now, let us see how matters fare when the ban on mixed billing is lifted, and a combination of treatments by a health insurance doctor (covered by health insurance) and advanced medical treatment (paid for by the patient) is permitted. One month's worth of Cetuximab costs US$5,680; one-third of

FIGURE 2.4

Cost of treatment including Olaparib

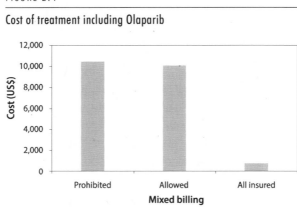

Source: National Cancer Center Japan 2014.

other treatments covered by health insurance amounts to US$262, for a total of US$5,942. This means that the difference in cost between when mixed billing is banned and when it is permitted amounts to a mere US$611 (Idegawa 2013).

Consider a different example. The National Cancer Center Japan did a similar study on the ovarian-cancer drug Olaparib, breaking down the costs into three categories. The difference in the cost to be borne by the patient one month after the commencement of its administration would look as follows (National Cancer Center Japan 2014):

- all paid out of pocket: US$10,463
- with combined use permitted (mixed billing): US$10,074
- with health insurance covering everything: US$781.

Because Olaparib is an expensive drug at US$9,907, lifting the ban on mixed billing and allowing its coverage within the scope of health insurance would make no major difference (see Figure 2.4).

While these cases are but examples that are not necessarily universally applicable, they do seem to indicate that in cases where patients get new medicines and advanced medical treatments, the cost of advanced medical services is normally disproportionately higher than that covered by health insurance.[10] This leads to the inference that, to put it bluntly, lifting the ban on mixed billing would mean a decrease only in the small proportion the patient has to pay of the costs. Prices for new medicines and high-level medical treatments are not controlled and are high; this would not change even if the ban on mixed billing were lifted. Consequently, the expenses borne by the patient would decrease only insignificantly compared with the status quo, and the enhanced access to medical care posited by the government and patients' groups advocating the relaxation of regulations would end up being quite trivial. Most patients who cannot access advanced medical treatment when mixed billing is banned would do no better even if the ban were lifted.

Alternatively, if new medicines and new forms of medical treatment were listed for universal health insurance, the impact of these changes on the costs borne by the patient would be much more noticeable. Specifically, patients would pay a mere one-tenth of the full cost for remarkably expanded access. Thus, from the patients' point of view, rather than lifting the ban on mixed billing, the best way to expand access to care would be to list new medicines and advanced medical treatments for the universal health insurance system.

As mentioned above, listing new forms of treatment for health insurance would impose price controls on the pharmaceutical industry and medical equipment manufacturers, cutting into their potential profits. Conversely, with mixed billing permitted, the market for free price setting would expand, however slightly, which would result in increased business profits. Yoshihiko Miyauchi, the chairperson of Prime Minister Koizumi's Regulatory Reform Council, has espoused the view that if people wanted expanded medical treatment, then "the health insurance (health plan) is only going to take you so far"; "please pay out of your own pocket for the rest." Faced with criticism that his proposals favoured the rich, he declared that "even if people who aren't well-off want advanced medical treatment, they can decide to sell their homes to get it" (Miyauchi 2002). The issue is complicated by the fact that the ORIX group, which Miyauchi heads, includes private health insurance companies. If the ban on mixed billing were lifted, industry would oppose the listing of therapies for health insurance as a matter of course. Private health insurance companies would also be able to create a new market.

Furthermore, because expanding the scope of insured medical services would strain public finances, one can reasonably expect the government to side with pharmaceutical and medical manufacturers in opposing the listing of new drugs and advanced medical treatments in the public insurance package – all the more because, as will be explained in greater detail below, the Japanese health insurance system already experiences a variety of financial challenges stemming from certain institutional inefficiencies as well as wasteful allocation of health care resources.

In the first place, because access to medical care is broadly available, it is possible, for example, to be examined by a doctor at a university hospital even for as trivial a matter as a cold. Nor is there anything to prevent a patient from having numerous consultations at different hospitals for the same medical problem. The guarantee of access to medical care that universal health care provides also leads to the excessive consumption of medical resources. Since 2016, self-referral (without a letter of referral) from small clinics to major hospitals for a medical exam has cost a patient a special levy of about US$40, but it is unclear whether this change in policy has had any significant effects. One can expect that controlling patients' behaviour in getting medical examinations will have a significant impact on eliminating waste in medical spending. Moreover, it is expected to have some effect on alleviating the work overload for doctors at major hospitals.

Second, there is a need to review the scope of health insurance coverage. Under Japan's system of universal coverage for medical treatments and medicines, everything from medicated compresses for stiff shoulders to cold medicines that one can easily pick up at a pharmacy is covered. From the patient's point of view, there is no sense in going to a drugstore to buy these things when one can go to hospital, get a medical exam, and pick up the medicines for a third of the price. In addition, patients who have multiple medical exams at different medical institutions can get a large number of prescriptions. There are countless cases of patients getting clearly unnecessary treatment from, for example, chiropractors, against doctors' advice, and then presenting the bill to the health insurance system. If the scope of treatments listed for health insurance is to be limited, it would be better to include new drugs for advanced medical treatment while excluding these kinds of treatment, which are simply a waste of money.

The problem, therefore, is not just that lifting the ban on mixed billing may not lead to enhanced access to care, as the medical profession and patients' groups fear. The odds are high that the listing of new therapies in the public health insurance package will be obstructed, and that access to high-level medical care will remain unattainable for many. Contrary to what the government claims, allowing mixed billing will likely impede access to medical care and create a system in which income-based disparities will persist.

The Issue of Sustained Access to Medical Care
There is a need for ongoing monitoring of the government's attempts to sweep aside the ban on mixed billing under the guise of a "medical treatment

system responsive to patients' requests." Essentially, the 2014 recommendations of the Regulatory Reform Council system proposed a total lifting of the ban. With those proposals stymied by major opposition on safety and other grounds, the system set to take effect in April 2016 was a revised system in a slightly different garb.[11]

The Ministry of Health is attempting to position this system as simply adding exceptional investigation procedures for new drugs and methods of medical treatment that are to be listed in the health insurance scheme – that is, it wants to keep the system of combined therapies under health insurance coverage in operation as it has been up to now, albeit in slightly expanded form. On the other hand, government and business see it as a transitional step toward outright lifting of the ban on mixed billing.

As we have seen, even if progress toward lifting the ban is made, as long as new drugs and methods of medical treatment remain expensive, the difference in costs to be borne by the patient will not vary greatly from the status quo ante, and so any change might not be so significant on the ground. Quite the contrary – if relaxation of the ban would entail diminished incentive for the government to broaden the scope of coverage of the health insurance system (universal health care), then patients' access to care will be compromised, potentially leading to the eventual collapse of the system. Aside from the superficial motivation to enhance access to health care, behind government and industry's pressure to lift the ban, there clearly lies a desire to limit public health spending by restricting the listing of new therapies in the health insurance package, and to increase business profits. So far, this 2016 system has not been used much, as the Ministry of Health, Labour and Welfare's attempt to resist and block the path to mixed practice have been successful. During the five years from April 2016 to December 2020, 145 applications were made and only 10 cases were approved.

Whether listing for health insurance will proceed more smoothly under this system, as the Ministry of Health hopes, or whether it will in fact slow down and lead to reduced access to care, is an issue that requires further examination of the dynamics of how the various actors, ranged in antagonistic coalitions, will compete and collude with each other for various forms of advantage.

Meanwhile, even if one believed that an expanded listing for health insurance would be a desirable thing, no one would want to see an inexhaustible amount of funding being poured into the health insurance system just to keep the system going. The fact is that, as mentioned above, a whole range of institutional inefficiencies as well as wasteful allocation of health care resources haunt the Japanese universal health care system.

In order to preserve access to high-quality and affordable medical care in Japan, as prescribed by SDG 3, it is necessary to take care of the health insurance system (universal health care) as the ongoing premise of health care, and to build around it protections against excessively expensive access to care. With regard to mixed billing, it does seem vital to position the "medical treatment system responsive to patients' requests" as a precursor to having new therapies listed for health insurance; mixed billing is then permitted only to the extent that it allows this to happen.

NOTES

1 https://sdgs.un.org/goals/goal3.

2 Also, more specific stipulations on medical treatment limited "the use of particular and new methods of treatment by health insurance doctors to those stipulated by the Minister of Health," and "Health insurance doctors are not to dispense or prescribe to patients medicines other than those designated by the Minister of Health."

3 This is Japan's largest patients' group, with sixty-six chapters and over 300,000 members, including those suffering from incurable diseases.

4 https://www.mfat.govt.nz/vn/trade/free-trade-agreements/free-trade-agreements -in-force/comprehensive-and-progressive-agreement-for-trans-pacific-partnership -cptpp/comprehensive-and-progressive-agreement-for-trans-pacific-partnership -text-and-resources/.

5 The heads of Tokyo, Kyoto, and Osaka University Hospitals submitted their request to the Council for Regulatory Reform and Privatization in 2004.

6 For a more detailed discussion of the emphasis on patient choice in Japanese health care policy, see Chapter 4.

7 Sunday Mainichi Dec. 19, 2004.

8 A wide range of medicines and treatments, from expensive authorized anti-cancer drugs to over-the-counter bandages and analgesics, are covered under Japan's universal health care system.

9 Cetuximab was approved in 2008 and is now covered by health insurance.

10 Fifty-three anti-cancer drugs are not yet authorized in Japan, including exceptionally expensive drugs such as dinutuximab (US$31,349), blinatumomab (US$63,133), Provenge (USD$80,984), and mifamurtide (US$165,452).

11 Unlike the "medical treatment system responsive to patients' requests," safety check procedures and restrictions on the medical facilities that can carry out new therapies, etc. are in place. So, if patients want to get new drugs or advanced medical treatment, the system permits mixed billing at around fifteen advanced medical facilities nationwide. At first, if the treatment to be done is unprecedented, these medical facilities apply to the government, expert advice is given, and confirmation on safety and effectiveness is supposed to be carried out in six weeks as a rule, with

approval following if appropriate. In current practice, the procedure of application and approval would take some six or seven months – a very significant speeding up. If the treatment has precedent, the decision to permit its practice at these medical facilities will take two weeks. In response to patients' groups' concerns about safety, the procedure may take over six weeks to firmly establish that the treatment in question is sound.

Health for All
Can India Meet Its International Human Rights Obligations?

TIFFANY CHUA, MARC McCRUM,
and ILAN VERTINSKY

International legal instruments have long recognized and supported the right of every human being to have access to health care and medicines. Key among these instruments is the 1946 constitution of the World Health Organization, which states that "the enjoyment of the highest attainable standard of health is one of the fundamental rights of every human being without distinction of race, religion, political belief, economic or social conditions" (WHO 1946). This view was echoed by the Universal Declaration of Human Rights two years later, which declared that every human being is entitled to "the right to a standard of living adequate for the health and well-being of himself and his family, including ... medical care" (UNGA 1948, Article 25, para. 46).

By conceptualizing health as a basic human right, international legal instruments acknowledge that health is essential to human survival and rooted in the notion of human dignity. As such, health takes precedence over other issues and claims, and emphasizes the good of each individual rather than the greater good. Access should be based on principles of equality and non-discrimination, and the lack of economic resources and costs of the access to treatment, albeit significant, are not adequate reasons to deny individuals the right to health (Helfer and Austin 2011).

A rights-based approach to health bestows legal and political legitimacy on the right to health and implies that governments have the responsibility to provide individuals with such entitlements (Helfer and Austin 2011). This principle has been emphasized in Article 12 of the International Covenant on Economic, Social and Cultural Rights (ICESCR), which highlights the responsibilities of states to take action to achieve the "full realization" of "the right of everyone to the enjoyment of the highest attainable standard of physical and mental health" (UNGA 1966, Article 12, para. 57). States' obligations to fulfill the right to health must address different elements, including the availability of a functioning public health care system, physical and economic accessibility, ethical and cultural acceptability, and quality (United Nations Human Rights Council 2011).

The United Nations Sustainable Development Goals (SDG) provide a framework for global health standards that reflects and substantiates these rights-based international obligations. SDG 3 specifies in particular that countries like India have an obligation to "ensure healthy lives and promote well-being for all at all ages," and sets the target to "achieve universal health coverage, including financial risk protection, access to quality essential health-care services and access to safe, effective, quality and affordable essential medicines and vaccines for all" (SDG 3.8).[1]

The obligations of governments in India to safeguard the health of their constituents have been incorporated into the Indian Constitution, which states that "the state shall regard the raising of the level of nutrition and the standard of living of its people and the improvement of public health as among its primary duties" (Ministry of Law and Justice 2007, Article 47, para. 76). These provisions were reflected in India's 1983 National Health Policy, which adopted the goal of "Health for All." The National Health Policy was updated in 2002, when it set out twenty strategies for increasing access and enhancing efficiency, affordability, and quality (Varatharajan 2003), and updated again in 2017 with a focus on providing comprehensive primary care and access to affordable health care (*Indian Express* 2017).

This chapter examines India's performance in providing for the right to health. We argue that although the central government has introduced numerous policies in an attempt to improve health standards in India, state governments play the most critical role in delivering local health services. The level of commitment of resources to health care and promotion services and the effectiveness of their management by state governments are the key determinants of the degree to which India is progressing toward its objective of improving the health of its population. Since an analysis of the policies and performance of each of India's twenty-nine states and its central government is beyond the scope of this chapter, we focus on the central government and on case studies of three states: Kerala, Tamil Nadu, and Gujarat.

Unlike many other states, these three have made the provision of health-related services a priority. However, their ideologies and approaches to the task of providing care and promoting health differ significantly, enabling us to gain some insight into the success factors that may move India toward its health objectives.

We first focus on India as a whole, and on the successes or failures and the prospects of health-related policies introduced by the central government. An evaluation of some of the health and health care challenges that India is facing is followed by an analysis of the major policies introduced by the central government in response to these challenges, and of the systemic failures and external barriers that reduce the effectiveness of such policies.

We then shift the focus to the states and their roles in India's path toward a healthier population. A brief description of the division of responsibilities between the central government and the states for the provision of health care and promotion services is followed by a comparative study of the governments of Kerala, Tamil Nadu, and Gujarat with regard to their commitments, policies, implementation of programs, and outcomes.

The chapter concludes with a summary of our analyses and conclusions with respect to the prospects for realizing India's health objectives and the conditions and strategies that might facilitate this.

Moving Toward a Healthy India: Central Government Policies and Their Performance

India's Health and Health Services Report Card

India's performance in raising health standards is mixed at best. India has made significant strides in increasing life expectancy and decreasing infant mortality rates. Life expectancy at birth rose from 58 years in 1990 to 68.3 years in 2015. During the same period, infant mortality rates fell by over 68%, from 88 per 1,000 live births in 1990 to 28 in 2015. Similarly, mortality rates for children under five years decreased from 126 per 1,000 live births in 1990 to 48 in 2015. India has also achieved significant improvements in battling tuberculosis, with the number of cases per 100,000 individuals falling from 438 in 2000 to 211 in 2016. As of 2015, around 72% of all new cases were treated successfully. Meanwhile, the percentage of communicable diseases and maternal, prenatal conditions as a cause of death fell from 39.8% in 2000 to 28% in 2015 (WHO 2017a). However, tuberculosis continues to be common in India, which accounts for approximately 26% of global tuberculosis deaths. In addition, as communicable diseases have decreased in importance as a cause of death, non-communicable diseases have grown in importance, rising from 48.4% in 2000 to 61% in 2015 (WHO 2017b).

Access to health care continues to be a challenge in India. Consider the following figures:

- Less than 5% of the 2 million Indians who need heart surgery are able to undergo it.
- Approximately 63 million and 2.5 million Indians suffer from diabetes and cancer, respectively, but they are neither formally diagnosed nor treated.
- Out of India's 12 million blind people, 70% have no access to a simple surgery that can cure them of blindness. (Govindarajan and Ramamurti 2013)

Physical access to health care facilities and hospitals also remains problematic, with reports showing that over 90% of the population has no access to a hospital and 87% has no access to primary health care facilities. India's health care infrastructure is woefully inadequate, even with the combined resources of both the public and private sector. Hospital bed density has failed to meet the World Health Organization (WHO) standard of 3.5 beds per 1,000 individuals. As of 2019, India had 0.93 doctors per 1,000 people, up only slightly from 0.6 in 2004 (World Bank 2022). Conditions also vary according to region, with approximately only 25% of qualified physicians practising in rural areas despite these areas being home to 72% of the entire population.

To a certain extent, many of India's health challenges can be traced to financing issues. The Indian government's financial contribution to health spending remains small compared with other countries. While government spending on health has grown continuously over the years, from US$18.60 per capita in 2000 all the way up to $63.30 per capita in 2015, India still ranked within the bottom thirty of countries surveyed with respect to health spending as a percentage of GDP. More specifically, in 2015 India spent 3.89% of GDP on health, compared with 5% for China, 10% for the European Union, and 16% for North America (World Bank 2018).

Inadequate public spending on health has translated into high private spending for those who can afford it.[2] Such private expenditures accounted for around 74% of total health expenditure in 2015, a small but not insignificant improvement from 2004, when private spending accounted for 80% of total health expenditures (World Bank 2018). Out-of-pocket expenditures put a heavy financial burden on many Indians, accounting for 65% of total health expenditures as of 2015, with millions more individuals falling under the poverty line annually due to health-related spending (ibid.).

Pharmaceutical-related expenses account for a big proportion of total health spending, with out-of-pocket spending on medicines constituting up to 50% of total health-related expenses, yet government spending on drugs continues to be low, accounting for only 0.1% of GDP per year (University College of London School of Pharmacy 2013). Most of India's population lacks sufficient access to essential medicines. With more than 270 million people below the poverty line as of 2016, India's population clearly does not have sufficient money to spend on medicine (World Bank 2016). Access also remains inequitable between urban and rural areas, with 25% of total pharmaceutical sales being traced to India's top twenty-three cities (Planning Commission, n.d.). As will be discussed later in this chapter, the introduction of "Modicare" in 2018 aimed to increase spending and improve coverage for health expenditures. Low levels of public spending on health give private insurance companies a bigger role to play, and the private health insurance sector is projected to grow at a compound annual growth rate of 10.1% from 2021 to 2027 (BlueWeave Consulting and Research, 2022).

Central Government Policies
Responsibility for fulfilling the Indian government's mandate to provide "health for all" as encapsulated in its National Health Policy rests primarily with the Ministry of Health and Family Welfare (MHFW). The MHFW has implemented a broad range of programs addressing different types of diseases across varying segments of the population. The National Health Mission (NHM) addresses a plethora of issues that affect the effective functioning of the health care system. First, the financial management component of the NHM addresses issues of planning, budgeting, monitoring, and procurement to ensure that enough resources are allocated to facilitate the smooth implementation of health programs. Second, the NHM focuses on strengthening health systems, recognizing that the effective delivery of health care would largely depend on human resources, existing infrastructure, and the provision of medicine. Third, the NHM targets specific segments of the population, highlighting the need to pursue improvements in reproductive and maternal health, child and adolescent health, and methods of family planning. Fourth, the NHM seeks to prevent and combat a variety of communicable and non-communicable diseases,

as well as address mental health challenges (Ministry of Health and Family Welfare 2013).

Acknowledging the large gap in levels of quality and accessibility between urban and rural areas, in 2005 the MHFW introduced the National Rural Health Mission (NRHM) as one of the major sub-missions under the NHM. Designed to address health concerns in underserved rural areas, the NRHM complements the NHM's objectives of combatting diseases and focusing on reproductive and child health. The NRHM has been lauded for achieving substantial progress, especially in the construction of new health facilities and improving access to medicines. It must be noted, however, that achievements have tended to vary according to state. Moreover, a key challenge remains, that of finding qualified medical personnel.

As access to medicines is a major dimension to the right to health, numerous policies have been introduced to ensure such access. These policies have been implemented by both the MHFW and other related agencies.

Under the MHFW, one of the key organizations is the Central Drugs Standard Control Organization (CDSCO), which serves as the primary regulatory authority for drugs at the central and state level. The CDSCO sets standards for medicines to ensure that they comply with safety, efficacy, and quality requirements (CUTS 2013). It also drafts the National List of Essential Medicines (NLEM) by adapting the WHO's List of Essential Medicines to the local context. Based on the types of widespread illnesses in India, the NLEM identifies essential medicines that the population should be able to access at affordable prices and of sufficient quality, and specifies the correct or prescribed dosage and strength. The organization also aims to promote the rational use of medicines and the utilization of generic drugs (CDSCO 2014). In 2011, the NLEM was published with a total of 348 medicines listed. The list serves as a guide for manufacturers and informs the formulation of lists of essential medicines at the state level (Gitanjali 2010).

The 2011 NLEM, however, was criticized by some experts who argued that the medicines were selected improperly. Not only were some obsolete drugs and those used to treat rare disorders included, but a number of life-saving drugs, including ones used to treat cardiac failure, were excluded. The list also contained some redundancies while excluding formulations and prescribed dosages for children. It provided wrong information concerning dosages and strengths (Manikandan and Gitanjali 2012). Given that the NLEM serves as the basis for state-level lists, or in many cases is replicated almost entirely, such mistakes were passed down to the state level (Gitanjali 2010).

To address the criticisms of the 2011 NLEM, a revised NLEM was published in 2015, with 106 new medicines added and 70 medicines deleted, for a total of 376 medicines in the list. It included medicines related to cancer and HIV/AIDs, among others, in order to cover life-saving drugs that had been excluded in the previous list (WHO 2017c).

While the MHFW addresses the public health aspect of drugs, the Ministry of Chemicals and Fertilizers (MCF) focuses on the pricing of medicines. Under the MCF, two departments – the Department of Pharmaceuticals and the Department of Chemicals and Petrochemicals – co-ordinate between themselves to determine pricing. The Department of Pharmaceuticals publishes the National Drug Policy, which the Department of Chemicals and Petrochemicals implements through the Drug Price Control Order (DPCO) (Sengupta et al. 2008).

Since the introduction of its first version in 1978, the National Drug Policy has strongly reflected the tension between public health concerns and the market. The 1978 National Drug Policy was considered a breakthrough in the sense that it laid the ground for a comprehensive graded price control mechanism for controlling drug prices. The Drug Price Control Order had the effect of placing 80 percent of the drug market, particularly essential life-saving medicines, under price control. Yet, this trend was eventually reversed through revisions to the National Drug Policy in 1986 and 1994. The movement toward liberalization signified that policy makers had chosen to rely on pressure from market competition as a mechanism for price control, and drugs were placed under price control on the basis of factors such as annual turnover, degree of market competition, and elasticity, rather than public health considerations. As a result, the percentage of the drug market covered by the DPCO had decreased to less than 40 percent of the market by 1995. Out of 74 drugs covered by the 1995 DPCO, only 37 were included in the NLEM, reflecting a lack of coordination between the MHFW and the MCF (CUTS 2006; Sengupta et al. 2008). In addition to the decreasing percentage of drugs covered by the DPCO, pharmaceutical companies have also found methods to circumvent the DPCO, choosing to focus on the production of expensive, non-life-saving medicines targeted toward the wealthier classes or concentrating on exports. Many companies have also chosen to halt the production of existing drugs and invent new drugs that replicated the functions of existing ones, since new drugs are not covered by the provisions of the DPCO (Sengupta et al. 2008).

In 2012, a legislative breakthrough led to the passage of the National Pharmaceuticals Pricing Policy, which was followed by the 2013 DPCO designed to implement it. The DPCO was lauded for including all 348 drugs listed in the 2011 NLEM and placing 60 percent of the drug market under price control. To address shortcomings in the earlier versions of the DPCO, the 2013 DPCO had provisions in place to ensure that production levels and the availability of medicines remained constant. The DPCO mandated that pharmaceutical companies not be allowed to halt the production of medicines unilaterally and abruptly, requiring instead that they submit a public notice six months before the target date of discontinuation. The government maintains the right to require companies to continue manufacturing the drug for up to a year from the proposed date of discontinuation. The government also has the right to require companies to increase drug production during national emergencies. In addition, the DPCO included provisions for covering new drugs. The list of price-controlled drugs can be revised periodically to prevent companies from making slight alterations to existing drugs and selling them as new drugs to escape price control (Ministry of Chemicals and Fertilizers 2012, 2013).

Even with these breakthroughs, the 2013 DPCO continues to reflect the contradiction between public health concerns and the market. The new method of calculation introduced by the 2013 DPCO, in which the ceiling price is computed by finding the simple average of all brands with at least 1% market share (Ministry of Chemicals and Fertilizers 2012), shows a disconnect between costs of production and prices. Critics claim that this will give some companies a profit margin as high as 1,000–3,000% (Srinivasan, Srikrishna, and Phadke 2013). Critics also believe that the DPCO will allow larger pharmaceutical companies to gain a larger share of the market and edge out small and medium-sized drug companies, as the narrowing price gap signifies that consumers are more likely to choose established brand names (Kesireddy 2013).

Both the MHFW and MCF enact policies that directly affect access to medicines. On the other hand, the Ministry of Commerce and Industry (MCI) indirectly affects access to medicines through its implementation of policies related to intellectual property rights (IPR) protection. Through the Office of the Controller General of Patents, Designs and Trademarks and the Indian Patent Office, the MCI implements the 1970 Patent Act and its 2005 revisions. While those who argue in favour of patents state that their granting stimulates innovation, patents bestow a monopoly on a drug manufacturer, allowing it to sell patented medicines at higher prices and lower quantities compared with a scenario of perfect competition. Patents therefore negatively affect availability and economic affordability.

India's Patent Act, revised in 2005, has often been cited as a promising model for other developing countries. While the Patent Act complies with the requirements of the Agreement on Trade-Related Aspects of Intellectual Property Rights (TRIPS Agreement),[3] it also leaves the government enough flexibility and discretion in the granting of patents. Setting higher criteria for patentability, the act banned "evergreening" practices (a strategy where manufacturers extend the lifetime of their patents through slight modifications of the original product), allowed the use of compulsory licences, sought to limit remedies and injunctions, provided for broad grounds for pre- and post-grant opposition, and complicated the patent application procedure, all of which made it more difficult for pharmaceutical companies to receive a patent (Kapcznski 2009). However, many of these flexibilities have not been fully utilized, owing to the lack of financial resources, the strong influence of a transnational legal culture predisposed toward IPR protection, and external pressures from developed countries (Kapcznski 2009; Drahos 2008; Sampat 2010).[4]

Health Insurance Penetration

In addition to a variety of health programs targeted at specific priority issues, the Indian government has introduced over the years a number of health insurance schemes to provide health coverage to its citizens. One of the oldest schemes is the Employees' State Insurance Corporation (ESIC), which provides social insurance to workers and their dependents. The ESIC is designed to provide full medical care from the first day of insurable employment, and offers cash payments in cases of illness or injury that leads to the temporary or permanent loss of capacity to work. Monthly pension is also received by dependents of workers who die as a result of work accidents or occupational hazards. The ESIC is implemented in thirty out of thirty-six states and union territories. Moreover, the scheme does not have an expenditure limit in terms of providing medical care and treatment to insured parties (Ministry of Labour and Employment, n.d.).

The ESIC is a self-financed scheme, with workers contributing 1.75% of their wages and employers contributing 4.75% of the amount of their employees' wages (Ministry of Labour and Employment, n.d.). Critics argue, however, that the funds collected by the ESIC are underutilized, with only 25% being devoted to medical care and 9% allocated to cash payments. Approximately 53% of the funds are not utilized optimally, invested instead in fixed deposits in banks instead of being used for services (Lobo 2011). At the same time, coverage is far from universal. Only 55 million Indians were covered by the ESIC in 2010, and an estimated 120 million Indians were projected to be covered by 2020 (India Brand Equity Foundation 2013). The prevalence of defaulting companies also contributes to lower coverage rates (Pawar 2014).

The central government's provision of health insurance only to formally employed workers also left a large gap that needed to be addressed. The National Health Insurance Scheme sought to serve this function by offering health insurance to informal workers and the poor at the national level. Launched in April 2008 and implemented in twenty-five of India's states and union territories, the scheme covered 100 million people by the middle of 2011 (Jain 2012) and was projected to cover 240 million by 2020 (India Brand Equity Foundation 2013). The scheme is financed primarily by the central government, which shoulders 75 percent of the costs, with the remaining portion shouldered by state governments (Jain 2012).

Problems abound, however. The scheme's complicated inclusion procedures risk excluding the very segment of the population the scheme was designed for, such as the working poor and informal workers. Gender inequalities are also rampant, with more women being excluded from the scheme, reflecting a predominance of demeaning attitudes toward women. Only a third of registered beneficiaries are women. Registration procedures often require the physical presence of the head of the household. In cases where the head of the household is sick or deceased, families are denied registration. At the same time, the scheme does not cover the costs of outpatient care and the costs of medicines – a rather unsound decision given that costs associated with outpatient care account for 79 percent of impoverishment caused by health-related expenditure. Moreover, the scheme highlights the lack of regulation in India's health sector. Instead of being implemented by the Ministry of Health and Family Welfare, the scheme is implemented by the Ministry of Labour and Employment, which lacks the necessary expertise. Huge disparities in the quality of health care provided by the public and private sectors signify that it is the poor who bear the brunt of low-quality health care (Jain 2012).

Modicare

In 2014, Prime Minister Narendra Modi proposed the National Health Assurance Mission (NHAM). The program aimed to provide affordable health care to the Indian population, by providing free essential medicines, free diagnostic treatments, and affordable insurance coverage to all citizens. The program was expected to be introduced in 2015 in some parts of India and completely implemented across the entire country by March 2019 (Kalra 2014; Chauhan 2014).

While the aims of the program are commendable, its implementation requires financial and human resources that the government is unwilling or unable to allocate. Budget concerns have delayed the implementation of the program since it was first announced. The program was projected to require US$25.5 billion in funding over four years. Although the budget had already been whittled down to $18.5 billion over five years at that point, the amount was still too much for Prime Minister Modi, who eventually ordered a revamp of the policy due to budgetary constraints (Rochan 2015). The number of essential drugs to which free access was promised was trimmed from 348 to 50 (Nagarajan 2015). In April 2015, it was reported that the aim of providing free drugs and diagnostic services had been quietly shelved (Mukherjee 2015). As a result of failure to receive funding, the National Health Assurance Mission was never launched.

Instead, in early 2018, the India Government announced the Ayushman Bharat-National Health Protection Mission, often dubbed as "Modicare." Despite doubts that the program would be launched, it was launched in September 2018, aiming to provide around 100 million families with insurance coverage of up to INR 500,000 or US$7,800 per year, which is over fifteen times the amount that poor families could claim. The program also aimed to set up 150,000 health and wellness centres by December 2022, to provide diagnosis and treatment, especially for rural communities where access has been significantly lower. Additionally, Modicare aimed to set up more government medical colleges and hospitals to address the shortage of health professionals (*Reuters* 2018).

With the official launch in 2018, the government allocated US$1.54 billion for the initial rollout of the program in 2018–19. The latest data published in June 2021 show that around 12.3 million people have availed themselves of the benefits under the program, amounting to less than 2 percent of the target 500 million (or 100 million families). In addition, beneficiaries under the scheme may lose their eligibility under other health care schemes.

Insurance coverage for citizens also does not adequately address many of the existing challenges in India's health care system. Poor health infrastructure, the lack of health care facilities, especially in rural areas, and inadequate health care staff are all problems that are likely to continue impeding access to health care despite insurance coverage.

Improving Public Health: Responsibilities, Policies, and Performance of States

The Responsibilities of States and the Diversity of Their Capacities to Deliver

The Indian Constitution assigns primary responsibility for health promotion and care to the states. It stipulates that the state government bears the primary responsibility of "raising the level of nutrition and the standard of living of its people and the improvement of public health" (Ministry of Law and Justice 2007, Article 47). The central government, however, attempts to provide leadership by establishing an overarching vision and targets for the entire country. It also identifies issues of national importance and develops and sponsors national programs to cope with them. The multiplicity of schemes initiated by the central government has constrained the flexibility of the states to respond to their special needs and deploy their resources in the most efficient manner (Planning Commission 2013). As we have seen above, the policies in place to deal with the provision of health care and medicine to some of the most vulnerable segments of the population were often bold and ambitious, but financial commitment was lacking and the effectiveness of their execution disappointing.

The enormous challenges that the states were left with included primary responsibility for the development of facilities and services and their operations within their territories. Throughout the country, poor literacy among women, low levels of health awareness, low incidence of hygiene, poor sanitation, socio-cultural norms leading to home birth, lack of access to antenatal and postnatal care, and backward and dangerous cultural traditions have been cited as major challenges to achieving improved health outcomes (Aga Khan Development Network 2007). The degree to which these factors affect health outcomes and the manner in which they are managed vary greatly from state to state, however, as do the economic capacities of the states to meet these challenges and their commitment to ensure a healthy population. Indeed, many states do little to augment the inadequate efforts of the central government.

Below, we focus on three states whose economic development enabled them to actively cope with the challenges presented by their constitutional responsibility to protect the health rights of their citizens – perhaps foreshadowing the paths that other states may choose as they develop. The period we are most interested in for our comparative case studies was the two decades ending in 2013, during which each of the three states developed and implemented its own distinct approach to promoting health and delivering health care to its people.

The Distinct Approaches of Kerala, Tamil Nadu, and Gujarat to Health Care Promotion and Delivery

We chose Kerala, Tamil Nadu, and Gujarat for our case studies because of their significant economic growth and rapid infrastructural improvements, particularly after 1991, when India's economy was opened to the global market by increasing the permitted amount of foreign direct investment in the country (Bhat and Mitter 2014). The three states took different approaches to improving the health of their populations, due in part to the influence of differing ideologies with respect to the role of government and the balance between social and economic objectives. As the following discussion will demonstrate, all three states have been cited as economic success stories in India (see Table 3.1.)

Gujarat, with an estimated population of 60,439,692 in 2011, is located in the northwest of India. Despite its urban-rural population split of 42.6% and 57.4%, it is considered an urbanized state by Indian standards and is one of India's major industrial hubs, home to some of the fastest-growing cities in the world. During the period of this study, Gujarat had gained international attention for its economic performance. Its former governor, Narendra Modi, was elected as India's prime minister in 2013, largely due to a campaign based on his model of business-friendly government focused on economic prosperity (*Economist* 2015). Through strong encouragement of private sector investment, Gross State Domestic Product (GSDP) in Gujarat grew considerably over the period of the study. Between 2000 and 2011, per capita GSDP increased at a consistent and nation-leading rate of 9.2% (Kalaiyarasan 2014). In 2011–12, Gujaratis earned on average INR 89,688 (Government of India 2013).

Tamil Nadu, a state of 72,147,030 residents in 2011, is found on the southeastern tip of India. It is the most urbanized of the three states in our case study, with 48.4% of the population living in cities. Like Gujarat, Tamil Nadu enjoyed a consistently high economic growth rate over the period of the study, with average annual per capita GSDP growing 5.1% annually between 1990 and 2001 and 7.5% annually between 2001 and 2011 (Drèze and Sen 2013). In 2012, Tamil Nadu recorded a per capita GSDP of INR 88697 (Government of India 2013).

Kerala is Tamil Nadu's western neighbour and, with 33,406,061 residents in 2011, has the smallest population of the three states. From an economic development standpoint, however, it made the most significant improvement over the study period. As with Gujarat and Tamil Nadu, Kerala enjoyed a high rate of annual economic growth, expanding 7.0% on average between

TABLE 3.1

Comparison of economic development in three Indian states

	Kerala	Tamil Nadu	Gujarat
Population (2011)	33,406,061	72,147,030	60,439,692
Urban/rural (%)	–	48.4/51.6	42.6/57.4
Per capita GSDP in rupees (2011–12)[1]	80,924	88,697	89,688
GSDP PPP Per-capita in US$ (2009)[2]	3,854	3,522	3,849
Life expectancy at birth, in years, female/male (2006–10)	76.9/71.5	70.9/67.1	69.0/64.9
Poverty estimates, rural/urban/total (%) (2009–10)	12.0/12.1/12.0	21.2/12.8/17.1	26.7/17.9/23.0

Notes:
1 Government of India 2013.
2 Gross State Domestic Product (at purchasing power parity) per capita. Muraleedharan, Dash, and Gilson 2011.
Source: Drèze and Sen 2013 unless otherwise noted.

2000 and 2011 (Drèze and Sen 2013). In M. Ghatak and S. Roy's study (2014) of sixteen major Indian states (including those discussed in this chapter), Kerala made the most significant improvement in per capita GSDP, jumping from tenth to fifth wealthiest between 1990–93 and 2008–10. In 2011–12, the per capita GSDP of the state grew to INR 80924 (Government of India 2013).

Health Indicators
One way in which health analysts gauge the state of health in India and other developing countries is through the United Nations Millennium Development Goals (MDG) framework. Millennium Development Goals "are a set of numerical and time bound targets to measure achievements in human and social development laid down by the UN" to be achieved by the year 2015 (Office of Registrar General 2011). The goals pertaining directly to performance in health are MDG 4 (Reducing Child Mortality) and MDG 5 (Improving Maternal Health) (United Nations Development Programme 2011). We will use these goals as the framework for our initial discussion.

Pediatric Health

MDG 4 committed nations to reducing their infant mortality rate (IMR) to 28 per 1,000 live births and their under-5 mortality rate (U5MR) to 42 per 1 by 2015. For both indicators, all three states made considerable improvements from 1990. Kerala performed best, recording an average IMR and average U5MR of 13. Tamil Nadu also achieved MDG 4, with an average IMR of 21 in 2010–12 and a U5MR of 24 in 2012. Gujarat, despite having made some strides over the earlier decade, did not achieve MDG 4 in both the IMR and U5MR measures before the Millennium Development Goal target of 2015.

In an attempt to explain why Tamil Nadu and Kerala achieved MDG 4 while Gujarat has not, analysts have pointed to other health indicators in which the states' performance differs considerably. These include areas such as vaccination coverage, full immunization, and the ratio of female infants born relative to males. In both Kerala and Tamil Nadu, vaccination coverage is high. Among children aged 12–23 months, 80.9% in Tamil Nadu and 75.3% in Kerala have been fully immunized. When children who have received some but not all of the scheduled immunizations are included, the numbers rise to 86.7%, and 79.3%, respectively. In contrast, immunization rates in Gujarat remain significantly lower despite increasing incomes

TABLE 3.2

Comparison of children's health in three Indian states

Child health indicators	Kerala	Tamil Nadu	Gujarat
IMR1 (total/urban/rural) (2010–12)	12/13/9 (compared to a total IMR of 13 in 2007)	21/24/18 (compared to a total IMR of 35 in 2007)	38/45/24 (compared to a total IMR of 52 in 2007)
U5MR2 (total/urban/rural) (2012)	13/13/10	24/28/20	48/56/32
Some vaccination coverage (%)	79.3	86.7	55.2
Full immunization (%)	75.3	80.9	45.2

Notes:
1 IMR = infant mortality rate: deaths per 1,000 live births.
2 U5MR = under-5 mortality rate: deaths per 1,000.
Source: Office of Registrar General, 2011.

among its residents, with less than half (45.2%) of children being fully immunized and only 55.2% receiving some vaccination coverage.

Maternal Health

In order to meet MDG 5, India was required to reduce its maternal mortality rate to 109 deaths per 100,000 live births countrywide by 2015. At the state level, both Kerala and Tamil Nadu achieved and surpassed this goal prior to 2015. Kerala led all Indian states in this measure, recording 66 deaths per 100,000 births in 2010. Although considerably higher than Kerala's, Tamil Nadu's statistic of 90 deaths per 100,000 births was below the UN Development Programme (UNDP) target and well below the national average of 190 deaths (United Nations, n.d.). Gujarat too performed better than most Indian states, but despite improving its statistics over the years, its maternal mortality rate remained above the MDG target, at 122 deaths per 100,000 births in 2010 (World Bank 2015).

One factor that analysts have associated with both positive and negative performance in maternal mortality is the presence of trained medical workers during childbirth. In case of unforeseen complications, it is believed (understandably so) that the mother's chances of avoiding harm are greater if a trained medical worker is in attendance. In this regard, a striking difference is observed in the number of assisted births taking place in Gujarat and those occurring in the two southern states. Nearly all births in Kerala and over 90% in Tamil Nadu are conducted in this manner. In contrast, trained medical workers assisted only 63% of women giving birth in Gujarat (Table 3.3). Although less marked, differences were also observed in the percentage of mothers receiving antenatal care visits. In this regard, both

TABLE 3.3

Comparison of maternal health in three Indian states

Maternal health indicators	Kerala	Tamil Nadu	Gujarat
Maternal mortality rate (deaths/100,000 live births) (2010–12)	66	90	122
Assisted birth (2005–06)	99.4	90.6	63.0
At least one antenatal care visit (%) (2005–06)	94.4	98.6	86.7

Source: Drèze and Sen 2013.

Kerala's and Tamil Nadu's statistics were high, at 94.4% and 98.6%, respectively, whereas Gujarat's was lower once again at 86.7% (see Table 3.3).

Assessment

As demonstrated by the health statistics of Gujarat, Tamil Nadu, and Kerala, not all states in India perform equally in terms of health indicators. Although all three states experienced considerable economic growth from the early 1990s and ranked among India's most wealthy states, this economic growth has not necessarily been accompanied by similar improvements to health and social development indicators. In the case of Gujarat in particular, it is apparent that improvements in the areas of maternal and pediatric health have not occurred on the same scale or speed as the state's economic growth. While certainly performing well compared with the national average, Gujarat has underperformed relative to its southern counterparts Kerala and Tamil Nadu on a variety of indicators.

While all three states are now among India's wealthiest in terms of per capita GSDP, their progress in terms of health indicators for their citizens has differed considerably. Kerala has garnered the most attention from foreign and domestic development analysts for the longest amount of time. Its ability to do "more with less" by providing better health outcomes to its residents despite limited economic capacity has been dubbed the "Kerala Model" and has been used as a blueprint for development for similarly poor countries and states around the world since the 1970s (Freund 2009).

For decades, Kerala has been India's best-performing state in most social and health development indicators. What has made this most noteworthy is that this feat was accomplished at a time when Kerala was experiencing below-average per capita income and rampant poverty (Brown 2013). Despite being ranked in the middle tier of state economic wealth, it still managed to record development indicator statistics that bore greater resemblance to those of developed nations than those of neighbouring states. For example, in 1990, when India's infant mortality rate stood at 85 deaths per 1,000 live births, Kerala recorded 17 (Brown 2013). In terms of life expectancy, Kerala has performed the best among the three states (and the rest of the country) over the past twenty-five years. In the early 1990s, it already enjoyed an average life expectancy at birth of 72.9 for females and 67.2 for males, figures much closer to those from developed countries than to the Indian average of 60 years (Ashokan 2010). By 2006, life expectancy for Keralans had improved further to 76.9 years for females and 71.5 for males.

Poverty levels also improved in Kerala: in 2013, an average of 12.0% of residents were considered to be below the poverty line (BPL), evenly balanced between rural and urban areas at 12.0% and 12.1%, respectively (Drèze and Sen 2013).

In comparison, Tamil Nadu and Gujarat have recorded higher BPL rates. Tamil Nadu's overall rate (in 2009–10) was 17.1% (21.2% rural, 12.8% urban), while Gujarat's was 23.0% (26.7% rural, 17.9% urban). Although better than the national average, Gujarat's life expectancy remained the lowest of the three states at 69.0 years for females and 64.9 for males (2006–10). Tamil Nadu's average life expectancy during the same period was 70.9 years for females and 67.1 years for males, a considerable improvement from the early 1990s. It is important to note that although Tamil Nadu started far behind Kerala, in terms of these indicators, it has made significant improvements during this period of time. In some areas – such as percentage of full child immunization (80.9 versus 75.3), percentage of children 0–3 years suffering from diarrhea (5.4 versus 5.6), percentage of women with at least one antenatal care visit (98.6 versus 94.4) – it outperformed its neighbour in terms of its residents' health (Drèze and Sen 2013).

Some observers, such as Bhagwati and Panagariya (2013) have argued that Kerala cannot be compared with Gujarat in terms of health status since Kerala's health statistics were already well beyond those of Gujarat in the early 1990s (Kalaiyarasan 2014). In fact, Gujarat made far greater improvements to its health statistics over the two decades of our study than Kerala, which, for the most part, maintained or improved only slightly its already strong statistics. Kerala also slipped marginally in certain areas, such as infant mortality. Tamil Nadu, on the other hand, was defined less by its rapidly improving health indicators than by its extreme poverty and glaring caste-based social inequality (Drèze and Sen 2013). At the beginning of the 1990s, its health statistics were similar to those of Gujarat. By 2013, however, it had outperformed Gujarat both in terms of its 2013 statistics and the rate at which those statistics had improved (Kalaiyarasan 2014). Furthermore, this was accomplished despite a slower rate of economic growth than Gujarat (Drèze and Sen 2013). So, while some may argue about the way the three states are compared, there is a general consensus that Gujarat underperformed in terms of delivering improved health outcomes. In other words, improved economic outcomes have not necessarily translated into proportionately better health and social outcomes for residents of states in India (Kalaiyarasan 2014).

Public Health Expenditure: Doing More with Less and Shifting Expenditures to the Private Sector as the Economy Grows
One might assume that Kerala's and Tamil Nadu's superior performance in health care outcomes would be the result of these states spending significantly more on health care than Gujarat. This, arguably, was not the case. In both Kerala and Tamil Nadu, state government expenditure remained small, and in fact had decreased significantly as a proportion of GSDP since the 1990s. In 2013, there was not much differentiating the state spending on health in Gujarat, Tamil Nadu, and Kerala. In all three states, public sector spending on health contributed less than the national average of INR 503 (Government of India 2013).

Although medical, public health, and family welfare comprise Tamil Nadu's largest area of expenditure next to education, only about a quarter of the approximately 4% of the state's GSDP spent on health was provided by the state government. The rest was covered by private expenditure and out-of-pocket spending (Muraleedharan, Dash, and Gilson 2011). In fact, state government spending on health in Tamil Nadu dropped steadily over the years, from 1.94% of GSDP in 1990 to 1.35% in 1998 and about 1% in 2011 (ibid.). Between 1990 and 2002, Tamil Nadu showed decreases in health care spending of 38.5% (Bhat and Jain 2014). Private funding of health care was also significant, accounting for financing of 80% of outpatient and 60% of inpatient care (Muraleedharan, Dash, and Gilson 2011).

Much the same can be said for Kerala. Although the state had become famous for achieving its high human development indicators despite limited financial means, state governmental financing of health relative to GSDP fell dramatically from 1990 to 2011. In 1998–99, 0.95% of GSDP was dedicated to health, a significant decrease from the 1.49% spent in 1990 and the 2.02% in 1980 (Ashokan 2010). In 2004–05, Kerala's public expenditure on health dropped even further, to 0.90% of GSDP (*Times of India* 2012). While the state's per capita public health expenditure as a proportion of GSDP was at one point among the highest for any Indian state, its public financing of health decreased by 35% between 1990 and 2002, making it "one of the States with the highest reduction in public contribution" (Daviadanam et al. 2012, 592). As a result, 90.3% of health care in Kerala was funded by the private sector, the highest of any state in India (ibid.).

Between 1990 and 2002, governmental per capita health expenditure in Gujarat decreased at an even greater rate than in Kerala and Tamil Nadu. In fact, the 46.2% cut represented the largest decrease in public spending on health among all states in India (Bhat and Jain 2014).

Despite low governmental funding of health care in all three states, it is clear that markedly different outcomes and rates of improvement of health indicators in Gujarat, Kerala, and Tamil Nadu have occurred during the time period of the study. A variety of factors have been cited to explain this disparity in outcomes over the years between Gujarat and the two southern states. Although exploring all of these factors is beyond the scope of this chapter, it is likely that important factors were the distinct policy choices made by each of the state governments and the way in which they chose to disburse their limited resources.

Universal Health Care and Policy Choices

Many observers have pointed to the implementation of policies in Kerala and Tamil Nadu aimed at affecting as many residents as possible as an important factor in these states' realization of significant improvements in health. According to Jean Drèze and Amartya Sen (2013, 79), for example, these states are among those in India that have "typically followed universalistic principles in the provision of essential public services." In these states, policies created for services like primary health care are targeted toward as many people as possible "on a non-discriminatory basis, instead of being 'targeted' to specific sections of the population" (ibid.). In committing to policies that aim to provide a fundamental suite of services to the largest number of residents possible, the states have established an "extensive network of lively and effective healthcare centres where people from all social backgrounds can get reasonably good healthcare" (ibid.). In aiming to provide access to equitable, affordable, and quality health care services to as many people as possible regardless of age, gender, religion, caste, or financial class, the two southern states have also made efforts to ensure that populations in both urban and rural areas receive access to essential health services. In Tamil Nadu, for example, successive governments have made a long-term commitment to improving primary care in rural areas (Muraleedharan, Dash, and Gilson 2011).

Tamil Nadu's commitment to providing fundamental services to as many of its residents as possible is demonstrated in the way in which it funds the three levels of health care. While the ratio of GSDP the state has spent on health has remained roughly the same as in most Indian states, since the late 1980s, Tamil Nadu invested substantial amounts into primary health care and capacity-building exercises: "Unlike most of India's large states, Tamil Nadu has a clear commitment to widespread access and affordability in healthcare. From the late 1980s, significant investments have transformed the state's health infrastructure. Initiatives that were launched by the central government were vigorously implemented, such as the large-scale expansion of primary health centres" (Parthasarathi and Sinha 2016). As M. Das Gupta and colleagues (2009, 4) explain, "the size of the public health budget [in Tamil Nadu] is large relative to spending on secondary/tertiary medical care and medical education." Since 1990 and throughout the period of the study, the state government had consistently devoted 45% of its annual health budget to primary health care, a proportion greater than that of most states in India (Muraleedharan, Dash, and Gilson 2011). Between 1990 and 2002, the government's funding of tertiary care decreased from 33% to 24%, with the difference being transferred to secondary services (ibid.). In contrast, policies in Gujarat were less universal in nature and were characterized by a more "targeted" approach toward certain sectors of society. While the state of Gujarat no doubt made significant gains in its overall socioeconomic indicators over the past quarter-century, especially compared with the national average, improvements were not experienced by all of its regions and subpopulations (Sanneving et al. 2013).

Efficiency and Reliability

The focus on treating fundamental ailments of as large a segment of their population as possible increased the efficiency and reliability of primary health centres in Tamil Nadu and Kerala. While both states experienced benefits from placing primary health care centres under the control of local governments (Varatharajan, Thankappan, and Jayapalan 2004), the results have been particularly pronounced in Tamil Nadu. Through the establishment of a "quasi-governmental organization" (Muraleedharan, Dash, and Gilson 2011, 170) at the substate level, continuity of policy in these centres was more easily maintained as civil servants equipped with management skills and sufficient discretion to create and implement meaningful reforms served as an effective mechanism for overcoming tardy bureaucratic procedures (ibid.). In addition to improving efficiency, the system also resulted in patients paying significantly less than patients of state-operated facilities in both Gujarat (Kalaiyarasan 2014) and Kerala (Ghosh 2011).

According to D. Varatharajan, R. Thankappan, and S. Jayapalan (2004), the success of the "Kerala Model" has been largely attributed to the universal availability and efficient delivery of the government-run health care system. While the system still functioned well compared with those of most other states, some have expressed concern that significant decreases in funding have resulted in a reduction of capacity and quality in essential facilities and services, causing a decrease in utilization (ibid.). With an increase in privatization, out-of-pocket expenses in Kerala have grown at one of the fastest rates in India (Ghosh 2011), with poor residents spending disproportionately on health care (upward of 40% of annual income, compared with the 2.4% spent by wealthier residents) (Varatharajan, Thankappan, and Jayapalan 2004).

Tamil Nadu was the only state in India that maintained a distinct public health management cadre at the district level (Muraleedharan, Dash, and Gilson 2011). This enabled trained health workers to work with their community to develop local solutions to health challenges. With this system in place, health officials were better able to understand the nuances in the communities they were serving, enabling them to address ailments and the spread of communicable diseases in a more efficient manner (ibid.). Furthermore, this autonomy empowered health care providers at the local level, enabling them to maintain a far more consistent quality of service than in states where the operation of primary health centres was more dependent on the changing priorities of the state government. Efficiency and quality of service were also strengthened by programs such as the Tribal Health Initiative, where trained local residents conducted education programs and established outreach clinics in more remote villages, resulting in greater access to and usage of antenatal care and significantly reduced infant mortality rates (Tribal Health Initiative 2015).

In contrast, continuity in health services remained a weakness of the health care system in Gujarat. Regarding challenges to the reduction of the maternal mortality ratio in Gujarat, D.V. Mavalankar and colleagues (2009) point to the lack of managerial capacity and a shortage of skilled human resources, in addition to infrastructural and supply bottlenecks. This, along with the complexity of coordination, lack of confidence in and underutilization of monitoring systems, and weak referral systems are further highlighted in Sanneving and colleagues' work (2013) on Gujarat's maternal health policy.

It would appear that in Gujarat, health care provision was much more reliant on "individual stakeholders than on sustainable structures and processes" (Sanneving et al. 2013). In this system, more emphasis was placed on implementing new policies with more visible, short-term solutions than on assessing the effectiveness, merit, and possibility of continuing or integrating previous initiatives (ibid.). As a result, the establishment of stable policies and planning to achieve long-term objectives became more difficult once changes in leadership occurred (ibid.). Also, while Gujarat made great efforts to maintain and update facilities and infrastructure, shortages of medical professionals and inadequately staffed public health facilities prevented it from providing quality and reliable services to its residents (Mavalankar et al. 2009).

Access to Medicines: The Tamil Nadu Model for Procurement

The development of transparent procurement systems for medicines and medical instruments in Kerala, Tamil Nadu, and Gujarat reduced the cost of public health care facilities, allowing for the care of a larger number of people. Once again, Tamil Nadu demonstrated leadership. In 1994, it became the first state in India to establish an essential medicines list (Kar, Pradhan, and Mohanta 2010). In 1995, it established the Tamil Nadu Medical Services Corporation (TNMSC), the operations of which were funded entirely by the state government (Baru et al. 2010). With the stated aim of "mak[ing] drugs and materials available to the poorest of the poor and 'Service to the Public'" (Velásquez, Madrid, and Quick 1998, 55), the TNMSC was the sole purchaser and supplier of medications for government-operated health facilities, and the drugs it supplied were among those included in the World Health Organization's Model List of Essential Drugs. The TNMSC list, including the prices of medicines and supplies, was published and distributed to doctors, nurses, and pharmacists practising in Tamil Nadu, as well as to the state's medical schools. In order to promote awareness of drug costs, the list was also made available to the public. To ensure regular supply to all facilities, TNMSC drugs were stored in warehouses spread throughout every district in the state. Passbooks were provided to institutions in order to log the amount available to be spent, expenses incurred from purchasing medicines and surgical supplies, and projected costs based on patient numbers and surgeries performed the previous year (Revikumar et al. 2013).

The result was a transparent online procurement system for medicine where all bidding was done at fixed-rate prices and all stocking and provisional information was openly available. The subsequent drop in drug prices saw the total number of people using public health care facilities in the state rise from 20% to 40%, compared with the rest of India, where the figure was less than 25% (Shepherd-Smith 2012). The effectiveness of this "Tamil Nadu Model" in the procurement and distribution of medicines led other Indian states to follow suit with similar systems, including Kerala, which established the Kerala Medical Services Corporation Ltd. (KMSCL) in 2007 (Kerala Medical Services Corporation 2015), and Gujarat, which incorporated its Gujarat Medical Services Corporation Ltd. (GMSCL) in 2012 (ZaubaCorp 2013).

The Role of the States in Modicare
With the launch of Modicare, a National Health Authority of India was set up to assist with smooth collaboration and coordination with state-run programs. The government announced that the burden would be split 60:40 between the government and the state, with states having flexibility in carrying out the implementation of the new scheme, including how they would work out the insurance model (Datta 2018). Tamil Nadu and Kerala have similar programs already in place, and Prime Minister Modi stated that Tamil Nadu's system was a successful one that could serve as an example for other states to emulate (*The Hindu* 2018). States have an increasingly important role in ensuring the success of Modicare, as developing many of the implementation details will fall on their shoulders.

The SDG agenda commits India to pursuing universal health coverage for access to quality necessary health care services and safe, effective medicines and vaccines. The Indian Constitution mandates that the states regard the improvement of public health as one of their primary duties. Despite their obligations, the central government and a majority of the states have failed to make a sufficient effort to ensure continuous improvement of the health system and access to affordable health care for a majority of their people.

An overwhelming majority of India's population has either no access or very limited access to essential medicines and health care services. While the private health insurance sector has been growing rapidly (about 23 percent a year) (Morder Intelligence 2020) serving the "haves," the limited expansion in public health insurance excludes essential services and drug costs that make up the bulk of the health-related expenditures of the "have nots." Far from realizing the promise of "health for all," the limited programs that are offered tend to exclude the most vulnerable segments of the population. The total financial commitment per capita by the governments of India is among the lowest in the world. Furthermore, while increased public commitment of financial resources to health care and promotion is crucial, it is not sufficient. The experience of states such as Tamil Nadu and Kerala suggests that more can be done with less with appropriate policies in place and a commitment and capacity to implement them.

Our analysis of the policies of the central government and their implementation indicates the existence of an ineffective bureaucracy mired in a gridlocked system of governance. For example, despite powerful legal instruments available to various government agencies to influence the price of medicines, the government is failing to ensure affordable, quality essential medicines for all. Price controls cannot make essential medicines affordable to significant segments of the population, i.e., the millions living at a bare subsistence level. Those who can afford to buy medicines at the regulated prices often face shortages and/or can find only low-quality drugs. "Flexibilities" in the patent law that provide the government with a variety of ways to lower the prices of medicines are rarely utilized; these include 1) reducing the ability of pharmaceutical companies to patent (and thus use their monopoly position to raise prices); 2) preventing "evergreening" (lengthening of the duration of patents by companies that introduce minor modifications and use them to get new patents); or 3) compelling the companies to license their production and sales to others so their prices are lowered. This is often due to lack of capacity in the patent office, the influence of private sector suppliers, or intervention by ministries pursuing economic development objectives.

An ineffective, highly bureaucratic, and inflexible civil service generates high transaction costs, slowing or stifling innovation in the health care system. Despite periodic long- and mid-term planning exercises focusing on the health care system by the central government and a recognition of inadequate physical infrastructure and insufficiently trained human resources, shortages of health care professionals and inadequate facilities persist and prevent the provision of quality care even when funds are available.

Besides implementation failures, policy failures abound. The experiences of Kerala, Tamil Nadu, and Gujarat highlight the importance of the appropriate design of policies and a commitment to implement them. They demonstrate the importance of shifting the balance of priorities between economic and social objectives as the economy grows. The Kerala Model is instructive. Early in its economic development, Kerala placed an emphasis on social objectives, including promotion of the health of its population, laying the foundation for eventual rapid economic growth. As it achieved higher levels of economic growth, it shifted more of the financial burden of the health care system to the private sector. It developed planning and implementation systems that emphasized a long-term view, universality of access to health care, efficiency, and transparency. It proved that more could be done with less. The experiences of Tamil Nadu echo those of Kerala with respect to managerial efficiency while highlighting the importance of a focus on primary care and regional autonomy.

Our overall assessment of India's ability to comply with its international commitments concerning the delivery of health to its people, at least in the short and medium term, is negative. As required by SDG 3.8, providing universal access to affordable essential health care and medicine to a population, a significant part of which lives in dire poverty, is a serious challenge, especially when faced with the utilization of traditional approaches to health care delivery. Using the current approaches to delivery of health care will require the investment of resources far beyond the levels that any level of government in India is likely to be able to afford or be willing to allocate. We argue that commitment to radical innovation in the delivery of health promotion and care, including the adoption of non-traditional methods of delivery and the deployment of new, less expensive types of health and allied professional services, is required if India is to make significant progress in the foreseeable future in improving the health of its people. Economic development must be accompanied by social development, including health education and promotion. Emphasis must be placed on investment in primary care and development of regional autonomous health care delivery systems. Management capacity must be developed and bureaucracies reformed to ensure an accommodating environment in which innovation may thrive in the Indian health care and promotion systems. Modicare may be a much-needed step in the direction of providing universal health care, but it comes with its own set of challenges that states and governments need to work together on, in order to ensure that it has a successful impact on the people of India.

NOTES

1 https://sdgs.un.org/goals/goal3.
2 Chapter 9 discusses in detail how India has created a market for the export of Japanese health care services.
3 https://www.wto.org/english/docs_e/legal_e/27-trips_01_e.htm.
4 Chapter 6 discusses how, despite efforts by the World Trade Organization, provisions by the Government of India to protect public health from unsafe food have been curtailed by international trade law.

PART 2

PROTECTING AND PROMOTING PUBLIC HEALTH

4

Linking Public Health Targets of the Sustainable Development Goals to Human Rights Performance in China

LESLEY A. JACOBS

China has consistently positioned itself within the international human rights community as a proponent of the view that while civil and political rights matter, its priorities are social and economic rights. This view was advanced by China at the outset of the establishment of the United Nations (UN) human rights system in the late 1940s and 1950s (Zhao 2015, 35–39). It is reflected today in the fact that although the People's Republic of China had signed both the International Covenant on Economic, Social and Cultural Rights (ICESCR) and the International Covenant on Civil and Political Rights (ICCPR) by the late 1990s, it has ratified only the former. The prioritizing of social and economic rights over fundamental civil and political rights is explicit in China's National Human Rights Action Plans, which the government began to issue in 2009. The 2016 Action Plan explains, "The Chinese government ... puts the protection of people's rights to subsistence and development in the first place, takes the people's well-being and all-around development as both the starting point and ultimate goal of China's human rights work" (Government of China 2016).[1] In practice, this sort of positioning by China has enabled it to represent itself in the international community as a strong performer on human rights, yet not in alignment with the human rights advocacy by governments of advanced industrial countries in the Global North or the leading international human rights organizations, such as Amnesty International and Human Rights Watch, that are based in those countries. Arguably, China has been a model in the Global

South for developing a public health system that has advanced global health security, without embracing other human rights centred on individual freedoms and liberties (Jacobs and Potter 2006; Jacobs 2019).

The establishment of the Sustainable Development Goals (SDG) agenda by the United Nations in 2015 provides a new lens for thinking about China's human rights performance affecting global health security. At the foundation of the SDG agenda, as explained in the Introduction to this book, is the idea that the right to health in international law has two distinct components, one centred on entitlements, the other centred on freedoms. The SDG agenda has embedded this concept into its public health targets, which suggests to me that it is worthwhile to revisit, and indeed reframe, China's approach to public health.

This chapter is designed to put pressure on the view that China can successfully realize progressively the right to public health and achieve the public health targets in the SDG without attending in tandem to issues of freedom such as reproductive health choices and treatment options for addiction and substance abuse. My point is not the common one based on the doctrine that because human rights are indivisible and seamless it is not possible to prioritize social and economic rights over civil and political rights, or vice versa (e.g., Toebes 1999). Nor is it the claim that in China the capacity to enjoy economic, social, and cultural rights is highly contingent on enjoying civil and political rights (Biddulph 2015). Instead, my argument is that the right to health in international human rights law is now formulated as having two components – entitlements and freedoms – and that these two components are embedded in the SDG, which means that respecting, protecting, and fulfilling the right to health requires attention to both of these components. Although this formulation of the right to health is quite recent, having emerged largely in the past twenty years, it is today virtually uncontested in the international human rights community. China's decades-old position that right to health performance requires attention only to entitlements and guarantees of a public health infrastructure is simply inconsistent with that formulation. The upshot is that for the public health targets in the SDG and international human rights in China, the performance record is a clear one of being stronger on entitlements but weaker on freedoms.

The Right to Health in China

China has readily embraced the right to health defined in the International Bill of Human Rights. [2] Indeed, China was one of the two countries – the other was Brazil – that initiated the establishment of the World Health Organization (WHO) in 1945 (Sze 1945–46, 3), and it maintains its enthusiasm for the WHO (Jacobs 2014). China has, however, also largely ignored the interpretation of the right to health in terms of entitlements and freedoms now prevalent in the international human rights community. The right to health is implemented in domestic constitutional law in Article 45 of the Constitution of the People's Republic of China – adopted in 1982 but amended since then – which states:

> Citizens of the People's Republic of China have the right to material assistance from the state and society when they are old, ill or disabled. The state develops social insurance, social relief and medical and health services that are required for citizens to enjoy this right.[3]

This constitutional article illustrates an earnest and sustained effort by the Chinese government to show commitment to the progressive realization of the entitlement provisions of the right to health, while at the same time giving far less priority to respecting, protecting, and fulfilling rights to certain basic liberties.

Two developments in the field of health and human rights are important for situating this discussion of the right to public health in China. The first revolves around concerns about the neglect of a human rights lens in public health epidemics. These concerns originate in the experiences of physicians and human rights activists responding to the AIDS epidemic in the late 1980s and early 1990s. Perhaps the best-known proponent of this view was Jonathan Mann, who served as the first head of the WHO Global Programme on AIDS (WHO/GPA). In the course of that role, Mann came to believe that the protection of basic human rights was not only compatible with the fight against AIDS but central to that struggle. In effect, what Mann argued was that the global AIDS epidemic had its origins not just in the contagion of a newly emerging infectious disease but also in social vulnerability. His point was that discrimination and stigma are a fundamental part of the problem, and that for this reason AIDS is also a human rights issue (Mann 1998, 143–49).

The second important development in the international field of health and human rights revolved around the growing recognition in the late 1990s of the so-called social determinants of health. At issue here is the view of health, most commonly identified with Richard Wilkinson and Michael Marmot, as dependent not simply on individual behaviour or exposure to risk but on how a population's economic and social structure shapes health (Marmot and Wilkinson 1999; Wilkinson 1996). The point is that the ambit of health concerns extends not just to medical care and public health measures but also to social issues such as poverty, housing, social exclusion, and the environment. The implication is that for all nations, including China, health and human rights performance should be linked to other social rights indicators in areas such as education, poverty reduction, and housing (Farmer 2005, 2010; Gruskin et al. 2005).

Significantly, the concept of social determinants of health gained global currency with the promotion of global development goals by the United Nations. The Millennium Development Goals (MDGs), which were adopted in 2000, targeted developing countries, including China and India. The MDGs made poverty reduction and the realization of the right to health the highest priorities. They set specific performance targets and dates organized around extreme poverty, primary education, maternal health, child mortality, gender equality, HIV/AIDS, and malaria. China was singled out by the United Nations in 2015 as the country that performed best on the MDGs (United Nations Development Programme 2015). In the period from 2000 to 2015, for example, China was especially effective at lifting people, particularly children, out of poverty, reducing infant and maternal mortality and increasing life expectancy. In its September 2017 White Paper on public health, the State Council Information Office of the People's Republic of China reported: "The average life expectancy of the Chinese rose to 76.5 years in 2016 from 67.9 years in 1981; maternal mortality dropped from 88.9 per 100,000 persons in 1990 to 19.9 per 100,000 persons in 2016; and infant mortality declined from 34.7 per 1,000 in 1981 to 7.5 per 1,000 in 2016" (State Council of the People's Republic of China 2017). These stunning improvements in health outcomes reflect in part escalating public investments in China's public health care system.

In 2015, the United Nations adopted the seventeen new Social Development Goals (SDGs). Health is at the centre of the SDGs, which, as we saw in the Introduction, provide global health standards. Health performance in the SDGs refers not just to the provision of health services and public health but also to protection from discrimination and other human rights concerns. The United Nations Development Programme (2016) initially suggested that China was well on the path to achieving the targets set out for it by the SDGs. This has recently been reinforced by an assessment of China's performance in the *Sustainable Development Report 2021* by J. Sachs and colleagues (2021). My argument here is to challenge that assessment on the basis that it fails to recognize the two components of the right to health.

Right to Health Entitlements in China

The entitlement component of the right to health centres on safeguarding public health. China has a well-established performance record on advancing its system of health protection, albeit with mixed results. For my purposes, I will focus on developments in two areas of public health: global infectious diseases and tobacco control. Both suggest that China is fulfilling to some degree its obligations with regard to the right to health entitlements.

China's Response to Global Infectious Diseases

A key target of the SDG agenda is SDG 3.3: "By 2030, end the epidemics of AIDS, tuberculosis, malaria and neglected tropical diseases and combat hepatitis, water-borne diseases and other communicable diseases."[4] China's handling of emerging communicable diseases such as COVID-19, severe acute respiratory syndrome (SARS), and AIDS during the twenty-first century, and the implications for global public health security, reflect a long history of concerns about the threats of foreign infectious diseases. Concerns about the spread of communicable diseases such as cholera, smallpox, and syphilis across international borders date to the early 1800s (Baldwin 1999). These concerns led to a series of International Sanitary Conferences in Europe over almost a century, designed to set norms and cooperation for dealing with the containment of infectious diseases. At the first of these conferences, in Paris in 1851, twelve major European countries adopted the international health sanitation rules, which contained 137 articles to guide them countries in dealing with epidemics. (China adopted these regulations in 1926.) The World Health Organization assumed responsibility for the International Sanitation Regulations when it was established in 1946. International human rights norms played no role in the initial adoption of these regulations.

Over the past three decades, emerging infectious diseases have increasingly come to be recognized as among the most pressing and difficult challenges to global security and international relations. They have the potential to destabilize governments, create havoc for national economies, and disrupt international trade. The global AIDS epidemic in the late twentieth century highlighted in particular the significance of emerging infectious diseases. Although the eruption of newly discovered infectious diseases has a long history, what is new is the greater vulnerability to the worldwide spread of these diseases caused by the rapid movement of people, goods, and resources (Garrett 1995). As the WHO (2007a, 5) observed, "Achieving international public health security is one of the main challenges arising from the new and complex landscape of public health." Although Africa has been the focal point for the global movement in the response to AIDS, the Asia-Pacific countries have been a major site for dealing with other new infectious diseases. China's role in global health crises is particularly important because of its immense population of 1.38 billion.

During crises involving infectious diseases, international obligations for states arise from the variety of international sanitary conventions that date, as noted above, originally to the mid-nineteenth century and were consolidated into the International Sanitation Regulations by the WHO in 1951 (Fidler 1999). These regulations, designed to prevent the international spread of infectious diseases, required states to notify the international community of outbreaks of certain diseases and maintain public health facilities that could regulate international points of entry and exit. In 1969, the WHO replaced these regulations with the International Health Regulations (IHR), which covered six "quarantinable" diseases (WHO 2008). The IHR for infectious diseases were revised in 1973 and again in 1983 so that they applied to only three diseases: cholera, plague, and yellow fever. This meant that the regulations did not address evolving contagions such as AIDS, SARS, avian flu, or H1N1. In 2005, the WHO formally adopted new International Health Regulations designed to apply to all public health risks, not just those stemming from cholera, plague, and yellow fever. The underlying logic of this new set of regulations is that they are better able to deal with new and emerging infectious diseases for the sake of international public health security (Fidler and Gostin 2006).

The new International Health Regulations came into force on June 15, 2007, and are legally binding on 194 countries, including all member states of the World Health Assembly. The aim of the IHR "is to help the international community prevent and respond to acute public health risks that have the potential to cross borders and threaten people worldwide" (WHO 2007b). They are designed to provide a public health response to the global spread of diseases and other public health risks while avoiding unnecessary interference with human rights, international travel, and international trade (WHO 2008). Unlike previous versions of the IHR, the new regulations are not limited to specific diseases, and in this way will maintain their relevance and applicability when new infectious diseases emerge. The new IHR also now extend beyond diseases to other global health risks, particularly dangers posed by food-borne diseases and disasters that can spill across borders, such as nuclear accidents and chemical leaks.

In addition to their greater reach, the 2005 IHR have a number of innovative features, including obligations for the state to develop certain basic public health capacities and to notify the WHO of public health emergencies that constitute international threats; allowing the WHO to utilize information sources other than official reports from member states; creating procedures and levels of risk for the determination of a global public health crisis; and embedding the protection of human rights in the regulations (WHO 2008).

From the perspective of member states, the WHO (2007a) is especially interested in supporting and strengthening national public health capacities along two dimensions. The first dimension is concerned with the so-called national disease prevention, surveillance, control, and response systems. The second involves public health security in travel and transport. The strengthening of these national capacities reflects a major shift in approach to international public health security by the WHO. As noted above, this is reflected partially in the broadening of the scope of the IHR from specific diseases to all health threats, but it is also significantly a shift from controlling contagions at borders to containment at their source, and a movement away from preset containment measures to "adapted response" (WHO 2007a, 11). The WHO envisions that the challenges of supporting and strengthening national public health capacities will be met not only through its own initiatives and those of other international institutions involved in public health capacity building, such as the World Bank and the Asian Development Bank, but also by fostering global partnerships between member states.

Prior to the introduction of the new IHR in 2007, China's record on responding to emerging infectious diseases such as HIV/AIDS and SARS was weak and subject to strong international criticism. Although HIV/AIDS was regarded as a disease of foreigners in the 1980s, by 2004 at least 1 million people were infected by the disease in China and infections were rising at a rate of 30 percent per year (Jacobs and Potter 2006). Some provinces with large ethnic minority populations, such as Yunnan, had a disproportionate number of people with HIV/AIDS (Hyde 2007). The State Council had released a series of strategic plans that had little effect in addressing the issue. In 2003, in an influential report that largely reflected the sort of health and human rights lens described above, Human Rights Watch (2003) issued a powerful indictment of Chinese HIV/AIDS policy, titled *Locked Doors: The Human Rights of People Living with HIV/AIDS in China*. Subsequent reports and studies questioned the absence of secure public funding for HIV/ AIDS anti-retroviral drugs, raising issues of discrimination and neglect. Eventually, under international pressure, China introduced a near-universal program for persons with HIV/AIDS that provided anti-retroviral drugs.

However, Joseph Amon, director of health and human rights at Human Rights Watch, reported in 2010 that "two-thirds of HIV-infected people in China have not sought treatment because of fear, ignorance and discrimination" (Amon 2010). In 2014, the UN Committee on Economic, Social and Cultural Rights reported in its periodic review that monitors China's performance on the ICESCR: "Despite the adoption of regulations to eliminate the persistent discrimination against persons affected by HIV/AIDS, the Committee is concerned that persons living with HIV/AIDS still face social stigmatization from the public at large, as well as discrimination in employment, in education and, particularly, in access to health care, including refusal of treatment" (para. 34). The number of persons with HIV/AIDS in China in 2016 was roughly the same as in 2004 (*FindChinaInfo* 2016). Moreover, the government continued to imprison prominent AIDS activists such as Hu Jia for publicly criticizing its actions. Similar international criticism was made of China in its response to SARS in 2003 (Fidler and Gostin 2006; Jacobs 2007).

The SARS crisis had a significant long-term impact on public health in China. Domestically, since 2003 China has been building its public health infrastructure (which for our purposes here is distinct from its system of primary health care delivery) in order to fill the gaps that became apparent during the SARS crisis. This has meant establishing a national network of centres for disease control, nurturing a vaccine immunization manufacturing industry, and improving the avenues of communication between the Ministry of Health, on the one hand, and local governments and their public health units, on the other. China also took on a leadership role in the WHO with the appointment of Margaret Chan as the director-general in 2006.

China's response to other emerging infectious diseases since 2003 revealed a much better infrastructure for disease monitoring, investments in drug development, and engagement with international health organizations such as the WHO. This was clearly evident in the H1N1 pandemic in 2009. Only two deaths were attributed to H1N1 in China. Moreover, China was the first country to develop a vaccination for H1N1 (Jacobs 2011). Other epidemics, such as Zika and Ebola since 2009, have had a minimal impact on China, in part, presumably, because of the new public health infrastructure the government has put in place.

The real test of that public health infrastructure was the COVID-19 pandemic, beginning in 2020. It originated in China in late 2019 and the country was the first to experience significant community spread of the disease. The Chinese government drew on its extensive resources to nimbly make immense investments into targeted health care facilities, such as new hospitals in cities like Wuhan and a national testing infrastructure, while at the same time imposing harsh, strictly enforced restrictions on basic civil liberties that are key to economic and social life – restrictions that are possible because of the lack of a firm commitment to human rights in its domestic politics and the prioritizing of social and political stability (Biddulph 2015). As public health historian Peter Baldwin (2021, 7) noted in his masterly global survey of responses to the first wave of COVID-19: "In some political systems, like authoritarian China, politicians could demand more and stricter measures than elsewhere. But even democratic leaders had marshalled impressive powers. And, ultimately, given the scale of action required by a global pandemic, sheer coercion was impossible anywhere, consensus was crucial." Ultimately, China limited its comprehensive lockdowns to Hubei Province, which was at the centre of the community spread of COVID-19 and included the city of Wuhan. At the same time, China held local officials in Hubei accountable for the pandemic by having them removed, or "reshuffled," from their positions (ibid., 84). China did not isolate itself from international institutions during the health crisis. Instead, it sought early in the pandemic to cooperate extensively – but selectively sharing information – with the WHO and ensure that it projected an image of complying with WHO directives on global public health security (WHO 2020). These responses to the COVID-19 crisis enabled China to become the first major economy to begin emerging from the first wave of the pandemic in the summer of 2020, albeit deeply scarred (World Bank 2020).

China's response to COVID-19 can be instructively compared with those of Japan and India. Although Japan was among the first nations outside China to be exposed to COVID-19 in January 2020, its response was remarkably different from China's, marked by a government hesitant to impose involuntary restraints on its citizens, embrace lockdowns, and restrict foreign travel. Instead, despite eventually declaring a state of emergency in April 2020 that lasted for seven weeks, the Japanese government focused on voluntary measures for citizens to prevent environmental transmission of the disease in the "3Cs": closed spaces, crowded places, and close-contact settings (Shimizu et al. 2020). This public health response was remarkably similar in tone to its good-manners approach to tobacco control health measures when smoking and lung cancer emerged as health crises at the beginning of the twenty-first century – it reflects a political culture that rejects state-enforced compliance on public health issues (Feldman and Bayer 2011). Moreover, Japan did not develop an extensive testing infrastructure for COVID-19. Despite widespread voluntary mask wearing, the result was successive waves of COVID-19 throughout 2020 and 2021 without the spread of the disease ever being fully controlled. Indeed, ultimately Japan experienced among the worst infection rates of any of the countries in East Asia. While the government kept the economy open and promoted domestic tourism throughout the pandemic, Japan did not see significant economic recovery in 2021, which makes for another contrast with China.

India, with its weak health care infrastructure and large population, has adopted measures to deal with COVID-19 that are much more similar to China's than Japan's – this is surprising because the country has a long history of being committed in principle to international human rights norms. In particular, India adopted among the most stringent lockdowns in the world for dealing with the pandemic. Unlike China, which targeted its lockdowns to geographical areas with a total population of 60 million people where there was significant community spread of the disease, India imposed a national lockdown on March 25, 2020, that ultimately lasted for more than two months for its entire population of 1.3 billion people. Partial lockdowns occurred in several Indian states, including Delhi, in 2021. The government also imposed nationwide measures such as mandatory mask wearing that have lasted throughout the pandemic. Without a robust public health infrastructure and an authoritarian policing culture, enforcement of the national lockdown was uneven at best, but there was nonetheless wide compliance among the general population. The two-month national lockdown was effective in containing initial community spread of COVID-19, with a significant increase in cases after the easing of the lockdown, but lower death rates (*New York Times* 2020). Declining fatality rates in India during the pandemic are generally attributed to expanded testing, early diagnosis of the disease, and effective treatment protocols in health care clinics, and not to lockdowns (*British Medical Journal* 2020). Following the national lockdown, the government adopted a gradual staged "unlocking" that had an explicit economic focus, intended to stimulate economic recovery. As the *New York Times* (2020) noted, "India is one of many developing nations where leaders feel they have no choice but to prioritize reopenings and accept the risks of surging coronavirus infections." Unlike China, India did not see its economy recover in 2021.

China's response to COVID-19 and its relationship to the World Health Organization have received careful scrutiny. As the first country to try to contain COVID-19, China adopted aggressive public health measures and invested heavily in building health care capacity. Following WHO guidelines, lockdowns were targeted at areas where there was significant community spread of the disease (Baldwin 2021). These lockdowns were harsh and constituted comprehensive restrictions on basic civil liberties; elsewhere in the country, there were severe limitations on travel and many aspects of social life, but they were far less intrusive than those in Hubei. Measures such as requirements to wear face masks and to quarantine were already widely practised in China, so there was little sense that broader public health directives were intrusive or controversial. Within months, China gained control over the spread of COVID-19, and eventually has had among the lowest incidence of the disease and mortality rate among G20 countries. Indeed, globally China's response to COVID-19 is viewed much more positively than America's (Baldwin 2021). The WHO continues to be hesitant to criticize China's actions during the pandemic. China's lightning-fast release of the genome sequence of COVID-19 in January 2020 made possible the eventual development of vaccines elsewhere in the world within twelve months of the disease's discovery – a major contribution to global health security. Objectively, China's new public health system passed the COVID-19 test with flying colours, but its role in creating the pandemic is in tension with the fundamental objective of SDG 3.3 – to end epidemics – to begin with. As Baldwin (2021, 278) concludes, "Yes, China dealt well with the coronavirus. But China was also its cause."

Tobacco Control in China
SDG 3 includes the target of "strengthen[ing] the implementation of the World Health Organization Framework Convention on Tobacco Control [FCTC] in all countries."[5] Tobacco control in China has been heavily impacted by this framework convention, which came into effect in 2005 and has provided global standards for tobacco control. In the mid-1990s, the WHO began to expand its traditional focus on infectious diseases to include chronic diseases. And it is in this context that the WHO has concentrated much of its efforts on tobacco control.

Globally, tobacco use is the single biggest cause of chronic disease, especially cancer, stroke, and heart disease. Tobacco use is not uniform across nations, however. In advanced industrial societies, cigarette users have been on a steady decline since the 1970s. By contrast, developing countries saw a dramatic increase in smokers from 1971 until 2001, followed by a levelling off.

There are at present about 1.2 billion smokers worldwide, and approximately 400 million of them live in China. It is estimated that at least 1 million people die annually from tobacco use in China (CDC 2012). China is the single largest producer of tobacco products, and there is a monopoly on that production through the China National Tobacco Corporation (CNTC), a company owned entirely by the Chinese government. China's tobacco industry has the lowest degree of foreign ownership in the world, at only 2.7 percent. (The question of whether the CNTC itself is a threat to global public health security is a separate issue. See Chapter 7.)

In 1998, the WHO began to explore the idea of meeting the global challenge of tobacco control through the development of international law. Cigarette companies have thrived in the neoliberal era of trade liberalization and the global movement of capital and goods. International treaty law is viewed by the WHO as an effective instrument for regulating trade liberalization and foreign investment. The FCTC states:

> The WHO FCTC was developed in response to the globalization of the tobacco epidemic. The spread of the tobacco epidemic is facilitated through a variety of complex factors with cross-border effects, including trade liberalization and direct foreign investment. Other factors such as global marketing, transnational tobacco advertising, promotion and sponsorship, and the international movement of contraband and counterfeit cigarettes have also contributed to the explosive increase in tobacco use. (WHO 2003, v)

The FCTC includes provisions on tobacco advertising, health warnings on cigarette packages, higher taxation, prohibition of sales to minors, regulations on illicit trade, and some commitments to supporting smoking cessation. The international law creates an obligation for member states to "reduce continually and substantially the prevalence of tobacco use and exposure to tobacco smoke" by adopting and implementing "effective legislative, executive, administrative and/or other measures" (WHO 2003, 6).

There are now 176 countries that are parties to the convention, and 10 more, including the United States, have signed the convention but not yet ratified it. This makes the FCTC one of the most successful international treaties in history. Despite owning China National Tobacco, China has been an early strong supporter of the FCTC. Cheng Li (2012, ix) notes, "The high prevalence of tobacco use in China is not only the country's single most serious public health problem, but also constitutes the ultimate test case for the global tobacco control campaign."

From a human rights perspective, the FCTC is significant because its preamble states clearly that the foundation for the legislation is the right to health, citing both the WHO constitution and the ICESCR statement of the right to the highest attainable standard of health provision. Tobacco control is presented, in other words, as a human rights issue (Crow 2004; Dresler and Marks 2006; Jacobs 2014). As the foreword to the convention states: "The FCTC is an evidence-based treaty that reaffirms the right of all people to the highest standard of health" (WHO 2003, iv).

Tobacco use affects men and women in many ways that are similar, for example, in terms of heart disease, stroke, vascular diseases, lung cancer, bronchial and digestive tract cancers, bronchitis, and emphysema. Men who smoke also risk distinctive sexual and fertility problems. Women are more at risk for cervical and breast cancer, cardiovascular disease, infertility, premature labour, low-weight births, early menopause, and bone fractures. There are also important gender differences in the prevalence of smoking. China currently has more smokers than any other country in the world, and the gap between male and female smokers is especially pronounced. The 2010 Global Adult Tobacco China Survey found that 52.9% of men smoked, but only 2.4% of women (Bettcher 2010). This suggests that the overwhelming harm done to women in China by tobacco usage at present is a consequence of second-hand smoke. Even though there has long been awareness of the differences in smoking rates between men and women in China, and of indications that foreign cigarette companies may have an interest in targeting Chinese women as a huge potential market, tobacco control in China was predominantly gender-neutral prior to the FCTC.

The gender-specific tobacco control measures in the FCTC have substantively enriched Chinese tobacco control policy, although at the time of writing it is far too early to judge the effects on chronic diseases. Two examples illustrate the point. Since the early 1990s, China has experimented with bans on tobacco advertising and smoking in public places but with little success or impact. In 2010, however, the WHO Representative Office in China released a special initiative titled "Protect Women from Tobacco Marketing and Smoke," which is linked explicitly to the FCTC's provision for gender-specific tobacco control measures. The initiative has a twofold focus: a comprehensive ban on tobacco advertising and a ban on smoking in public places. The rationale for the first ban is explained in the following way: "Advertisements falsely link tobacco use with female beauty, empowerment and health. In fact, addiction to tobacco enslaves and disfigures women" (WHO China 2010). The rationale for the ban on smoking in public places is that "the bigger threat to women is from exposure to the smoke of others, particularly men ... in China more than 97 percent of smokers are men. Yet more than half of Chinese women of reproductive age are regularly exposed to second-hand smoke, which puts themselves and their unborn babies at risk" (ibid.). This new way to rationalize advertising bans and prohibitions on smoking in public places has helped reinvigorate tobacco control policies. Hundreds of Chinese cities have introduced bans on smoking in at least some public places, such as public transportation, and there is much more rigorous enforcement of the advertisement bans, especially on billboards.

From a different angle, China is also narrowing its focus for smoking cessation on men. The challenge, explains Douglas Bettcher (2010) is that "among men [in China], there is enormous social pressure to smoke, and this is facilitated by the policy environment." This pressure comes in the form of business practices as well as socializing with friends. His point is that tobacco control must address the social pressure on men to smoke and the business and social culture for men in China. The WHO office in China holds that this change can come with the sort of tobacco control measures mandated in the FCTC, but these should be implemented with a special focus on changing male norms around tobacco usage – in effect, using gender-specific measures.

How impactful have these tobacco control policies? In a 2019 report on the global tobacco pandemic, the WHO found that as of December 31, 2016, 52.1% of adult men and 2.7% of adult women in China smoked tobacco (WHO, 2019). This means that there has been a small reduction in the number of men smoking compared with 2010, but a significant increase in smoking among women – an increase from 2.4% to 2.7%, reflecting a net increase of over 10%. This does not mean that the tobacco control measures have not had an impact, however. Without those measures, the increase in the number of women smoking in China might have been much greater.

The upshot in general is that the FCTC has been successfully integrated into China's public health system, as envisioned by SDG 3.a. There is clear evidence that this rights-based international agreement has had a positive effect on tobacco control in China. Over time, the benefits of these tobacco control measures will be evident in health outcomes.

Right to Health Freedoms in China

Although China has made considerable achievements in advancing public health entitlements, it has a much poorer record when it comes to basic freedoms that are a component of the right to health and reflected in many targets of the SDG agenda. The freedoms component of the right to health centres on giving people control over their bodies, which includes freedom from non-consensual medical treatment, the right to be free from interference, discrimination, and harassment, and the right to express concerns about public health and to gain redress for abuses of these rights.

We focus now on developments in two areas of Chinese health care: the reliance on administrative detention for treating drug use, and accountability measures that allow rightsholders to address grievances about health care. Both areas suggest that China's performance is weak in terms of its obligation to respect and protect the right to health freedoms.

Administrative Detention for Drug Use and Addiction

By international public health norms, China's performance in its treatment of drug dependency and addiction is much weaker than its response to infectious diseases and tobacco control. SDG 3.5 sets the following as a global standard: "Strengthen the prevention and treatment of substance abuse, including narcotic drug abuse and harmful use of alcohol."[6] The emergence of international norms and standards for the treatment of drug dependency and addiction – what is generally labelled as drug use disorders by the United Nations – is very recent. In 2016, the WHO and the United Nations Office on Drugs and Crime (UNODC) issued its first set of standards, founded on international human rights norms, which are designed

> to support Member States in the development and expansion of treatment services that offer effective and ethical treatment. The goal of such treatment is to reverse the negative impact that persisting drug use disorders have on the individual and to help them achieve as full recovery from the disorder as possible and to become a productive member of their society. (WHO-UNODC 2016)

The international standards for drug dependency and addiction flow from seven basic principles. For the purposes of this chapter, it is instructive to focus on three of those principles:

Principle 1. Treatment must be available, accessible, attractive, and appropriate for needs

Principle 2. Ensuring ethical standards in treatment services

Principle 3. Promoting treatment of drug use disorders by effective coordination between the criminal justice system and health and social services. (WHO-UNODC 2016)

These three principles are all significant for assessing China's drug treatment public health policy.

China has a long history of placing drug addicts in administrative detention, meaning that these individuals are held for extended periods of time, without judicial oversight of their detention. This form of detention functions as a complement to criminal detention – in effect, drug addicts are jailed instead of hospitalized. China's complex system of administration detention as a complement to criminal detention is a familiar site for human rights concerns arising from basic civil rights such as due process, access to justice, and fair trials (Biddulph 2007). The most familiar and controversial use of administrative detention concerned the use of "re-education through labour" to detain and punish political dissenters – including, as noted earlier, AIDS activists such as Hu Jia – drug users, and minor criminals. China officially abolished re-education through labour in 2013, but retains other forms of administrative detention. It should be noted that the UN Committee on Economic, Social and Cultural Rights (2014, para. 22) "remains concerned about the lack of effective implementation of this decision, particularly at the municipal and provincial levels."

It has been estimated that half of those subject to re-education through labour were detained for drug use (Biddulph 2016). *China Daily* (2018) reported the growing incidence of drug addiction in China: "By the end of 2017, there were 2,553,000 known drug addicts in China, a growth of 1.9 per cent year-on-year. Those aged 18–35 made up 55.6 per cent of that population, with the 36–59 age group a further 43 per cent." Human Rights Watch estimated that in China in 2011, there were 171,000 individuals detained in facilities for drug dependency that were neither prisons nor hospitals (Amon et al. 2013, 125). Sarah Biddulph and Chuanyu Xie (2011, 982) suggested that the numbers might be much greater, perhaps even 500,000.

According to Human Rights Watch, drug users in China reported that "their history of drug use was electronically linked to their national identity card" (Amon et al. 2013, 127). Everyone in the study reported being forced to exercise as well as work for no pay. The study also chronicled abuse, discrimination, and harassment in detention. All drug users were compelled to take urine tests. The facilities where they were held did not provide medical care for drug addiction. No one "reported having received any evidence-based drug dependency treatment, and detention centers had few, if any, trained health professional on staff. Routine health care of any kind was often denied" (ibid., 133).

Furthermore, "the use of administrative law ... masks an approach to drug use that sees dependency as a moral failing, rather than a medical condition" (ibid., 124). Biddulph and Xie (2011) link this moralizing approach to the state ideology of an ideal socialist state where the failings of drug addiction have no place. They observe that legislation in 2009, despite not criminalizing drug use, allows for "the interlocking coercive powers of registration, surveillance and administrative detention of drug-dependent people ... [so] a person may be subject to coercive drug rehabilitation orders, custodial and non-custodial, for a total of nine years" (ibid., 983). Decisions about these orders are made principally by the police without judicial oversight, and there is evident arbitrariness in many such decisions, especially distinctions between drug use and drug dependency and the length of detention (Biddulph 2015).

Administrative detention, especially re-education through labour, is in fundamental tension with WHO-UNODC Principles 2 and 3 listed above. Principle 2 requires that "treatment of drug use disorders should be based on the universal ethical standards – respect for human rights and dignity ... Informed consent should be obtained from a patient before initiating treatment and guarantee the option to withdraw from treatment at any time" (WHO-UNODC 2016, 9). Detention is not subject to any sort of basic judicial oversight or due process; there is no opportunity for the individual to consent or to withdraw from the detention. Principle 3 states that "drug use disorders should be seen primarily as a health problem rather than a criminal behavior and wherever possible, drug users should be treated in the health care system rather than in the criminal justice system" (ibid., 10). Clearly, administrative detention in the form of re-education through labour or anything similar is in practice treating the individual as a criminal, not a patient.

Principle 1 requires that "essential treatment services for drug use disorders should be available through organization of treatment interventions at different levels of health systems: from primary health care to tertiary health services with specialized treatment programs for drug use disorders" (ibid., 8). The finding by Human Rights Watch (Amon et al. 2013) that administrative detention in China for drug dependency and addiction generally involves no medical services violates this basic principle.

Accountability to Protect the Right to Health

SDG 16.6 sets the following as a target for all countries: "Develop effective, accountable and transparent institutions at all levels."[7] Accountability, in the sense of mechanisms to enable rightsholders to seek remedies for violations of their human rights (Gruskin et al. 2005; Qiu and MacNaughton 2017) is, in my view, fundamental to protecting and respecting the freedom components of the human right to health (Jacobs 1993). Mechanisms in China for the protection of the right to health are an ongoing challenge, and framing issues regarding public health in China around rights-based mechanisms of accountability is still largely in its infancy. Although there is a catalogue of formal mechanisms of accountability – judicial, political, administrative – these mechanisms are quite weak (Qiu and MacNaughton 2017).

Judicial accountability involves the courts acting to protect human rights and is one potential avenue for redress in China. As noted above, Article 45 of China's constitution provides for a right to health, but this has not strengthened judicial accountability. In practice, this constitutional right has not been the explicit basis for any claim in the Chinese courts. As Shengnan Qiu and Gillian MacNaughton (2017) note, the rights claims brought in the courts are based on more specific statutes and regulations concerned with health issues. There have been some successful malpractice claims brought against physicians and hospitals, especially when the hospital is privately owned (Ho 2014). There have also been some recent successful court cases involving air and water pollution (Qiu and MacNaughton 2017), and after the SARS crisis in 2003 (Jacobs 2007). But the frequency and significance of litigation around the right to health has been limited.

Political accountability in the context of the right to health has been defined by Qiu and MacNaughton (2017, 283): "the government is required to ensure participatory processes for the adoption of health policies and strategies." Participants in participatory processes should include rightsholders. The lack of democracy in its core governing institutions, such as the National People's Congress, the State Council, and the Chinese Communist Party, makes it difficult to be optimistic about political accountability for any infringements of basic freedoms. It should be noted, however, that an important positive example of political accountability in China arose in 2009 in the context of the comprehensive health care reform (discussed above). The government undertook a set of consultations, principally with stakeholders (Kornreich, Vertinsky, and Potter 2012), and in 2008 invited the general public to provide input on some reform proposals through an online portal, fax, or mail. It received 35,260 responses, 27,892 of which were online; half were from people working in health care. In practice, many of the responses expressed general grievances about the public health care system. Yoel Kornreich, Ilan Vertinsky, and Pitman Potter (2012) argue that the government responded to these grievances with substantive policy changes to the proposed reforms. For example, in response to complaints that the existing system was inaccessible and too costly, the government shortened its timeline for implementing key reforms by two years, and in this way showed sensitivity to the concerns of those who complained. As a response to the findings of the participatory process, the Chinese government also increased the subsidies for individuals joining insurance schemes and allowed for more insurance choices for retired citizens who had moved from rural areas to cities (ibid.).

Social accountability differs from formal accountability because it lacks direct enforcement mechanisms. Qiu and MacNaughton (2017, 288) explain that social accountability instead "draws its authority from social moral values ... in China where the contemporary goal of the central government is to achieve a harmonious society ... the main mechanism is public exposure through the media." Public health scandals, especially around food safety, that lead to resignations of responsible officials and even criminal prosecutions are good examples. I noted above that in response to the COVID-19 outbreak, the government "reshuffled" some officials in Hubei Province. The government's tolerance of and response to social accountability mechanisms can provide some measure of China's respect for some of the freedoms associated with the right to health.

Medical disputes at Chinese hospitals provide an interesting context for thinking about social accountability. These disputes have risen dramatically over the past decade. Biddulph (2015, 29) observes that "privatization of China's health care system laid the groundwork for the steadily growing public anger about availability and quality of medical care." In 2014, there were an estimated 120,000 disputes between patients and their hospital-based health care provider; only 17 percent of these centred on lawsuits (He and Qian 2016, 362). In other words, only a small proportion of patients in these disputes turned to the courts for judicial accountability. The Ministry

of Health estimates that a very similar number of these disputes led to violence (ibid., 362). A powerful explanation in part for why there are so many
of these disputes is the perverse financial incentives and moral hazards in
hospitals around the prescription of drugs, noted above in the discussion of
entitlements and access to health care.

Most medical disputes at Chinese hospitals involve neither litigation
nor violence but rather protests, either in person outside the hospital gates,
traditional petitioning, or on social media.[8] According to the Chinese Medical Association, "more than 80 percent of medical disputes nationwide are
resolved by under-the-table settlement, a majority of cases involving private
compensation of patients" (He and Qian 2016, 373). From the perspective
of social accountability, protests appear at times to be very effective for addressing rights-based medical disputes at hospitals in China. However, this
form of social accountability does not meet the requirements of transparency required by SDG 16.6. Moreover, as Biddulph (2015) argues, although
protests have been met by efforts on the part of the government or public
hospitals to address the problems that fuel them, this occurs in tandem with
efforts to regulate and curtail protests that are too disruptive or threaten-
ing to the status quo. These efforts to regulate and curtail protests suggest
that there are clear limits on the respect for the freedoms component of the
right to health by the government of China. Moreover, the informal character of social accountability means that patients and their families cannot
reliably depend on protests to address their rights concerns.

This chapter provides a new lens for thinking about China's human rights
performance on global health security by establishing a link to SDG targets.
China's performance on public health entitlements over the past decade is
moving progressively toward realization of the SDG goals. There are clear
indicators that support the case that the government is fulfilling its obligations on entitlements and will meet SDG targets. The measures to deal with
emerging infectious diseases and tobacco control reflect committed efforts
to advance global public health security in alignment with the SDG targets.

China's recent performance on the freedoms that comprise the right to
health is much weaker and there are good reasons to be skeptical about the
government's commitment to other SDG targets. The continued reliance
on administrative detention for mental health and addiction issues is a
violation of basic freedoms that are a component of the right to health.
Moreover, formal accountability mechanisms remain weak. Social accountability mechanisms, such as protests outside hospitals, which are generally

tolerated, are too informal to provide a reliable indicator of a strong performance on the part of the government of China.

At the outset, I argued that under international human rights law, entitlements and freedoms are both integral components of the human right to health and that for this reason countries cannot excuse weak performance on freedoms because they prioritize economic and social development over civil and political rights. China has received a lot of credit internationally for its successes in achieving the UN Millennium Development Goals related to health care entitlements and its progress on the Sustainable Development Goals. However, the fact that China's performance is weak on the freedoms that are also a component of the right to health means that from a global health security perspective, significant progress on protecting and respecting those freedoms is required before China should be strongly praised for its record by rights-based international organizations such as the World Health Organization.

NOTES

1 The 2009 National Health Action Plan explains in a similar fashion:

> While respecting the universal principles of human rights, the Chinese government in the light of the basic realities of China, gives priority to the protection of the people's rights to subsistence and development, and lawfully guarantees the rights of all members of society to equal participation and development on the basis of facilitating sound and rapid economic and social development. (Government of China 2009)

2 The International Bill of Human Rights consists of the United Nations Declaration of Human Rights (1948), the International Covenant on Economic, Social and Cultural Rights (1966), and the International Covenant on Civil and Political Rights (1966) and its two Optional Protocols.

3 https://www.elegislation.gov.hk/hk/A1!en.assist.pdf.

4 https://sdgs.un.org/goals/goal3.

5 Ibid.

6 Ibid.

7 https://sdgs.un.org/goals/goal16.

8 Alex He and Jingwei Qian (2016, 374) claim, "Despite the fairly high chances of winning compensation via legal channels, litigation appears not to be favored by Chinese patients. This is arguably because of the availability of greater compensation through non-legal channels, such as staging a protest, which also require much less time and expense."

Moving Japan toward the Global Standard for Vaccines

TOSHIMI NAKANASHI

Vaccination policies are a model in public health for effective initiatives that have contributed significantly to the improvement of global health security. These polices have countered the threat of infectious diseases by promptly providing artificially acquired immunity to a large number of people and reduce the burden of dangerous infections. For example, the incidence of smallpox was reduced so drastically with systematic and widespread smallpox vaccination that in 1980 the World Health Organization (WHO) declared the disease eradicated on a global scale. Vaccines are also a vital strategy for advancing global health security during the COVID-19 pandemic. The importance of vaccines is reflected in several Sustainable Development Goals (SDG) targets, including "access to safe, effective, quality and affordable essential medicines and vaccines for all" (SDG 3.8) and "support[ing] the research and development of vaccines and medicines for the communicable and non-communicable diseases that primarily affect developing countries" (SDG 3.b).[1]

No wonder, then, that in most countries, including Japan, there is a history of compulsory immunization for the sake of protecting society from dangerous infections. However, despite the well-recognized benefits for global health of vaccinations against infectious diseases, Japan is often described as having a "backward vaccination policy" (*Japan Times* 2018). For certain common vaccinations, such as that for the human papilloma virus (HPV), Japan has the lowest rates among of all Organisation for Economic

Co-operation and Development (OECD) countries, pointing to a vaccination gap between Japan and the other countries. Indeed, Rumiko Shimaza and Masayuki Ikeda (2012, 312) note that "from the perspective of global public health, Japan is cited as an exporter of infectious diseases to countries that have those diseases under better control through vaccination." This means that although Japan is a world leader generally in its health services, as indicated in Chapter 2, its vaccination policy is deeply flawed. Why, despite being an advanced developed country, are Japan's vaccination rates so low?

There are at least two important inter-related explanations for the vaccination gap in Japan. One revolves around the fact that while immunization efforts are laudable and necessary for global health, the approval of new vaccines by individual countries typically faces a tension between public safety and the commercial interests of the maker of the vaccine. On the one hand, the global pharmaceutical industry seeks prompt approval of new vaccines in order to generate significant revenue; on the other hand, individual countries are concerned about the safety of their own populations and require drug approval through their own national process. For instance, even drugs that have been developed and approved in Europe cannot be released on the market in Japan until they have gone through an approval process. This process can considerably delay the entry of drugs into the market. Such delays, which are deemed to be an invisible barrier to free trade in the pharmaceutical industry (Kawabuchi and Talcott 2010) are caused by risk considerations as well as assessment of the pros and cons of approval in light of international standards. With regard to vaccines, these considerations encompass concerns pertaining not only to the health of individuals but also the health needs of *Japanese society as a whole*. In practice, for example, Shimaza and Ikeda (2012) found that Japan had approved only four of the twenty most common vaccinations for children available in the United Kingdom.

The other explanation for the vaccination gap in Japan concerns the weight given to the so-called malpractice avoidance dilemma (Tezuka 2010). The benefits of new medicines, including vaccines, are often accompanied by the risk of adverse effects. An important legal and policy question arises about which party – the agency that approved the vaccine, the physician who prescribed the vaccine, or the individual who received the vaccine – should bear principal responsibility for any adverse effects as well as the cost of treatment. Japan has adopted a unique legal paradigm for the allocation of risk and responsibility regarding the adverse effects of vaccines, one that differs from that embraced by other developed countries. This paradigm has been a major, albeit little understood, catalyst for the vaccination gap in Japan.

This chapter focuses on how Japan's current vaccination gap stems from the malpractice avoidance dilemma. We begin by examining the global health norms for vaccination policy, noting that the global standard for effective national vaccination policies involves balancing these different norms. We then clarify certain features of Japan's vaccination policy, which have evolved over the course of various epidemics since the Second World War, particularly the impact of litigation over adverse side effects of vaccines on policy development. This is followed by an examination of rights and risks associated with vaccines, and of responses to the conflicts pertaining to vaccination decision-making. Then, it will discuss risk management regarding risk consideration and approval in light of international standards in Japan's immunization policy, as well as conflict management concerning the dilemma of avoiding medical errors in vaccine policy. Finally, it maps out how vaccination policy in Japan can move toward the global standard.

Global Norms for Vaccination Policy

Three global norms for vaccination policy are important to keep in mind when thinking about Japan's vaccination gap: 1) the establishment and maintenance of herd immunity; 2) the weighing of patients' rights; and 3) the alleviation of the individual patient's financial burden for accessing vaccines. The global standard for effective national vaccination policies is to strike a balance between these three norms. Japan does not strike such a balance.

Herd (Group) Immunity as Infection Prevention

The purpose of vaccination is to maintain the population immunity level against certain infections. To this end, it is essential to provide safe vaccination opportunities and to ensure broad immunization coverage. As long as the coverage level reaches a particular threshold proportion of immune individuals, the risk of infection among susceptible individuals in a population is reduced by the presence and proximity of immune individuals (Fine, Eames, and Heymann 2011, 911). This phenomenon is usually called "herd immunity."

From the perspective of herd immunity, as indicated in Figure 5.1, it is essential to focus on potential carriers of pathogens rather than infected carriers. For example, if one person out of 200 develops polio, the remaining

199 become potential *carriers*. Every time a potential carrier comes into contact with an uninfected person, a new opportunity for infection is created. One of main goals of vaccination is to eliminate these potential carriers. If, due to vaccination, a certain number of people in a group are not affected by disease, then those not eligible for vaccinations, or children for whom vaccination is not effective, as well as people who cannot get vaccinated due to economic, social, or cultural reasons, are also protected from infection.

If we were to weigh the risks of potential side effects against the benefits obtained from vaccines, in situations with established herd immunity the benefits greatly exceed the risks, as it becomes possible to avoid infection outbreaks, reduce social and individual anxiety, contain potential economic losses due to outbreak occurrence, and also indirectly protect the small number of people who cannot get vaccinated. It should be noted, however, that for the small number of people who actually experience vaccine side effects, not only is there no benefit but great losses are incurred.

Patient Rights to Self-Determination

A vaccination policy must give weight to patients' rights in any deliberations about access to vaccines. The World Medical Association (WMA) Declaration of Lisbon on the Rights of the Patient enumerates the following eleven rights (World Medical Association 2018):

- the right to good-quality medical care
- the right to freedom of choice
- the right to self-determination
- the rights of the unconscious patient
- the rights of the legally incompetent patient
- the right to refuse procedures that go against the patient's will
- the right to information
- the right to confidentiality
- the right to health education
- the right to dignity
- the right to religious assistance.

Based on this declaration of rights, vaccinated persons have needs related to six rights that vaccination policy writers need to address: 1) good-quality medical care, 2) freedom of choice, 3) self-determination, 4) refusal of procedures that go against the patient's will, 5) information, and 6) health

FIGURE 5.1.

A model for community or "herd" immunity

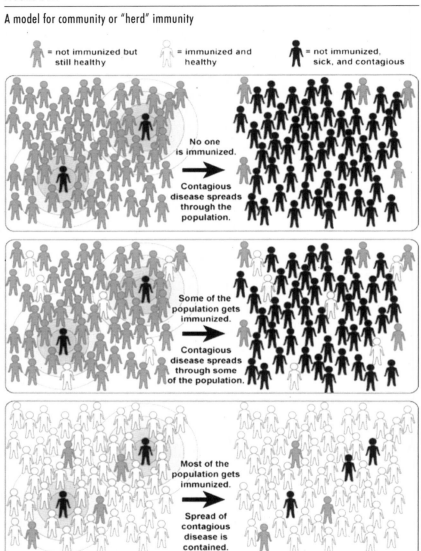

Source: Anthony S. Fauci, "Building Trust in Vaccines," December 4, 2019, National Institute of Allergy and Infectious Diseases, National Institutes of Health, NIH PIO Network. https://www.nih.gov/about-nih/what-we-do/science-health-public-trust/perspectives/science-health-public-trust/building-trust-vaccines.

education. There may be a tension between the objective of increasing herd immunity against certain infections and patient self-determination, especially when vaccines present risks of adverse side effects for some individuals.

The Cost of Vaccines

Who should pay for vaccines? Most private health insurance plans in the United States cover the cost of vaccinations. If vaccines are not covered by private health insurance, they are implemented by the Centers for Disease Control and Prevention (CDC)'s Vaccines for Children (VFC) program (CDC-VFC 2015). In Germany, 90% of vaccines are purchased by the private sector and 90% of those costs are paid by statutory insurance policies. The remaining 10% of vaccine cost paid by the private sector is reimbursed by supplementary private insurance policies. In France, 85% of pediatric vaccines are provided by private practice physicians (GPs, especially pediatricians), and 15% are provided by public mother-child clinics (MCH). At public clinics, required vaccines are free, as are some recommended vaccines. In Canada, each province decides which vaccinations to make free, and vaccines are free for high-risk individuals. In England, all regular vaccinations are free, paid for by the government. The general point is that individuals do not carry the burden of paying for vaccines.

In Japan, there is some uncertainty about who pays, which complicates achieving herd immunity. Half of the financial resources come from the national government, one fourth from prefectures, and one fourth from municipalities. With regards to vaccination costs in Japan, according to nationwide data from 3,017 facilities, the cost of influenza vaccine per adult for the 2020–21 season averages JPY 3,500 (Tokyo Midtown Clinic 2021). The prices of other vaccinations in Japan can be found in the data from the Ministry of Health, Labour and Welfare (2021b).

Rights and Risks Surrounding Health Damages

Because vaccines are administered to healthy people, drug administration for disease treatment requires judgment based on different criteria, and the range of acceptable side effects is narrower than for disease-treatment drugs. As indicated in Figure 5.2, the occurrence of unexpected adverse event cases is also possible. The more active, routine vaccines are strengthened, the greater the risk becomes. Therefore, it is essential for policy makers and mass media to cooperate with experts (scientists) and publicly report trustworthy, reliable information based on scientific evidence. It is

TABLE 5.1.

Manufacturer/seller's suggested retail prices of vaccines in major countries

Country	Cervical cancer		Bacterial meningitis	Meningitis/sepsis/otitis media	Adult pneumococcal infection	Hepatitis		Rotavirus infection	
	Cervical cancer vaccine (HPV)		Hib vaccine (HibV)	Pneumococcal vaccine (for children)	Pneumococcal vaccine (for adults)	Hepatitis B vaccine (0.5 mL)		Rotavirus vaccine	
	Cervarix (GSK)	Gardasil (MSD)	ActHIB[2] (Sanofi)	7-valent Prevnar[3] (Pfizer)	Prevnar 7[3] (Pfizer)	Bimmugen[4] (GSK)	Heptavax (MSD)	Rotarix (GSK)	Rota Teq
Japan	¥12,000	¥12,000	¥4,500	¥6,800	¥4,664	¥2,481	¥2,408	¥10,000	Undecided
United States	$128.75 ¥10,236	$130.27 ¥10,356	$30.41 ¥2,418	$100.51 ¥7,990	$61.94 ¥4,924	– –	$59.70 ¥4,746	$106.57 ¥8,472	$72.34 ¥5,751
US CDC[1]	$96.08 ¥7,638	$95.75 ¥7,612	$9 ¥716	– –	$34.54 ¥2,746	– –	$24.04 ¥1,911	$89.25 ¥7,095	$59.76 ¥4,751
United Kingdom	£80.50 ¥10,290	£86.50 ¥11,056	– –	£34.50 ¥4,410	£8.32 ¥1,063	– –	£8.95 ¥1,144	£41.38 ¥5,289	– –

France €111.82 ¥12,427	€123.66 ¥13,742	— —	€57.34 ¥6,372	€13.56 ¥1,507	€10.15 ¥1,128	Not disclosed[5] —	Not disclosed —
Germany €111.82 ¥17,542	€157.85 ¥17,542	— —	€80.40 ¥8,935	€38.45 ¥4,273	€45.97 ¥5,109	€67.50 ¥7,501	€45.09 ¥5,011
Immunization status in Japan Routine immunization (discontinued since June 2013)		Routine immunization with inactivated vaccine	Routine immunization	Routine immunization since October 2014	Voluntary immunization	Voluntary immunization	

Notes:

The manufacturer/seller's suggested retail prices in each country were obtained from each manufacturer/seller. The prices in Japanese currency are as of 2011, except for the price of Cervarix in countries other than Japan, which is as of 2009. The prices were converted into Japanese yen using the mean foreign exchange closing rate in 2011: $1 = ¥79.5, £1 = ¥127.82, €1 = ¥111.3.

1 The US Centers for Disease Control and Prevention prices are contract prices for the *Vaccines for Children* (VFC) program.

2 Hib vaccine has been replaced by combination vaccines in many European Union countries, Canada, and Australia.

3 Currently, not 7-valent but 13-valent conjugate vaccine is on the market in the United States, the United Kingdom, France, and Germany. (The date of this change was 2013 in the United States and the United Kingdom, June 2010 in France, and December 2009 in Germany.)

4 There is no history of Bimmugen being exported to major countries.

5 In France, rotavirus vaccine is not covered by health insurance, and the price is determined by individual negotiation with medical institutions; consequently, the prices are not disclosed.

Source: Masabayashi, 2021.

FIGURE 5.2

Adverse drug reactions

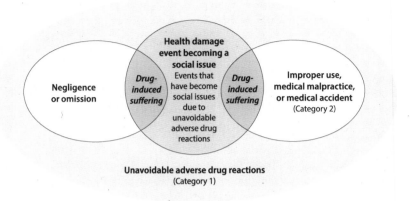

Negligence or omission

Drug-induced suffering

Health damage event becoming a social issue
Events that have become social issues due to unavoidable adverse drug reactions

Drug-induced suffering

Improper use, medical malpractice, or medical accident
(Category 2)

Unavoidable adverse drug reactions
(Category 1)

Source: Pharmaceutical and Medical Device Regulatory Science Society of Japan 2013, 4–5.

especially essential that the government continue gathering information on side effects and periodically disclose vaccine safety information.

Despite the fact that vaccine side effects can never be predicted with certainty, the mechanism for rectifying the inflicted damage is always essential. As shown in Figure 5.2, health damages caused by drug-related disasters are typically addressed as a social problem. Every time a policy in Japan reaches a dead end, it is transformed, and this pattern perpetuates itself. Because of the absence of an adequate damage management system, vaccine victims file a lawsuit in court in an effort to seek legal relief.

Characteristics of Japan's vaccination policies link to the principal of individual vaccination. The phenomenon of the vaccine gap illustrates the fact that compared to other developed countries, Japan's variety of available vaccines is insufficient. For example, 1) vaccines used in other countries cannot be used in Japan; 2) safer vaccines cannot be used; and 3) with incomplete usage, the disease cannot be fought off.

Currently, a variety of forward-looking policies are being taken to overcome these problems, such as accelerating the safety-verification procedures for vaccines, providing subsidies for vaccines, aiming a health-damages relief system at relief for victims, creating an environment for promoting research developments on safe vaccines, and improving vaccine production and distribution systems. This cycle is a vicious one that leads to further constriction of manufacturing (Tezuka 2010, 32–36).

Vaccination is an important means of saving people's lives; it plays a crucial role in protecting children of the next generation, especially infants, from infections. Japan should try to eliminate its vaccination gap with other developed countries. To do so, it is necessary to build an adequate damage management and relief system from the perspective of conflict management and crisis management.

The Dichotomous Structure of Individual Risk and Social Risk

Risk perception of side effects at the *individual level* is composed of 1) the fear factor, 2) the uncertainty factor, and 3) scale and size factors. It goes without saying that evaluations of these factors differ based on individual and cultural backgrounds (Suzuki 2012). Meanwhile, when side effects and drug-related disasters occur, they are first investigated from an expert's viewpoint, and there will be a judgment regarding which drugs caused the damages. S. Suzuki (2012) states that initially this judgment must reference individual causal relationships and utilize drug epidemiology research. Further, in order to evaluate individual side effects, a causal relationship assessment must be conducted based on causal association assessment. These investigation results will constitute specific content for social risk evaluation.

The danger of conflict arising during the evaluation of these two risks is always present, as the very foundations of perception are different. Keeping in mind the difference in the foundations of risk evaluation and the potential for conflict as a premise (in other words, understanding the multi-dimensional structure of vaccination risk evaluation) is key in both aspects – sharing prior preventive knowledge about vaccinations and eliminating conflict at the time of side-effect occurrence.

Conflict and Vaccination Decision-making

A big problem for stakeholders involved in vaccinations is how to interpret risk messages, both when determining the suitability of a vaccination and when recognizing problems before adverse events occur. Even in the mid-90s, Japan's vaccination target was referred to as the "vaccination gap" compared to developed countries overseas, and it remained in a very limit state. As a result, in 2013, three diseases, the Hib infection, pneumococcal infections in children, and human papillomavirus infection, were finally chosen as routine vaccinations (the HPV vaccine uses a virus involved in cervical cancer). The next year, by March 2014, there were significant movements toward vaccination expansion, such as the announcement of a plan for promoting the prevention of diseases that are avoidable by vaccines and the promotion of vaccine research and development. However, around that time, 176 cases of side-effect reactions among 3.38 million people vaccinated with the HPV vaccine were reported, about which the popular media produced a series of sensational stories. In June 2014, the Ministry of Health, Labor, and Welfare (MHLW) reacted by shifting from encouraging the HPV vaccine to in effect ending its widespread use.

Thus, Japan's vaccination policies have wavered between aggressive policies of compulsory vaccination and obligatory efforts, which are desirable from the perspective of social defence against viruses, and passive policies that make vaccines optional and weight the risk of potential side effects for individuals who receive vaccines. This "malpractice dilemma," to quote Tezuka, directly reflects the dilemma between social risk and individual risk that surrounds vaccines (Falcaro et al. 2012; Nicol et al. 2016).

As shown in the HPV vaccine example, when non-expert, unvaccinated persons receive expert information before the secondary-response information gap has been eliminated among experts, it can create confusion during the decision-making process. Although my analysis appreciated the phenomenon of information and decision-making by means of the concept of "cross-multiplying issues phenomenon" in this process, danger and fear are added to the existing reference points of safety and security, and it is highly likely that heuristic decision-making is performed. That is, in situations of emotional danger and urgency, people do not make decisions based on careful deliberation, but rather tend to make instant, superficial judgments, and this is the heuristic decision-making model. With heuristic decision-making, people are more susceptible to emotional content than to knowledge-based elements of information. In the case of the HPV vaccine, the mass media distributed images of victims and information indicating the risk of chronic pain and brought about more hysteria. During vaccination decision-making, science-backed information on medical drug safety and effectiveness should be appropriately communicated rather than emotion-raising content, and establishing understanding must become the prerequisite for this decision-making.

When vaccinations must be tested, even with a lack of scientific evidence on safety, it is even more essential to anticipate the potential for adverse events and investigate a model that will address these in a timely and appropriate manner. Along with the Precautionary Principle, introducing regulatory science becomes important for policies clouded by uncertainty. Regulatory science aims to control typical drug-related disasters.

N. Luhmann's "risk evaluation conflict" becomes a reference for cases in which side effects occur.[2] Luhmann (1996) suggests that there is a need to clearly distinguish the dichotomous conflict of "risk evaluation conflict" and "attribution conflict." "Risk evaluation conflict" involves the difference in risk evaluation from the standpoint of the subject. Decision makers who observe potential damage as a "risk" produced by them tend to underestimate its severity and seriousness. On the other hand, affected persons who observe the potential damage as a "danger" inflicted by others (decision makers) tend to overestimate it. Conflict arises from this difference in evaluations. According to Luhmann (1996), damages occur from decision makers' decisions, and therefore with regards to assigning legal responsibility for the decision, implicit common understanding between decision makers and affected persons needs to be established in "risk evaluation conflict." Causal attribution itself, or attributing responsibility for damage to decision makers is not in any way suspected or opposed, and under that premise, the conflict that arises is over whether to evaluate the risks that occur from this decision.

"Attribution conflict" manifests itself in the form of disagreement between decision makers and affected persons over whom damages should be attributed to, including how much responsibility for such damages. Here points of conflict arise over whether potential damages are "artificial risks" or "natural dangers," and exactly who the decision makers and the affected persons are, and it can be considered a deeper-level conflict than risk evaluation conflict. Japan's vaccination policies have avoided assigning responsibility for adverse side effects by making vaccines optional and diluting compulsory elements, which results in further intensifying the attribution conflict.

Management Examples from One Pharmaceutical Company
The Tylenol incident is an example of effective management of drug-related adverse effects that illustrates the importance of corporate social responsibility and prompt disclosure of information that, basically, saved Johnson & Johnson. In 1982, Chicago police reported that seven people who died mysteriously from cyanide poisoning on Chicago's West Side had taken Tylenol – a drug popular enough in the United States to be termed a national drug. This announcement caused great anxiety among many Americans. At the time, however, the hypothesis that cyanide was mixed into Tylenol amounted

to no more than suspicion, and the cause of the deaths was unclear. This uncertainty notwithstanding, the CEO of Johnson & Johnson issued a warning at a press conference that people "not take Tylenol," and announced a recall of all suspected contaminated products. To reiterate, at that juncture the causal relationship between cyanide and deaths had not yet been scientifically proven. Nonetheless, Johnson & Johnson introduced a consumer hotline and committed to providing exhaustive information to its customers. Vouchers were issued to recover products from consumers, and exchanges were made with new drugs that did not contain cyanide. The recovery cost at the time is said to have been over $100 million.

This case showed that corporations' economic interests should be implemented within certain social and cultural frameworks, that is, it explicitly showed the importance of corporate governance. The WHO goes even further and advocates pharmacovigilance with regard to adverse events involving pharmaceuticals. Pharmacovigilance is defined as "the science and activities relating to the detection, assessment, understanding and prevention of adverse effects or any other drug-related problem" (WHO, n.d.).

Wingspread Statement on the Precautionary Principle
We can also see social responsibility for adverse events in the January 1998 Precautionary Principle described in the Wingspread Statement as follows:

> The Wingspread Conference on the Precautionary Principle is a historic meeting of scientists, philosophers, lawyers, and environmental activists that took place last weekend at Wingspread, the headquarters of the Johnson Foundation, to discuss public health and environmental decision-making. It refers to the principle of reaching consensus on the need for the precautionary principle in decision making. A key element of this principle is to encourage people to take precautionary action in the absence of scientific certainty. This meeting was also held on August 5, 2013. This precautionary principle is considered a place for collaborative decision-making as an integration of risk management and conflict management across stakeholders.

The Precautionary Principle is based on the premise that even if one confirms the potentially dangerous impact of a phenomenon, product, or process, risk occurrence cannot be determined with sufficient certainty by scientific evaluation. Even in cases like the HPV vaccine's adverse events, if the Precautionary Principle is appropriately upheld, and a specific process for conflict management is incorporated in advance, there can still be more appropriate crisis management. It is necessary to implement the Precautionary Principle: When an activity raises threats of harm to human health or the environment, precautionary measures should be taken even if some cause-and-effect relationships are not fully established scientifically. In this context the proponent of an activity, rather than the public, should bear the burden of proof. The process of applying the Precautionary Principle must be open, informed and democratic and must include potentially affected parties. It must also involve an examination of the full range of alternatives, including no action. To heighten herd immunity in Japan, first, key vaccination stakeholders should begin by implementing a value share for the potential occurrence of adverse events in a vaccine administration plan and relief measures. This could be initiated by holding discussions among experts as well as relevant stakeholders in various fields and providing a forum for sharing this information with the public. The government and pharmaceutical industries should adhere to the Precautionary Principle, keeping in mind the potential for serious adverse events.

The Vaccination Gap in Japan

Japan's national vaccination policy fails to strike an effective balance between the three global norms. This is evident from the fact that Japan has failed to achieve three major objectives: 1) to increase vaccination rates for particular infectious diseases, 2) establish and maintain herd immunity, and 3) lower mortality rates for certain common infectious diseases. Why, despite being an advanced, developed country, are Japan's vaccination rates so low?

Japan's Preventive Vaccination Law

It is helpful to begin with the observation that the history of immunization in Japan can be traced as far back as 1849, when the smallpox vaccine was first used for immunization purposes. The Preventive Vaccination Law, enacted in 1948, introduced a compulsory vaccination system with penalties, which was rated as one of the world's leading strict legal systems (Pharmaceutical and Medical Device Regulatory Science Society of Japan 2013).[3] This resulted in a remarkable decrease in tuberculosis morbidity and success in eradicating acute poliomyelitis (polio).

The current Japanese immunization system divides vaccinations into two categories: so-called routine vaccinations and optional vaccinations. While some routine vaccinations are not, strictly speaking, compulsory, they are strongly encouraged by national and local governments as an obligatory effort. The costs of vaccines defined as an obligatory effort are covered by local governments. In contrast, optional vaccinations are available to individuals not included in the list of those who should receive routine vaccinations as well as to those receiving routine vaccines outside the regular vaccination period. In these cases, whether to receive a vaccine or not is left up to the individual, and the cost becomes a personal responsibility.

Diseases for which routine vaccinations are intended are further classified into Class-I and Class-II diseases. Class-I diseases are diseases for which it is necessary to get a routine vaccination in order to prevent occurrence and spread; these include diseases such as diphtheria, pertussis, and polio. Class-I diseases have serious implications for social safety, and the corresponding vaccines are defined as obligatory efforts. Class-II diseases are considered diseases for which it is necessary to prevent individual onset or reduce severity as well as spread; such diseases include diphtheria, pertussis, tetanus, polio, measles, rubella, Japanese encephalitis, tuberculosis, Hib infection, pneumococcal infections in children, varicella, human papilloma virus infection, and influenza. Obligatory efforts for these diseases are not established, and the decision on whether or not to get vaccinated is an individual choice.

In Japan in 2014, there were twelve types of routine vaccinations; obligatory efforts had not been imposed for five of them: chickenpox, mumps, hepatitis B, rotavirus, and adult pneumococcal infection. As we saw earlier, routine vaccinations for which obligatory efforts are imposed are generally free, whereas the other vaccines are generally paid for entirely by the individual, unless there is assistance from the local government. Therefore, regional differences occur in individual vaccination rates implemented by municipalities (Tezuka 2010, 264).

Initially, Japan's vaccination policies were based on compulsory vaccinations. However, following a lawsuit in 1992, the legal landscape underwent drastic changes and the system was transformed into obligatory effort and optional vaccination. Victims who suffered side effects from various vaccines that were either mandated or strongly encouraged by the government filed the lawsuit against the government and sought compensation. This will be covered in more detail below. For our present purposes, suffice it to say that even in the mid-1990s, Japan's vaccination target was referred to as the "vaccination gap" compared with developed countries overseas.

In the case of the HPV vaccine, eight years after the government temporarily stopped supporting the use of the vaccine in 2013, obstetricians and gynecologists, Diet members, and others began calling for the resumption of an active campaign to use the "uterine cancer vaccine." The vaccine to prevent infection with a portion of the HPV virus will be available from the fall of 2022 onward. The MHLW has categorized the vaccination as a routine vaccination, and girls starting from the sixth grade of elementary school to the equivalent of the first grade of high school will be able to receive it free of charge (Ministry of Health, Labour and Welfare, 2021a).

In summary, Japan's vaccination policies have wavered between aggressive compulsory vaccination and obligatory efforts (which are desirable from the perspective of social safety), on the one hand, and passive policies that make vaccines optional due to risks of possible side effects, on the other. This reflects the dilemma between social risk and individual risk that surrounds vaccines. We will now examine this in more detail with reference to Y. Tezuka's concept (2010) of the "malpractice avoidance dilemma."

The Transformation of Vaccination Policy and Responses to Adverse Events

Figure 5.3 summarizes the history of drug-related disasters in Japan. Tezuka (2010) claims that drafters of Japan's vaccination policies (bureaucrats) have promoted vaccination policy from the standpoint of having to avoid "malpractice" problems. He classifies malpractice into "error malpractice," or "doing things that shouldn't have been done," and "omission malpractice," or "not doing things that should have been done." Historically, in Japan, vaccination policies have faced the "malpractice avoidance dilemma," and the process of avoiding this dilemma has defined the characteristics of Japan's vaccination policies. This viewpoint can be divided into three main periods.

First, during the Invisible Responsibility Period (1945 to the early 1960s), since error malpractice was a latent potential problem, policy emphasis was placed on avoidance of "omission malpractice." Without error-related problems occurring on the surface, it was difficult for responsibility to be socially accepted. Next, during the Responsibility Dilution Period (late 1960s to early 1980s), error malpractice began appearing in various areas, as seen in public hazards such as cases of Minamata disease, and there was heightened social criticism of policy responsibility. Policies during this period focused on responsibility for "remedying" side-effect damages, rather than responsibility for occurrence of side effects – thus, responsibility was diluted. During the third period, Responsibility Distribution Period (late 1980s to present), informed consent and deregulation became major social trends, and it became widely recognized that side effects were not inevitable but

FIGURE 5.3

The history of vaccine-related disasters in Japan

YEAR	INCIDENT — Major health damage incidents related to drugs and medical devices in the past	Evaluation of immunization by the Ministry of Health, Labor, and Welfare	Evaluation of the ways of taking responsibility for national immunization by Sugizuka
1948	The Diphtheria Immunization Tragedy incident	In 1948, protection of the society against infections was strongly promoted. Immunization became mandatory with a penalty.	1948–the early 1960s: Responsibilities disappeared. Outbreaks of infection.
1956	Anaphylactic deaths from penicillin		
1962	Impairment including limb defects caused by thalidomide (The Thalidomide incident)		
1965	Anaphylactic deaths from a cold remedy with an ampule		
1967	Hearing disorders caused by antibiotics including streptomycin and kanamycin		The late 1960s–the early 1980s: Responsibilities were weakened.
1968	Aplastic anemia caused by chloramphenicol		
1969	Retinopathy caused by chloroquine		
1970	Subacute myelo-optico-neuropathy caused by quinoform (The SMON incident) Suits against smallpox vaccination tragedy (post vaccination)		
1973	Incidents of smallpox vaccination	In 1976, health damages caused by immunization became a social problem. Immunization became mandatory without a penalty. A relief system for health damage was established.	
1975	Quadriceps contracture caused by intra-muscular injection solution Deaths after DPT vaccination		
1982	Ophthalmopathy caused by dialyzers		
1983	HIV infection caused by blood products (blood coagulation factor preparations) (The AIDS incident)		
1987	HCV infection caused by blood products (fibrinogen preparations) (The Hepatitis C incident)		

Year	Incident	Policy
		1980s–current responsibilities were created.
1988	Uterine rupture/fetal distress caused by oxytocin	In 1994, individuals gained respect in medical care. Lawsuits over immunization tragedies were adjudicated. Mandatory requirements were changed to a making-efforts requirement.
1992	*Aseptic meningitis caused by MMR vaccine (The MMR incident) 1989–1992*	
1993	Myelosuppression caused by concomitant use of sorivudine and 5-FU, anti-cancer drug (The Sorivudine incident)	
1994	Myelosuppresion/diarrhea caused by irinotecan hydrochloride	*In 2001, public health and medical service were dramatically improved. Severe symptoms assocated with the influenza virus in the elderly became a social problem. Immunization requirements were changed to obligation with efforts (immun-ization recommended) and without efforts (immunization determined by individuals).*
	An issue of gelatin allergy in live vaccines	
1997	Prion infection caused by the human dry endocranium (The CJD incident)	
2000	Mycobacterium infection caused by the cattle pericardium	In 2009 and 2011, new types of influenza viruses (A/FIN1) emerged. A temporary immunization was created.
	Hepatopathy caused by troglitazone	
2002	Interstitial pneumonia caused by gefitinib (The Iressa incident)	
2005	*Acute disseminated encephalomyelitis (ADEM) after Japanese encephalitis vaccination*	In 2013, there was a "vaccination gap" from other developed countries. The immunization program was broadly revised. Hib infection, child pneumococcal infection, and human papillomavirus infection were added to the list of immun-izations. The basic plan for immunization was formulated. A reporting system of side reactions was designated by law.
2011	Deaths after concomitant vaccination including Hib and pneumococcus vaccines	
2012	Vaccine-associated paralytic poliomyelitis (VAPP) after live polio vaccination	
2013	*Complaints of chronic pain after human papillomavirus vaccination*	

Notes:

DPT: Diphtheria, Pertussis, and Tetanus / MMR: Measles, Mumps, and Rubella / HCV: Hepatitis C virus

Immunization-associated health damages are shown in *italics*.

Incidents where the casual relationships were unclear and those caused by improper use were included.

Source: From "Instructive lessons about drug-induced incidents we need to know – voices from victims wishing to prevent recurrence" Yakuji Nippo Press, 2013

rather should be avoided. It is assumed that the above-mentioned vaccination epidemic lawsuit strongly influenced this revision. During this period, there was also a great policy shift from obligatory vaccines to optional
vaccines (or suggested vaccines), and from mass vaccination – such as collective vaccination of children at schools and similar places – to mainly individual vaccinations, with individuals receiving vaccinations at their own
family physician's office and other such places.

It can be said that this policy transformation process involved a gradual
shift from the social safety standpoint, which emphasized avoiding omission malpractice linked to the spread of infectious diseases, to passive or
responsibility-avoidance policies that emphasize avoiding error malpractice, which takes the form of individual-level side effects.

The Impact of Lawsuits on Japan's Vaccination Policy

Since the enactment of the Preventive Vaccination Law in 1948, lawsuits
seeking state compensation for adverse reactions caused by vaccinations
have occasioned the most significant changes to vaccination policy, which,
despite some minor changes, had previously been premised on compulsory
inoculation. In response to a 1992 Tokyo High Court decision, the Preventive Vaccination Law was amended in 1994, which led to the transition from
a compulsory model to one entailing the obligation to make an effort, as well
as to the abolition of occasional intake for influenza vaccinations. Here, I
would like to examine a lawsuit seeking compensation from the state that
brought about a unique Japanese vaccination policy, one that has not been
seen in other developed countries.

While lawsuits seeking compensation for adverse reactions caused by
vaccinations have arisen all over Japan, the earliest case in which a Tokyo
High Court ruling was issued was a Tokyo-based class action lawsuit. This
case involved 159 people seeking compensation from the state, composed
of patients and parents from sixty-two families that had experienced the
death of a child or whose members suffered from residual physical or psych-
ological disorders as the result of side effects from having received vaccinations against smallpox and other diseases between 1952 and 1974. As the
court of first instance, the Tokyo District Court, after acknowledging the
causal relationships for all victims, recognized negligence on the part of
the physicians in charge (e.g., for overdosing) and affirmed state liability
for two plaintiffs, but rejected the responsibility of the state for the other
affected children. On that basis, however, the court recognized the claim

for indemnity by "analogically inferring the Constitutional provision that 'Private property may be taken for public use upon just compensation therefore.'" In other words, while not recognizing negligence under the framework of the principle of liability, the ruling sought to provide de facto relief by analogical application of the Constitution.

The government appealed this ruling, and the Tokyo High Court handed down an even more severe judgment against it. The court held that "in the case of serious adverse reactions arising due to vaccination, compulsory vaccination is illegal in the sense that vaccination should not by right have been forced upon the individual in question." The court also explained that to eliminate the danger of serious adverse reactions, it was necessary that a system be created for physicians to carry out sufficient preliminary examinations to precisely identify and exclude contraindicated persons. The court found that, for a long time, the country had placed emphasis on raising vaccination rates in order to prevent infectious diseases, had not paid sufficient attention to the issue of adverse reactions to vaccinations, and had been negligent in fulfilling its obligation. In addition, "it was presumed that the on-site official [i.e., physician] responsible for performing vaccinations misidentified the contraindication and inoculated the children affected in this case, even though they corresponded to the contraindications." Therefore, if the state (i.e., minister of health and welfare) had taken sufficient steps to identify contraindications and exclude corresponding children from being inoculated, the occurrence of the incidents involving adverse reactions in question could have been avoided. Based on the above, the state acknowledged its responsibility under the State Redress Law as having been negligent by failing to take adequate measures to prevent contraindicated individuals from undergoing vaccination.

In other words, the Tokyo High Court advanced a strong interpretation regarding the obligation to identify contraindicated individuals and acknowledged negligence and liability for compensation on the part of the state, which had failed to develop a system for that purpose. Unlike the district court ruling, it may be said that this decision took the first step toward recognizing the state's liability for negligence.

A variety of views have been advanced regarding this ruling, which has been the subject of considerable debate. In fact, there has been strong opposition from the medical community in terms of whether it is possible for them to fulfill the level of obligations sought in this ruling. Such reasons include the fact that during preliminary examination at the time of inoculation, especially for subjects who have not presented with fever or other major symptoms, it is practically impossible, medically speaking, to predict what and how much should be asked during the preliminary examination. Even if such questions are asked, it is unclear whether it is possible to identify contraindicated individuals based on parents' responses, or whether a preventative vaccination will result an adverse reaction. Thus, there are plausible grounds for the critique that this is an unrealistic obligation to impose on physicians on the front lines. Regarding state responsibility, beyond the fact that it is extremely difficult to predict adverse reactions, the view could also be expressed that, even if a system was established, no matter how much budget and personnel are allocated, the difficulty of identifying contraindicated individuals would effectively remain unchanged. Moreover, the country's emphasis on improving the vaccination rate in an effort to improve public hygiene and protect its citizens from infectious disease does not in itself seem worthy of criticism.

While one cannot deny that vaccinations engender a certain number of adverse reactions, they also have the social effect of preventing infectious disease and securing the health and hygiene of society as a whole. On the other hand, it is also necessary to think about helping those who suffer from the adverse reactions that have a certain probability of occurring, and about the responsibility of the nation, which benefits as a whole. While this is a natural challenge, the 1992 ruling of the Tokyo High Court was arguably an attempt to respond to this challenge within the framework of the principle of liability for negligence through a finding of the country's negligence.

In this case, however, after the country has been found liable for negligence, it could also be expected that the country attempt to adopt policies designed to avoid this. This means that rather than simply considering the financial burden of paying compensation, the country must also consider how to avoid being labelled as negligent. The Japanese government is vulnerable to popular criticism and tends to adopt policies that will avoid criticism as much as possible. This tendency to easily alter principles in an effort to show consideration for others reflects behavioural principles inherent in Japanese culture.

As a result, Japan transformed its vaccination policy at a fundamental level. In the Revised Preventive Vaccination Law of 1994, as well as the shift from a compulsory model of imposing regular vaccinations to one entailing the obligation to make an effort, occasional vaccinations for illnesses such as influenza were also abolished. In a way that showed consideration for

public opinion, which was sympathetic toward victims, the national regulations on "mass vaccinations" were relaxed, with a major shift toward "individual vaccinations," in which individuals (i.e., parents) agreed to vaccinations
after understanding the significance and risks they entailed.

Vaccination is fraught with conflict between the public health and welfare of an entire nation and the rights and choices of individuals, and a variety of policy options have been adopted by different countries in an attempt
to solve this dilemma; it was in response to this dilemma that the Japanese
government abolished the compulsory model on the basis of public opinion
and that the courts found fault with the state – in other words, the response
was a retreat from vaccinations that had originally been deemed necessary
for public health. This policy of retreat, on its face, might seem like a public
health shift toward a position that shows more respect for the rights of individuals. However, the judgments in question are largely silent about the
rights of individuals, and the country's policy change contains little from the
perspective of respect for individual rights. As shown earlier, it would seem
that this policy was a reaction to public opinion and an attempt to avoid
liability.

In addition, it may also be said that this policy is one that shifts the responsibility of damages from unavoidable adverse reactions from the country to the parents of those who receive vaccinations. While it sounds good to
say that the decision is being left to the autonomous choice of individuals, in
actual practice, it must be said that, as well as evading responsibility by shifting it onto the shoulders of recipients, this measure could end up compromising the public's welfare. We could also say that this policy is consistent with
Japanese behavioural principles, which, with regard to the inextricable components of rights and responsibilities, tend to take the latter aspect into account at the expense of the former. For the court, rather than relying on a
logical argument that directly recognized the country's negligence, a judgment that provided relief by analogy to the provisions of the Constitution,
as in the district court ruling, might have been more appropriate not only in
jurisprudential terms but also in view of its social impact.

Many developed countries have established systems that, rather than
being informed by the principle of liability for negligence, instead seek to
provide no-fault guarantees for secondary and adverse reactions from preventative vaccinations. These systems do not inquire into the question of
who was negligent, but rather provide relief to any and all who have experienced injury for the sake of public welfare. In Japan, a system of guarantees

for providing relief for vaccination-related injury also exists for the time being, but its scope and the amount of compensation provided is extremely low, and the system cannot be said to fulfill its intended function. Thus, based on this background, there is a barren cyclical relationship whereby courts, adhering stubbornly to the premise of the principle of liability for negligence, find liability for negligence using a logic that is arguably inappropriate, and then governments respond by moving to an ineffective no-fault relief system.

Acknowledgment of negligence by the government in subsequent legal cases continued. Over the course of four years, beginning in 1993, the measles, mumps, and rubella (MMR) and diphtheria, pertussis, and tetanus (DPT) vaccines were administered to 1.8 million people, 1,800 of whom subsequently contracted aseptic meningitis. Consequently, lawsuits were launched over 1) defective vaccines, 2) the responsibility of the manufacturer, the Osaka University Research Foundation for Microbial Diseases, and 3) the national government's inaction. In 2003, the Osaka District Court indicated that the delay in halting usage of the MMR vaccine despite side effects being foreseen increased overall damages, and rendered a decision recognizing the national government's responsibility for harm. The court further observed that the defendant nation had, at the very least, responsibility for negligently produced harm, due to the failure to comply with its supervisory obligations as the negative side effects of vaccines in question could have been foreseen (Osaka District Court Judgment Wa 12535, Wa 4262, March 13, 2003). In response to this decision, policies shifted toward the total ban of the MMR vaccine. At the same time, the statement of omission malpractice (that is, the measles outbreak) was pardoned. As a result of leaving vaccination to the discretion of individuals in an attempt to avoid the error of omission that could result in the occurrence of side effects, the original purpose of vaccination, "to prevent the outbreak and spread of potentially contagious diseases, to contribute to the improvement and promotion of public health, and to provide prompt relief from health damage caused by vaccination," has deviated significantly from its goal. Thus, vaccination policies during the third period were far from the world standards of the 1980s.

Consequently, the attempts by the government to avoid the occurrence of side effects by making vaccines an individual's choice has drastically changed policy priorities, which in the 1948 Preventive Vaccination Law were "to provide vaccines in order to prevent the occurrence and spread of potentially infectious diseases, and contribute to the improvement and enhancement of public health while also working toward quick relief of health damages caused by vaccines."

Recent Cases of Health Damage Caused by Vaccinations

After a period of relative inaction, the efforts to close the vaccination gap resumed. For instance, consider the responses to secondary reactions of the HPV vaccine (cervical cancer vaccine). This vaccination was initially recommended for girls in grades 6 through 10. According to the vaccination schedule, the first vaccine is to be given in grade 7, followed by the second vaccine one to two months later, and the third vaccine six months after the first.

The HPV vaccine was released internationally in 2006, and vaccination in Japan began in April 2013. Shortly thereafter, however, there was an outbreak of HPV-associated adverse events that had not been anticipated before the start of the vaccination campaign. Cases of secondary reactions as well as complaints of chronic pain in a wide range of areas around the body besides the injection site were reported successively throughout the country. According to the Representatives of Japan Cervical Cancer Vaccine Sufferers Organization, although pain around the injection site was light, there were various other symptoms, such as "severe pain," "convulsions," "learning disabilities," and "psychology symptoms that prevented me from being able to go to school and obstructed daily life." Furthermore, compared with other countries with cases of a "wide range of pain beyond the vaccination site," Japan had 1.1 cases per 100,000 vaccinations, which was 2 to 10 times more frequent than other countries, such as the United States with 0.1 cases, England with 0.6 cases, and South Korea with 0.1 cases.[4]

As noted above, in 2013, MHLW announced its intent to "temporarily suspend active vaccination encouragement" for the HPV vaccine because of community concerns about its safety. The number of vaccinations administered decreased compared with 2012, when vaccinations had been performed at public expense. The MHLW announced that it would temporarily refrain from issuing aggressive vaccination recommendations. As a result, the number of inoculated persons dropped drastically in 2014 compared to the previous year. Presumably, many people interpreted this shift by the MHLW to mean that the vaccine was considered dangerous. Even today, despite the fact that the MHLW has resumed its encouragement of the HPV, vaccination rates remain low.

It is noted in the WHO's safety statement (2014), as well as in the Japan Pediatric Society petition and joint statements from the Japan Society of Obstetrics and Gynecology, that the high safety and efficacy of the HPV vaccine (product name: Cervarix and Gardasil) have been scientifically verified. If this is the case, should policy management not try to explain why the occurrence of side effects was high only in Japan, as well as seek to promote unbiased perspective and deep understanding of the risks surrounding the vaccine, rather than focus on malpractice avoidance? One would think that it would be necessary to fulfill this responsibility by calling for investigation on a global scale, beginning with drug epidemiology, causal relationship assessment, and recurrence prevention. However, that opportunity has been lost with the shift to passive policies. The implications of this shift included, among other things, the dilution of responsibility for creating relief policies targeting vaccine victims who suffered health damages.

Furthermore, there have been problems with Japan's mass media reporting. Without waiting for verification from experts on HPV vaccine secondary reactions, the mass media's reporting fuelled the perception that there was a clear cause-and-effect relationship between the vaccine and the damages. This became one factor leading to responsibility dilution as a result of a decrease in vaccinations and policy makers' passive avoidance.

Patient Self-Determination and Risk Taking

Currently, Japan's vaccination policies are predicated on the principle of patient self-determination and informed consent to vaccine risk taking. One reason that can account for the phenomenon of the vaccination gap in Japan is the fact that, compared with other developed countries, there is insufficient supply of necessary vaccines. Specifically, some of the vaccines used in other countries cannot be used in Japan due to safety concerns. The downside of such strict requirements, however, is that many infectious diseases cannot be efficiently and adequately controlled. This was especially evident as Japan struggled to contain COVID-19 infections in 2020.

A variety of forward-looking policies are being drafted to overcome these problems, such as acceleration of the safety verification procedures for vaccines, cost assistance for vaccines, a health-damages relief system aimed at relief for victims, the creation of a supportive environment for promoting research developments on safe vaccines, and improvement of vaccine production and distribution systems. Some parents may avoid vaccines because they do not know about the potential threats of disease, and public communication on the significance of vaccines is an important issue.

The outcome remains unclear, but the need to meet world standards is a pressing issue in Japan, a developed country.

Common Understanding of the Safety and Risks Surrounding Vaccines

Because vaccines are administered to healthy people, the range of acceptable side effects is narrower than for disease-treatment drugs. Naturally, the stronger routine immunization is, the greater the risk of adverse effects. Therefore, it is essential for policy makers and mass media to cooperate with experts (scientists) and publicly report trustworthy, reliable information based on scientific evidence. It is especially essential that the government continue gathering information on side effects and periodically disclose vaccine safety information.

Disclosure of experts' open discussion process is effective for deepening the understanding of unvaccinated people and their caregivers about various issues, beginning with side-effect reactions associated with vaccinations. As stated in the WMA Lisbon Declaration, the right to information, the right to receive health education, the right to self-determination, the right to freedom of choice, and the right to good-quality medical care lead to the exercise of consented decision-making by the unvaccinated person. In Japan, where the prevalence of optional vaccination is high, the sharing of accurate information becomes all the more important. Furthermore, the information gathered from experts' discussions could improve evaluation of side effects from vaccines as well as enable policy makers to solve vaccine-associated problems more quickly and efficiently.

To sum up, trust in policy makers should arise not from the appearance of fairness (i.e., responsibility distribution and dilution) but from an evidence-informed understanding of causal relationship in vaccination as well as from the promotion of the benefits of immunization.

Moving toward the Global Standard for Vaccines

Eliminating the Vaccination Gap

The term "vaccination gap" is used in the United States to refer to the difference between the targeted vaccination for herd immunity and the actual vaccination rate. In Japan, however, it is used to refer to the vaccine strains that are not being implemented yet are recommended by the WHO. Behind this conceptual discrepancy lies a difference between the two countries with regard to thinking about the concept of herd immunity.

The WHO recommends ten types of vaccines for implementation in all regions of the world, and in 2013, Japan finally began administering all of them, moving toward eventual elimination of the vaccination gap. Rotavirus and HPV vaccines have finally become routine, partly due to the impact of the new corona vaccine that became a pandemic. As mentioned above, a recommendation for routine vaccination was made in November 2021, but the number of people who wish to be vaccinated and those who have been administered the vaccination are few.

Breaking Away from the Constriction of Vaccination Policy

To achieve the aims of the Preventive Vaccination Law, the government must re-examine its policies from the perspectives of herd immunity, the Precautionary Principle, and patient rights. The original mission of drug administration is to protect the lives and health of the people. Another objective is to ensure prompt decision-making and compensation for adverse events based on the Precautionary Principle.

Various laws and regulations, especially pharmaceutical laws, must clearly state the responsibility for preventing damage occurrence in involved parties, and it is necessary to promptly carry out pharmacovigilance. Specific areas for examination include activating medical institutions' reporting of side effects, creating mechanisms for utilizing side-effect information reported by patients, and strengthening international cooperation on dispatches from resident staff to foreign regulatory agencies.

It is also important to encourage the building of a system for consistent analysis and evaluation of safety information for each vaccine that will be performed by a team of experts in medicine, pharmaceuticals, drug epidemiology, and biostatistics, both post-marketing and at the time of approval-review promotion (methods to analyze and approach the patient's genomic information or genetic characteristics) of pharmacogenomics research.[5] Based on the Precautionary Principle for adverse events, it is essential that safety information be publicly released, even when cause-and-effect relationships are still uncertain.

Information regarding vaccination risk, the health-damage relief system, as well as the range of relief should be made available to the public. A special education campaign on vaccinations and herd immunity should also be carried out. The most important areas of focus are public debates among experts, and disclosure and sharing of information on debates taking place among governments, beneficiaries, experts, academics, and pharmaceutical companies.

Ensuring a Transparent, Comprehensive Policy
Formation Process

Since 1948, Japan's vaccination policies have been caught between a social mission of "protecting the population from infection" at one end of the spectrum and the incidents of drug-associated health damages at the other. Consequently, the government opted for a path of avoiding the malpractice dilemma – in other words, abandoning a position of main responsibility. It increased the number of optional vaccines and shifted responsibility to unvaccinated persons, though it is hard to say whether this is the appropriate allocation of risk. Under the pretext of respecting individual rights to avoid side-effect damages, the significance of unvaccinated persons' right to relief and right to social safety became ambiguous. Then, each stakeholder involved in the implementation of vaccination policy ended up engaging in responsibility avoidance in instances of adverse events, based on their own interests and perspectives.

In the future, it is desirable to acknowledge that vaccine side effects are always accompanied by uncertainty and anxiety among the unvaccinated. It is likewise advisable to consider implementation of a vaccination policy that states in advance the risk of side effects. For example, when examining adverse effects, it is desirable for all stakeholders to clarify their individual standpoints and interests, whether 1) the elimination of the public-health immunization gap, 2) economic strategies under the pretext of bridging the "vaccination gap," or 3) the main interest of expert groups.

Prospective vaccination policies in Japan should be premised on the following objectives, based on the Ministry of Health, Labour and Welfare's review of the vaccination system in 2014:

- confirming the basic direction of vaccination measures (significance and collaboration with stakeholders, awareness-raising activities, research promotion, guidelines for a safe supply of vaccines)
- delineating stakeholders' roles (confirming the individual roles of national and regional government bodies, medical personnel, vaccine manufacturers and distributors, and the public)
- setting targets for the promotion of vaccine measures (continuous examination of the vaccination rates and cost burden of each vaccine)
- spreading awareness of and knowledge about vaccines (knowledge dissemination and awareness activities for stakeholders, collaboration with related organizations, promotion of individual vaccines, etc.)

- ensuring vaccine supply and promoting vaccine research and development (research promotion, strengthening of the domestic vaccine production system, scrutinized testing of vaccine compounds, etc.)
- implementing risk, conflict, and crisis management for proper vaccine implementation (ensuring a vaccine implementation system, implementing rapid damages relief, promoting information disclosure)
- improving vaccine safety and effectiveness (reporting secondary reactions, ensuring a system for implementing infection surveillance, etc.)
- engaging in international collaboration on vaccinations (exchanging and gathering information from international organizations and other countries)
- holding consensus meetings to evaluate and examine vaccines according to social circumstances on a regular basis
- examining and evaluating vaccine policy from anthropological, social, cultural, and economic viewpoints. (Ministry of Health, Labour and Welfare [of Japan] 2014)

Instead of a traditional examination of adverse effects performed exclusively by experts and the government, we recommend that new emphasis be placed on the process of risk assessment and distribution of responsibility through social consensus by publicly disclosing all pertinent information. Responsibility distribution is not static but rather a consensus process. Once this fact is acknowledged, a new approach to risk and responsibility in Japan's vaccination policies can be developed in order to break away from the dichotomous conflict of the malpractice dilemma. This will also bring Japan closer to global standards for vaccination policy, reflected in the targets of SDG 3.8 and 3.b, and better enable it to meet global health security challenges such as COVID-19.

NOTES

1 https://sdgs.un.org/goals/goal3.
2 Luhmann (1996) introduced the distinction between "risk" and "danger." "Risk" is the potential for future danger for which one (or one's own decision) is responsible, while "danger" is defined as something attributable to the external environment and others.
3 In 1948, a national civil servant's monthly salary was JPY 13,000, and the penalty imposed by the law was JPY 3,000.
4 A. Yagi et al., "Cervical Cancer Protection in Japan: Where Are We?" *Vaccines* 9, 11 (2021): 1263–75. https://doi.org/10.3390/vaccines9111263.

5 Pharmacogenomics is a term coined from "pharmacology" and "genomics." It refers to an approach whereby genomic information (genetic traits) of patients is analyzed in order to explore and develop effective and safe drugs for a specific group of diseases, which aims at individual medical treatment (administration of drugs) and research leading to the creation of drugs. Specifically, it points to the development of optimal drugs for a certain disease by identifying common genetic traits among patients with that specific disease.

Global Health Standards and Food Security
Exploring the Double Science Standard of Review under the SPS Agreement after India – Agricultural Products

MARIELA de AMSTALDEN

Trade and public health are two distinctive yet highly intertwined concepts that bear increasing relevance for global economic governance. From an international law perspective, public health refers to a state's right and obligation to ensure the conditions for the population within its territory to be healthy, aiming at the highest possible level of health that is consistent with principles of social justice, with particular emphasis on the fair treatment of the most disadvantaged (Gostin 2008). Arguably, protecting public health is a national regulatory imperative that has been at times limited by some of the obligations imposed on signatory states in international trade agreements. Attempting to reconcile the tension between trade facilitation and national autonomy in protecting public health, the World Trade Organization (WTO) adopted the Agreement on the Application of Sanitary and Phytosanitary Measures (SPS Agreement) at its inception in 1994. The SPS Agreement promised to make available regulatory space for science-based domestic legislation on public health. However, despite the undeniable extension of sovereignty afforded to the protection of public health under the law of the WTO, participation in the rules-based trading system remains at odds with the pursuit of domestic science-based public health standards. This chapter analyzes the impact of the SPS Agreement on certain domestic legislation in India that seeks to strengthen food safety and security by imposing restrictions on the trade of certain agricultural goods. The relevant global health standard is set out in Sustainable Development Goal (SDG) 2.1, which seeks to "ensure access by all people, in particular the poor and people in vulnerable situations, including infants, to safe, nutritious and sufficient food all year round."[1] While engaging in a legal analysis of the role of science in international economic law, this chapter ultimately asks whether WTO law, and the SPS Agreement in particular, is well-equipped to engage with non-trade concerns in assessing the appropriateness of domestic measures with the potential to display trade-distorting effects.

As noted in Chapter 3, India has been an innovative leader in the developing world in utilizing provisions in international trade law, such as the Agreement on Trade-Related Aspects of Intellectual Property Rights (TRIPS Agreement), to protect its public health initiatives, especially with regard to pharmaceuticals. I posit here that scientifically unfounded public health measures impose significant non-tariff barriers to trade in cases where they are not based on an international standard. In order to support this point, I will determine whether and to what extent public health measures that are not based on science may potentially constitute disguised non-tariff barriers to trade.[2] I will begin by presenting what I have called the "double-science standard" as established under Article 2.2 of the SPS Agreement to identify the legal standard of review that domestic measures must meet in order to comply with trade obligations.[3] This will be followed by a study of the appropriate levels of public health protection and whether and to what extent domestic public health measures may or may not constitute non-tariff barriers to trade. The significance of risk assessments and their symbiotic relationship with scientific principles will be addressed. The chapter concludes with some thoughts on the legal implications of the use of scientific evidence in regulation aimed at protecting public health.

The Double Science Standard of Review under the SPS Agreement

The context for my discussion is a recent WTO dispute over interpretation of the SPS Agreement, namely, *India – Measures Concerning the Importation of Certain Agricultural Products* (*India – Agricultural Products*) (WTO 2015). Brought against India by the United States, the case was eventually appealed to the WTO Appellate Body. In essence, the dispute concerned India's import prohibition affecting certain agricultural products, such as poultry meats, eggs, and feathers, from countries reporting Notifiable Avian Influenza (NAI) —more commonly known as "bird flu" – to the World Organisation for Animal Health (formerly the Office International des

FIGURE 6.1

Double science standard as provided for in Article 2.2 of the SPS Agreement

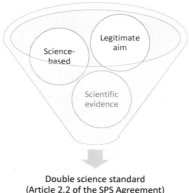

Double science standard
(Article 2.2 of the SPS Agreement)

Epizooties [OIE]). According to the United States, these measures were not based on the relevant international standard (the Terrestrial Animal Health Code) or on a scientific risk assessment, and thus unjustifiably encumbered international trade.

This dispute raises many important issues, but the present analysis will focus on the relationship between scientific principles and risk assessment by identifying a legal threshold imposed by Article 2.2 of the SPS Agreement. I will call this legal threshold the "double science standard."

As Figure 6.1 shows, a domestic measure will not be considered a non-tariff barrier if it is demonstrated that three subsequent requirements are fulfilled. First, the respondent party will have to show that the adopted measure is necessary to attain a legitimate aim of protecting human health, such as reducing deaths (A). Second, the measure must be science-based in accordance with the principles set out for risk assessments in Article 5 of the SPS Agreement. Both provisions, Article 2.2 and Article 5 of the SPS Agreement, have a symbiotic relationship that informs their interpretation. This element constitutes the first science standard. For instance, the adopted regulatory framework has to identify the potential effects on human health and evaluate their likelihood of occurrence (B). And third, the measure must not be maintained without sufficient scientific evidence, which constitutes the second science standard (C). As a result, the double science standard imposed by the SPS Agreement will be met in cases where all three elements are present.

Public Health Protection and the Double Science Standard

The SPS Agreement applies to all sanitary and phytosanitary (SPS) measures that may affect, directly or indirectly, international trade (SPS Agreement, Article 1). The first step in determining whether the SPS Agreement will serve as a backdrop to assessing compliance with international trade obligations is to identify the nature of the domestic measures being challenged. In other words, the scope of application of the SPS Agreement will be established only after a domestic measure is identified as an SPS measure.

Conceptualizing SPS Measures

The SPS Agreement defines SPS measures in its Annex A as any measure applied:

- to protect animal or plant life or health within the territory of the Member from risks arising from the entry, establishment, or spread of pests, diseases, disease-carrying organisms, or disease-causing organisms;
- to protect human or animal life or health within the territory of the Member from risks arising from additives, contaminants, toxins or disease-causing organisms in foods, beverages or feedstuffs;
- to protect human life or health within the territory of the Member from risks arising from diseases carried by animals, plants or products thereof, or from the entry, establishment or spread of pests; or
- to prevent or limit any other damage within the territory of the Member from entry, establishment or spread of pests. (See also Charnovitz 2007.)

I have argued elsewhere (Maidana-Eletti de Amstalden 2014, 2015) that measures requiring the disclosure of nutritional information on the packaging, such as labelling measures, may not prima facie fall within the ambit of the SPS Agreement. Rather, these type of measures are likely to constitute a technical regulation related to a product, and thus the 1995 Agreement on Technical Barriers to Trade (TBT Agreement) – and its arguably less stringent requirements (Pauwelyn 1999, 644; Downes 2015) – may apply. However, paragraph 2 of Annex A establishes that a domestic measure adopted to protect human health from risks arising from additives, contaminants, toxins, or disease-causing organisms in foods, beverages, or feedstuffs shall be considered an SPS measure, to the exclusion of other WTO agreements. Thus, it is also conceivable that product regulation measures addressing nutritional requirements may fall within the scope of the SPS Agreement in cases where they have been adopted with the aim of protecting human health from risks arising from repeated exposure to elements considered unhealthy in large quantities, such as saturated fats, sugars, or salt. In other words, the legality of measures on the nutritional composition of food-stuffs could become subject to SPS scrutiny to the extent that 1) those risk management measures are adopted with the aim of protecting human health from additives and 2) saturated fats, sugars, and salt are classified as additives.

Identifying International Health Standards

In establishing the concept of food additive for the purposes of WTO law, the Codex Alimentarius Commission (CAC) standard setting forth the conditions for the use of permitted food additives is relevant. The CAC is the most influential food standard–setting body at the international level.[4] Its main objective is to set international food standards for the protection of public health and the promotion of fair practice in food trade (WHO and FAO 2010, Articles 1[c], [d], and [e]). Unlike more recent WTO instruments, the CAC was established in 1962 by the Joint Food and Agriculture Organization (FAO)/World Health Organization (WHO) Food Standards Programme as their subsidiary body to respond to the increased trade in food.[5] It elaborates on international standards, codes of practice, guidelines, and related texts addressing food safety and quality with a view to facilitating international trade (CAC 2006). For many decades, the legal relevance of CAC standards was dismissed because of their non-binding nature and merely advisory role.[6] It was only upon the adoption of the WTO agreements that the Codex Alimentarius was upgraded to semi-binding status (Arcuri 2014; Veggeland and Borgen 2005). Articles 3.4 and 12.3 of the SPS Agreement explicitly refer to the adoption of the CAC standards as a way to sustain a presumption of compliance with food safety rules.[7]

The CAC defines additives as "any substance not normally consumed as food by itself and not normally used as an ingredient of the food, whether or not it has nutritional value ... the intentional addition of which ... may be reasonably expected to result in it or its by-products becoming a component of or otherwise affecting the characteristics of such foods."[8] Paradoxically, the CAC definition further specifies that the term "food additive" does *not* include substances added to food for *improving nutritional qualities*. A WTO Panel Report, *European Communities – Measures Affecting the Approval and Marketing of Biotech Products* (*EC – Biotech*) (Peel 2007, 1031), has given some general indication of the manner in which the term "food additive" may be interpreted in accordance with WTO law.[9] This description emphasizes the role of the CAC in providing scientific advice, a matter to which I return below. However, *EC – Biotech*, for all its textually focused reading, does little to clarify the meaning of food additive in the context of measures establishing nutritional composition requirements.

Against this backdrop, saturated fats, sugars, and salt can be considered food additives for the purposes of the SPS Agreement in cases where the following requirements are fulfilled:

1 The substance is not normally consumed as food by itself.
2 The substance is not normally used as an ingredient of the food.
3 Intentionally adding the substance results in its incorporation to the foodstuff or otherwise affects the characteristics of such foodstuff.
4 The substance does not improve the nutritional quality of the foodstuff.

A grammatical interpretation of this threshold – as favoured by the WTO Appellate Body in *Australia – Measures Affecting the Importation of Salmon* (*Australia – Salmon*) (WTO 1998, 1999a) – will undoubtedly lead to an unsatisfactory result, with high evidentiary challenges for both parties to the dispute. First, what constitutes normal consumption in country A is likely to differ from the *normality* standard in country B. This suggests that no clear-cut interpretation is possible and therefore a case-by-case analysis must be conducted. The notion of normality, which by definition excludes perceived risks, is strongly related to the right of Members to adopt an appropriate level of protection (ALOP), as established in Article 5.3 of the SPS Agreement.

The Controversial Nexus between Risk Assessment and Scientific Evidence

In *India – Agricultural Products* (WTO 2015), India contended that eight out of ten challenged measures were based on an international standard. However, the panel still found a violation of Article 3.1 of the SPS Agreement because the challenged measure was not "based on" an international standard, i.e., it was not based on a risk assessment as established in Article 5, and so it failed to benefit from the rebuttable presumption of compliance as provided for in Article 3.2. The lack of sufficient scientific evidence supporting the implementation of the challenged measure was instrumental in determining its (lack of) legality under the SPS Agreement. In other words, even in cases where a domestic measure is based on an international standard, this fact alone does not release Members from their obligation to conduct a risk assessment. Only in cases where the measure has been found to "conform to" an international standard is the respondent party's burden of conducting a risk assessment lifted.

The SPS Agreement provides various instruments for determining whether a domestic SPS measure has been adopted as a disguised non-tariff barrier. The umbrella provision establishing the basic obligations for Members adopting SPS measures is found in Article 2.2 of the SPS Agreement, which provides for the double science standard, as elaborated above. This provision imposes a triple threshold to assess the compatibility of domestic measures with the SPS Agreement. Adopted measures that

1 shall apply only to the extent necessary to protect human health
2 are science-based
3 are not maintained without sufficient scientific evidence.

As the WTO Appellate Body clarified, many elements of Article 2.2 are later elaborated in more detail in Article 5 and the interpretation of one should inform the interpretation of the other (WTO 2015, para. 5.12).

First Element of the Double Science Standard: Legitimate Aim
The first element of the double science standard of review demands the execution of a necessity test to assess whether the aim is legitimate, i.e., SPS measures must not arbitrarily or unjustifiably discriminate between Members where identical or similar conditions prevail. The necessity test further requires that SPS measures not be applied in a manner that restricts international trade. In many ways, the novelty of this test is limited, since it reflects the necessity requirement in Article XX(b) of the General Agreement on Tariffs and Trade (GATT) 1994 (GATT 1994). Unlike the general exceptions clause under Article XX of the GATT 1994, however, Article 2.2 of the SPS Agreement will always be applicable, even in cases where other violations of the SPS Agreement could not be established. Article 2.2 also reflects the obligations established in Article III(4) of the GATT 1994, which imposes upon Members the duty to accord nationals of other members any treatment that is not less favourable than that accorded to its own nationals.

In other words, imported goods must be treated no less favourably than like products of national origin. The national treatment prohibition in the GATT 1994 also aims at requiring equality of competitive conditions and protecting expectations of equal competitive relationships.[10] Unlike other instruments, however, the national treatment principle in the SPS Agreement has been interpreted as also prohibiting discrimination between different products (*Australia – Salmon:* WTO 1998, para. 252). Thus, a measure will be in violation of WTO obligations where there is evidence that it detrimentally affects competition in a given market.

Second Element of the Double Science Standard: Science-Based Rules

The second element of the double science standard of review requires SPS measures to be based on scientific principles. At its core, the SPS Agreement aims at guaranteeing human, animal, and plant life and health in all Member States (SPS Agreement, Preamble, recital 1), while minimizing the negative trade effect of SPS measures and promoting international trade (*EC – Hormones* 1998, para. 177).[11] As mentioned earlier, although Members retain their right to choose their own adequate level of SPS protection (ALOP),[12] Articles 2 and 5 of the SPS Agreement provide a legal backdrop for assessing whether challenged SPS measures establishing domestic thresholds for the protection of public health are unjustifiably impeding trade. In other words, Members can still determine the level of risk they are willing to accept, for the establishment of an ALOP is both "a privilege and an obligation" (WTO 2015, para. 5.221) in exercising regulatory autonomy.

Article 5.1 establishes that domestic SPS measures must be based on an assessment of the risks to human, animal, or plant life or health, taking into account risk assessment techniques developed by the relevant international organizations. Risk assessments evaluate the likelihood of entry, establishment, or spread of a pest or disease within the territory of an importing Member and of the associated potential biological and economic consequences (SPS Agreement, Annex A, para. 4). It also refers to the evaluation of the potential for adverse effects on human or animal health arising from the presence of additives, contaminants, toxins, or disease-causing organisms in food, beverages, or animal feed (ibid.). A measure is based on a risk assessment under Article 2.2 of the SPS Agreement in cases where there exists an objective relationship between the former and the latter (*EC – Hormones* 1998, para. 189), that is, the result of the risk assessment is rationally related to the measure.

The WTO Panel found in *Australia – Salmon* that a measure that is not based on a risk assessment (as in Article 5) will suggest that it is not based on scientific principles (as in the second tier of Article 2.2), leading to a violation of both provisions (*Australia – Salmon* 1998, para. 8.52). The WTO Appellate Body upheld this reasoning, stating that a violation of Articles 5.1 and 5.2 will lead to an inconsistency with Article 2.2 of the SPS Agreement *by implication* (WTO 1998, para. 138). In other words, there will be a rebuttable presumption of non-compliance with Article 2.2 in cases where a violation of Articles 5.1 and 5.2 of the SPS Agreement is established.

The same legal analysis was put forward once again by the WTO Panel in *India –Agricultural Products:* "Where an SPS measure is not based on a risk assessment as required by Articles 5.1 and 5.2 of the SPS Agreement, this measure is presumed not to be based on scientific principles and to be maintained without sufficient scientific evidence, in contravention of Article 2.2 of the SPS Agreement (WTO 2014, para. 7.331, with further references)." In this case too, the Appellate Body upheld the findings of the Panel (WTO 2015, para 5.15). It also shed light on the manner in which the symbiotic relationship between the basic rights and obligations of Article 2.2 and the more specific requirements of Article 5 of the SPS Agreement should be understood to determine SPS compliance. Furthermore, the Appellate Body clarified that an analysis of whether a violation of Article 5 would lead to a violation of Article 2.2 can be established only on a case-by-case basis (ibid.), and so no clear-cut interpretative guidance is available to date. In other words, could an objective and rational relationship between the SPS measure and the scientific evidence be established with resort to science?

The short answer is yes. The rationality of the relationship will have to be established on a case-by-case basis, taking into account the characteristics of the measure at issue and the quantity and quality of the available scientific evidence that possesses the *"necessary scientific and methodological rigor to be considered reputable science"* (WTO 2015, para 5.28). The risk assessment would further entail an inquiry into evidence adduced by the parties regarding the particular risks that the challenged measure is set to protect against, and to whom the risk is posed (ibid., para 5.27). Hence, the risk assessment will have to 1) identify potential effects on health and 2) evaluate the likelihood of those potential effects to occur.

Third Element of the Double Science Standard: Scientific Evidence
The third element of the double science standard of review requires that SPS measures are not maintained without sufficient scientific evidence in order to avoid becoming a non-tariff barrier. A careful reading of *India –*

FIGURE 6.2

Scientific evidence under the double science standard of review

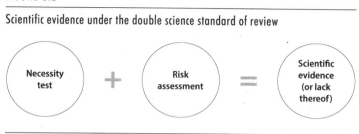

Agricultural Products (WTO 2015, para 5.27) suggests that the establishment of a sufficient level of scientific evidence can be pursued by weighing the outcome of the necessity test carried out under the first element of the double science standard of review (A) against the scientific basis as identified in the second element of the same standard (B). The result of this equation will determine whether an SPS measure is being maintained with or without sufficient scientific evidence (C) – that is, there must be a rational relationship between A and B in order to produce C.

Figure 6.2 shows that the double science standard of review will be met in cases where scientific evidence is established after weighing the outcomes from the necessity test and the risk assessment. Equally, a domestic measure will be WTO-compliant in cases where all three elements of the double science standard are cumulatively fulfilled. It is apparent that the SPS threshold is much more stringent than those standards of review established under other WTO agreements.

Implications of the Double Science Standard for Public Health Measures

In the aftermath of *India – Agricultural Products*, the United States requested authorization[13] from the Dispute Settlement Body (DSB) to suspend concessions and other obligations to India in the amount of US$450 million in 2016, to be updated annually.[14] The argument put forward by the United States indicated that the revised Indian measure was still inconsistent with WTO obligations, since it provided for a domestic public health standard that was substantially more restrictive than that suggested by the World Organisation for Animal Health (OIE).

In this chapter, I have focused my analysis on the impact of the SPS Agreement on measures addressing public health. As evidenced in some recent SPS disputes, divergent public health standards of protection arising out of different regulatory approaches among WTO members have the

FIGURE 6.3

The double science standard of review in context

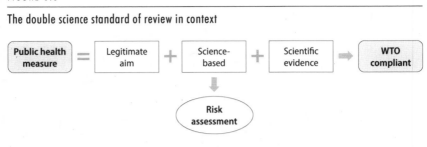

potential to impose important non-tariff barriers to trade. The *India – Agricultural Products* case shows that the use of international standards, such as those adopted by the OIE, as the basis for domestic SPS regulation does not allow Members to deviate from their obligation to conduct a risk assessment. Risk assessments (or lack thereof) will also inform the interpretation of whether a challenged measure can be considered to be based on scientific principles. This line of enquiry suggests that there is a "double-science standard of review" under the SPS Agreement. The double-science standard of review provides that a domestic measure will not be considered a non-tariff barrier to trade if three successive elements are fulfilled (Figure 6.3).

First, the respondent party will have to show that the adopted measure is necessary to attain a legitimate aim of protecting human health (i.e., reducing deaths caused by non-communicable diseases) (A). Second, the measure must be science-based in accordance with the principles set out for risk assessments in Article 5 of the SPS Agreement. Both provisions, Art. 2.2 and Art. 5 of the SPS Agreement have a symbiotic relationship that informs their interpretation, i.e., it will have to identify the potential effects on human health and evaluate whether they are likely to occur (B). Third, the measure must not be maintained without sufficient scientific evidence (C). Thus, it can be presumed that, based on the equation described earlier (A + B = C), a measure is maintained with sufficient scientific evidence whereas the first and second elements are established. The analysis has shown that a legitimate aim to protect public health alone does not suffice to show compliance with international trade obligations. These domestic measures must be based on sound science, that is, they must be in accordance with scientific principles of risk assessment and cannot be maintained without sufficient scientific evidence proving that the measure continues to be necessary to protect public health.

It poses the question, however, of whether, in light of the United Nations Sustainable Development Goals, India is entitled to impose measures that are more trade-restrictive than necessary due to its own societal concerns, particularly with regard to food insecurity and the economic and social inequality within its jurisdiction. Pursuing what one member state deems as an appropriate level of public health protection entails a certain degree of distribution of a variety of available resources – legislative, financial, and social. Arguably, containing a public health risk or protecting food safety and security may take precedence over the free flow of goods in a rules-based trading system. Whether the WTO dispute settlement system is equipped to deal with such legal and policy considerations of the SDG agenda is a topic for another study.

NOTES

1 https://sdgs.un.org/goals/goal2.
2 This chapter is partly based on Maidana-Eletti de Amstalden, 2015.
3 https://www.wto.org/english/tratop_e/sps_e/spsagr_e.htm.
4 Other international institutions also devote their work to setting standards in the area of food safety, e.g., the Organisation for Economic Co-operation and Development (OECD).
5 As a subsidiary organ, the CAC depends financially and institutionally on the FAO and the WHO, a dependence that impairs its ability to rapidly and effectively adopt standards.
6 Prior to the adoption of the SPS Agreement, CAC standards were binding only when voluntarily transposed into national legislation; thus, they remained untouched by national or international political interests. See generally Herdegen 2001; Veggeland and Borgen 2002.
7 Article 3.4 of the SPS Agreement reads, "Members shall play a full part, within the limits of their resources, in the relevant international organizations and their subsidiary bodies, in particular the Codex Alimentarius Commission ... to promote within these organization(s) the development and periodic review of standards, guidelines and recommendations with respect to all aspects of sanitary and phytosanitary measures."
    Article 12.3 of the SPS Agreement reads, "The Committee shall maintain close contact with the relevant international organizations in the field of sanitary and phytosanitary protection, especially with the Codex Alimentarius Commission ... with the objective of securing the best available scientific and technical advice for the administration of this Agreement."

8 General Standard for Food Additives, Codex Standard 1992-1995, 2, https://
   www.fao.org/fao-who-codexalimentarius/sh-proxy/en/?lnk=1&url=https
   %253A%252F%252Fworkspace.fao.org%252Fsites%252Fcodex%252FStandards
   %252FCXS%2B192-1995%252FCXS_192e.pdf.
9 WTO 2006, para. 7.301, where the panel referred to the definition provided by
   the CAC, and in doing so, failed to provide substantive guidance on the matter
   at hand, largely limiting its interpretation to the ordinary meaning of the terms.
10 See, e.g., WTO 1999b, para. 120; WTO 1997, para. 464; WTO 2000, para.
   11.182.
11 European Communities – EC Measures Concerning Meat and Meat Products
   (Hormones) – Report of the Appellate Body, 16 January 1998, WT/DS48/AB/R.
12 Annex A, para. 5 of the SPS Agreement states that the appropriate level of
   sanitary or phytosanitary protection is the level of protection deemed appropriate by the Member establishing those sanitary or phytosanitary measures to
   protect human, animal, or plant life or health within its territory.
13 Based on Article 22.2 of the Understanding on Rules and Procedures Governing
   the Settlement of Disputes, 1869 UNTS 401 (DSU), which reads, "If no satisfactory compensation has been agreed within 20 days after the date of expiry
   of the reasonable period of time, any party having invoked the dispute settlement procedures may request authorization from the DSB to suspend the application to the Member concerned of concessions or other obligations under
   the covered agreements."
14 "Recourse to Article 22.2 of the DSU by the United States," WT/DS430/16,
   circulated on July 8, 2016.

PART 3

ENGAGING GLOBAL MARKETS IN PRIMARY HEALTH CARE AND PUBLIC HEALTH

7
Does the China National Tobacco Corporation Threaten Global Public Health?

JENNIFER FANG, KELLEY LEE, and
NIDHI SEJPAL POURANIK

The implementation of tobacco control measures is among the highest public health priorities of the World Health Organization (WHO) to advance global public health. This is also reflected in the United Nations Sustainable Development Goals (SDG). SDG 3.a requires member states to "strengthen the implementation of the World Health Organization Framework Convention on Tobacco Control [FCTC] in all countries, as appropriate."[1] With nearly one-third of the world's smokers (300 million) and 40% of global tobacco production (2.5 trillion cigarettes), China has the largest tobacco industry in the world (Jacobs 2018). The state-owned monopoly China National Tobacco Corporation (CNTC) is the fourth-largest Chinese company in terms of profit (Li 2012), employing 510,000 people across thirty-three provinces (China Tobacco, n.d.), and accounting for 7–11% of government tax revenues annually (Han 2013). Following China's accession to the World Trade Organisation (WTO) in 2001, and facing growing saturation of the domestic market, the CNTC declared its ambition to "go global" (*EuroMonitor International* 2008). On a global scale, CNTC profits exceed British American Tobacco (BAT), Philip Morris International (PMI), and Altria combined (Bloomberg News 2012).

This chapter examines the global business strategy of the CNTC as a global public health challenge. Using Chinese- and English-language sources, it describes the CNTC's globalization ambitions and its global business strategy focused on internal restructuring, brand development, and expansion of overseas operations in selected markets. It assesses the extent to which this strategy has been successful to date, the likely prospect that this Chinese firm will join the ranks of existing global tobacco companies, and the implications for the SDG target of strengthening the Framework Convention on Tobacco Control.

Background

Tobacco was brought to China by trading merchants during the sixteenth century. Leaf cultivation was firmly established by the mid-1800s, and smoking from the late nineteenth century with the automation of cigarette manufacturing. During the first half of the twentieth century, the industry was dominated by BAT, with 82% of market share (Tong et. al. 2008), and a handful of domestic companies (Benedict 2011). Political instability and conflict over decades undermined attempts to regulate the industry (STMA 1997).

BAT was required to leave China in 1953 following the industry's nationalization after the establishment of the People's Republic of China (Lee, Gilmore, and Collin 2004). The domestic industry grew rapidly, with the building of many small factories, and annual cigarette production grew on average 11% annually between 1949 and 1958 (Benedict 2011). However, the industry was also highly uncoordinated, controlled at the provincial level by local monopoly offices reporting to ministries of light industries, commerce, and other financial entities (STMA 1997). The Great Leap Forward (1958–60) and ensuing famine (1959–61) slowed cigarette production to 5.1% annually (Benedict 2011). In 1963, the China Tobacco Industrial Corporation was established in an effort to achieve greater efficiencies through centralized management of procurement, production, and sales (STMA 1997). Production and revenues rose dramatically, and tobacco taxes remitted increased from CNY 4.1 billion from 1958 to 1962 to CNY 5.6 billion from 1963 to 1966 (ibid.). The corporation was dismantled in the wake of the Cultural Revolution in 1966 (ibid.) and the industry reverted to its former fragmented structure.

Economic reforms under the Open Door Policy, from the late 1970s, allowed imports of new technology and know-how (STMA 1997). To reassert central control, the CNTC was formed in 1981 to manage the twenty-eight provincial companies (State Council of the People's Republic of China 1981). Profits and tax revenues were distributed among the central and provincial governments, the CNTC, and various subsidiaries (ibid.). In 1983, the State Council established the State Tobacco Monopoly Administration (STMA) as the industry's administrative and regulatory body (State Council of the

FIGURE 7.1

Structure of the Chinese tobacco industry

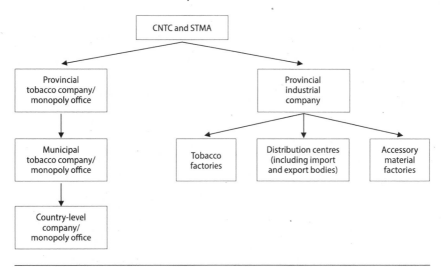

Note: The CNTC and STMA also manage other tobacco-related entities, including leaf, machinery, accessory materials, research institutes, technology centres, and tobacco museums.
Source: Compiled from STMA 1997; Zhou 2004.

People's Republic of China 1983). Formally separate entities, in practice the CNTC and STMA are "one institution with two name plates" (STMA 1997). The CNTC undertakes central planning, manages raw materials, sets regional production quotas for tobacco leaf and products, and is the umbrella company for provincial firms. The STMA administers and regulates the national monopoly, with parallel structures at the provincial level governed by municipal and provincial authorities (Zhou 2004) (Figure 7.1).

Methods

The study adopts the framework set out in Lee and Eckhardt (2017) to organize and analyze the factors affecting the global business strategy of the CNTC, including the key factors driving the strategy, key tactics used, and the extent to which the company has succeeded to date. The primary and secondary data sources were compiled into a chronological narrative according to these three questions.

We began by searching Google Scholar and Baidu Scholar to review the limited scholarly literature on the Chinese tobacco industry from public health, business studies, and other relevant fields. Chinese-language secondary literature (dissertations, articles, and industry reports) was identified through the China Knowledge Network. These sources were used to map the industry's history and the changes to its structure over time.

To understand the global business strategy of the Chinese industry, we searched CNTC public announcements and international tobacco industry media. To triangulate Chinese source data, we searched Google and Baidu for news on the globalization ambitions of the Chinese tobacco industry. We also searched other English-language business news sources, notably *EuroMonitor, Tobacco Journal International,* and *Tobacco Reporter.* We sought information on industry restructuring, mergers and acquisitions (M&A), joint ventures (JV), foreign direct investment (FDI), target markets, and product development.

Although English- and Chinese-language sources were consulted, the available data have three limitations. First, as a government-controlled monopoly, the CNTC is not required to report as a public company (e.g., annual report to shareholders). Chinese data is thus limited in scope and content. Second, official Chinese data is government-controlled and not verified by independent sources. Much secondary analyses, in turn, are based on official sources. Third, we found inconsistencies in data on key indicators from different sources. To address these three caveats, triangulation of multiple data sources was undertaken where possible. The compiling of trend data drew on the same sources where available for consistency.

Findings

What Are the Key Factors behind the CNTC's Global Business Strategy?

China's export-led growth and its status as the "world's factory" (Zhang 2013) faced growing competition from lower-wage emerging economies by the late 1990s. In 1998, President Jiang Zemin called on Chinese companies (including state-owned enterprises) to improve product development, pursue foreign markets, and establish manufacturing abroad (CCPIT 2007). This policy was named the "Go Global" strategy in 2000 (ibid.).

Tobacco industry interest in foreign expansion was first raised following China's signing of the General Agreement on Tariffs and Trade (GATT) in 1993. As STMA director Jiang Ming stated, to ensure long-term development of the tobacco industry, "we must follow a 'Big Tobacco' strategy" (Huang 1993). Ming envisioned the establishment of overseas companies and diversification into non-tobacco sectors (ibid.). Similarly, CNTC director Xun

TABLE 7.1

Value and quantity of tobacco product imports into China, 2001–15

Year	Import value (US$)	Growth (%)	Import quantity (tons)	Growth (%)
2001	33,353		1,788	
2002	25,866	−22.45	1,374	−23.15
2003	38,460	48.69	1,883	37.05
2004	51,734	34.51	2,568	36.38
2005	52,448	1.38	2,836	10.44
2006	50,275	−4.14	2,715	−4.27
2007	60,573	20.48	3,843	41.55
2008	67,212	10.96	4,010	4.35
2009	76,345	13.59	4,513	12.54
2010	75,464	−1.15	3,534	−21.69
2011	78,442	3.95	3,658	3.51
2012	75,819	−3.34	3,742	2.30
2013	101,120	33.37	5,065	35.36
2014	117,781	16.48	5,704	12.62
2015	551,162	367.95	26,940	372.30

Source: Trade Map 2015. China tobacco imports [data file].

Xinghua declared that the industry was "seizing all opportunities to expand and occupy foreign markets" (Anonymous 1993). Given continued exclusion of competition from international tobacco companies by the Chinese import quota system (Lee, Gilmore, and Collin 2004) and size of the domestic market, initial industry efforts were limited.

The industry anticipated change following China's accession to the WTO. As C. Holden and colleagues (2010) describe, global tobacco companies from outside China pressed hard to access the closed Chinese market during accession negotiations. Import quotas remained in place, but import tariffs were reduced from 70% in 1996 to 25% in 2004, and there were opportunities for wider distribution of foreign brands. Tobacco imports rose in value and quantity from 2001 (Table 7.1). Given potential erosion of the CNTC's domestic market share, the industry was called upon to "actively implement the 'go global' strategy to establish stable international markets" (STMA 2004), coinciding with the removal of the requirement for retail permits to sell foreign cigarettes in China (Tong et al. 2008).

The Chinese tobacco industry can be seen to have shifted sharply since the mid-2000s, from largely domestic-focused to increasingly outward-looking, in four ways. First, the CNTC is a "natural resource seeker," as the industry aims to source quality leaf to bring its products in line with international brands. Establishing local leaf procurement companies in key tobacco-growing regions of Brazil, Zimbabwe, and the United States ensures a steady supply to feed growing industry needs both domestically and abroad. Second, the CNTC is a "market seeker." It has been exporting since the 1980s, but the scale and reach of exports since the late 2000s suggests a more concerted strategy. Third, the CNTC is an "efficiency seeker," setting up overseas operations in key strategic areas to target specific markets. To further reduce operational costs for greater profit margins, the CNTC's overseas operations strive to use locally grown tobacco leaf and hire locals where possible, thereby increasing efficiency through the removal of cultural and language barriers. The strategic location of major offshore production bases in each region is a clear indication of efficiency seeking. Fourth, the CNTC is a "strategic asset seeker," as it monitors foreign markets, seeking investment opportunities for business growth through mergers and acquisitions. The CNTC's globalization efforts are expected to intensify.

Which Global Business Strategies Has the CNTC Pursued?

Restructuring of the Chinese Tobacco Industry

In China, high profits and tax revenues sustained government support for cigarette manufacturing at the provincial, municipal, and county levels over many decades. Provincial governments also introduced protectionist measures in the 1990s, including near-monopolies, to protect local companies regardless of productivity and efficiency. The result, a crowded and fragmented industry, was seen by the STMA as problematic ahead of WTO accession and foreign competition. Structural reforms were introduced to boost efficiency, productivity, and product quality. Tobacco companies were placed in four categories:

- large firms, with annual profits of over CNY 100 million (US$12.08 million) and production of more than 500,000 cases of cigarettes (major interprovincial/regional enterprises)
- medium firms, with potential production of more than 300,000 cases annually (major provincial/regional companies)
- small firms, with production of 100,000–300,000 cases annually (to merge with other firms or close, depending on performance)
- poorly performing firms, with production of less than 100,000 cases annually (to declare bankruptcy).

FIGURE 7.2

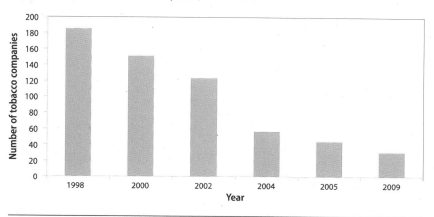

Total number of Chinese tobacco companies, 1998–2009

Source: Compiled from STMA 2000, 2002, 2003, 2005, 2006, and 2009.

Between 1998 and 2009, this consolidation reduced the number of companies to one-sixth (Figure 7.2).

The industry at the provincial level was also restructured into three distinct entities: industrial companies, tobacco companies, and local monopoly bureaus (Zhou 2004). *Industrial companies* centralize the management of manufacturing and allow pooling of resources among factories (Tong et al. 2008). *Tobacco companies* are concerned with the sale and distribution within the province of all tobacco products, regardless of where they are produced. *Local monopoly bureaus* regulate and administer the industry at the provincial level (Xu and He 2003). This restructuring supported the STMA's vision of fostering "large-scale enterprises, big brands and large markets" (Zhou 2004). For example, the removal of provincial protectionism allowed provincial manufacturers to sell their brands nationally, fuelling domestic competition and, in turn, product and brand development, and the expansion of successful companies. Provincial tobacco companies, delinked from manufacturing and now reliant on sales, purchased only products that sold well (Xie 2003).

In 2003, Anhui became the first province to implement these reforms, establishing Anhui Tobacco Industrial to manage the assets of five manufacturers (Zhou 2004). The same year, the first interprovincial industrial company was formed, between Sichuan Province and Chongqing city, consolidating their manufacturing into Chuanyu Industrial. In 2003, the Beijing

Cigarette Factory split from the Beijing Tobacco Company to merge, along with the Tianjin Cigarette Factory, with the Shanghai Tobacco Group (Zhou 2004). In 2008, a "merger of two giants" occurred between Yunnan's Hongyun and Honghe Groups, forming the Hongyun Honghe Tobacco Group. With annual sales of over 4 million cases, Hongyun Honghe is the world's fourth-largest by sales volume after PMI, BAT, and Japan Tobacco International (JTI) (Anonymous 2008).

The overall vision of provincial reforms has been to establish a three-tiered system, with municipal factories becoming subsidiaries (with legal authority) or branches (without legal authority) of provincial industrial companies, and the latter acting as CNTC subsidiaries. The aim has been to reduce local government power over the industry, and increase competition across the same tiers in the industry, by dismantling its vertical structure and bureaucracy. However, given the economic and political importance of the industry, including its significant contribution to public revenues, wholesale privatization is unlikely to precede the pursuit of a global business strategy in the near future.

Overall, restructuring of the Chinese tobacco industry since the early 2000s has been seen by industry sources as a key strategy in order for the CNTC to become globally competitive. It is believed that the CNTC may follow in the footsteps of JTI, eventually pursuing public listing for the most successful firms but remaining partly owned by government (Anonymous 2003). Five domestic giants from three regions have emerged through these reforms: Hongta Group and Hongyun Honghe Tobacco Group in Yunnan Province; Shanghai Tobacco Group (STG); and Changsha Tobacco Group and Changde Group in Hunan Province.

Product Development: Brand Consolidation and Premiumization
To enhance global competitiveness, Chinese product development involved three strategies: consolidation of brands into a smaller number with mass appeal; adaptation to appeal to foreign markets; and higher-value-added premium products. First, historically, a large number of Chinese companies manufactured thousands of local brands at many different price points (Anonymous 2014). The number of brands was dramatically reduced, to a few with broader appeal, to improve economies of scale and enable marketing abroad. In 2001, STMA selected thirty-six brands to support through advantageous policies such as priority access to raw materials and technology. The result was an increase to 11 percent market share within two years (Zeng 2010).

In 2004, STMA announced plans to limit mid- and higher-priced brands to 100 within three years (STMA 2004). In 2006, this became known as the "two by ten" strategy, with plans to have *ten* large-scale manufacturers produce *ten* key brands. In 2007, the so-called two leaps was emphasized, whereby leading provincial brands were encouraged to enter the national market, and strong national brands to enter the global market (Zeng 2010). This was followed in 2010 by the "235" strategy, to develop *two* brands selling over 5 million cases; *three* brands selling over 3 million cases; and *five* brands selling over 2 million cases (ibid.); and the "461" strategy, with twelve brands to earn revenues over CNY 40 billion (US$5.87 billion), six brands over CN¥60 billion (US$8.80 billion), and one brand over CNY 100 billion (US$14.7 billion) by 2015 (ibid.).

By 2013, consolidation had reduced the number of cigarette brands from around 2,000 in the late 1990s to 90 (Figure 7.3). These remaining brands held larger domestic market share. By 2010, seven brands exceeded US$4.4 billion in annual sales, with five brands – Hongtashan, Baisha, Double Happiness, Furongwang, and Chungwa – aiming to sell over 5 million cases (US$14.7 billion) annually (Zeng 2010). Besides fending off global brands such as Marlboro in the domestic market, consolidation aimed to create global Chinese brands for foreign markets. In 2013, the CNTC sold 70 billion sticks overseas, comprising seventy-four brands. This was reduced to thirty brands by 2014, with many tailored to key markets (Feng Junxia 2014).

FIGURE 7.3

Number of CNTC brands, 1990–2013

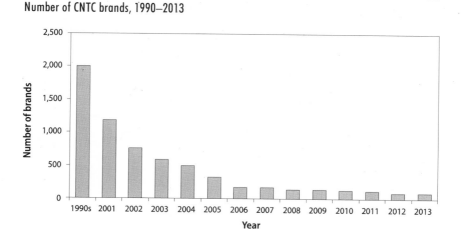

Alongside consolidation, the CNTC has pursued a strategy of premium-ization since 2008. In China, luxury brand cigarettes are an important cur-rency of *guanxi* (a system of social networks and influential relationships to facilitate business and other dealings). Premium brands enjoyed rising sales as the economy boomed, with manufacturers releasing luxury versions of familiar brands or new brands. In 2012, luxury brands sold over 2 million cases and enjoyed a 20% growth from the previous year (Anonymous 2013b). Despite an STMA price cap, anti-corruption measures, and public smoking ban for government officials, production and sale of luxury brands con-tinued to rise. Market share grew, from 6% in 2007 to 25.2% in 2014, the only segment to see growth in 2014. Mid-priced products saw modest growth, while the economy segment fell dramatically from 59.7% to 28.3% during the same period (*EuroMonitor International* 2013, 2015).

Expansion of Chinese Cigarette Exports

Chinese cigarette exports date from the creation of the China Shenzhen Tobacco Trading Centre in 1984. In 1985, the China National Tobacco Im-port Export Corporation (CNTIEC) was then formed to oversee trade of tobacco products, technology, and accessories, as well as international eco-nomic cooperation (STMA 1997). However, exports remained small-scale and distributed across many different companies. From 1991 to 1995, the CNTC exported over 100 brands to thirty-seven countries, including Virginia (flue-cured) cigarettes to Southeast Asia; blended cigarettes to Europe, the United States, Russia, and Africa; and herbal cigarettes to Korea and Japan (STMA 1996). The restructuring of the industry from the mid-1990s saw the closure of several export arms of provincial companies (STMA 1998). Focusing on quality over quantity, underperforming brands and markets were subsequently dropped, and exports declined to an all-time low in 1998–99 (STMA 2000).

China's looming WTO accession prompted a more strategic approach to exports. In 2000, the CNTIEC was reorganized and renamed the China Tobacco Import Export Group (CNTIEG). The CNTIEG became the parent company of all CNTC overseas operations and export branches of provin-cial companies (STMA 2005). In 2008, the CNTIEG became China Tobacco International (CTI), focused on supporting the company going global. It adopted a three-step strategy for tobacco market expansion: 1) market entry and establishment of a distribution network, 2) licensed production by local manufacturers, and 3) establishment of local production facili-ties. Five export manufacturing facilities in Shanghai, Guangdong, Yunnan,

FIGURE 7.4

Value of China's tobacco product exports, 1992–2013

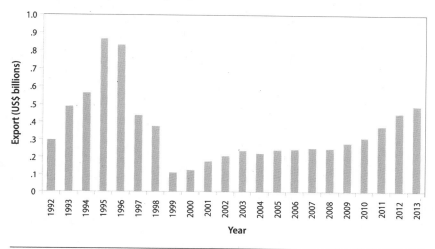

Source: Compiled from UN Comtrade Database 2015. China tobacco export data file (2015), http://comtrade.un.org/data/.

Hunan, Zhejiang, and Jilin were announced in 2013 (Anonymous 2013a), each focused on nearby regions and "cultural advantage." For example, Yunnan Tobacco would target Southeast Asia.

Chinese exports as a proportion of total production remain relatively small but have grown from 4.35% in 2004 to 5.08% by 2013. By volume, this represents a 60% increase from 16.3 to 26 billion sticks (STMA 2005, 2014). Export value (unadjusted) has also increased, from US$100 million in 1999 to US$500 million in 2013 (Figure 7.4). In 2015, a link between the "One Belt, One Road" and "Go Global" strategies was announced to improve the CNTC's access foreign markets. This initiative refers to the extension of the so-called Belt and Road Initiative, linking western China with Europe through Central Asia, to the new Maritime Silk Road from China's southern coast to Europe via North Africa and Southeast Asia (Knowler 2015).

Gaining Access to Foreign Technology and Know-How

International tobacco companies have sought to negotiate a return to the Chinese market. While they pressed for full or part ownership of local manufacturing, the STMA limited joint ventures to leaf production and manufacturing of foreign brands by Chinese companies (Lee, Gilmore, and Collin 2004). For example, the R.J. Reynolds Tobacco Company (RJR) licensed the Xiamen Cigarette Factory to produce Camel cigarettes in 1980 (Lin 1984). In 1991, BAT agreed to license manufacturing of Derby by the Wuhu Cigarette Factory, while Rothmans was licensed by the Shandong-Rothmans joint venture (Lai 2009). In 1993, PMI signed licensing agreements for Marlboro (Shanghai Cigarette Factory) and other brands (Lai 2009; PMI 1993). In 1999, JTI licensed production of Mild Seven to Shanghai Gaoyang International Tobacco Company (Lai 2009). Imperial Tobacco's West brand was licensed to the Hongta Group.

From a Chinese perspective, licensing enabled local firms to access new technology and know-how (Lai 2009), while keeping the industry under Chinese control. This strategy is evident in agreements with foreign tobacco companies supporting the development of Chinese brands. In 1986, Huamei was established in Xiamen's Special Economic Zone (SEZ) as an equity joint venture between Xiamen Cigarette Factory and RJR, developing Golden Bridge as a leading brand by 1989 (ibid.). In 1996, BAT agreed to support brand development (Lovell, White, and Durrant 1996) of Guangzhou Cigarette Factory's Cocopalm and Guiyang Cigarette Factory's Huangguoshu Waterfalls (Lai 2009). BAT and Yunnan Tobacco Company agreed in 1999 to "jointly develop and produce blended cigarettes," in addition to leaf cultivation and training (BAT 1999). In 2000, RJR agreed to develop a jointly owned brand for sale in China and the United States (RJ Reynolds 2000). Foreign tobacco companies hoped that these agreements would lead to greater market access, but were disappointed in 2006 when the government announced a ban on all new manufacturing facilities, including joint ventures with foreign companies, as part of stronger tobacco control measures (Ding 2006). As PMI realized, the CNTC only wants "to acquire foreign technology and management skills without giving away much to foreigners" (PMI 2002).

Establishing Foreign-Based Operations

Foreign operations established during the early 1990s were limited in scope and focused on Asia, notably Laos, Cambodia, and Myanmar. Hong Kong and Macau received substantial investment due to their SEZ status and proximity to the mainland. This began to change in the mid-2000s as the CNTC looked to expand foreign production and distribution of Chinese brands. Lacking its own networks, it formed joint ventures with foreign tobacco companies to produce and distribute Chinese cigarettes abroad (CTI

2014c). In 2003, the Shanghai Tobacco Group and Gallaher signed reciprocal trademark licence agreements and, the following year, launched each
other's brands in China and Russia (Gallaher 2004). A "long-term strategic
cooperative partnership" with PMI in 2005 involves licensed production
and distribution of Marlboro in China, and the establishment of the jointly
owned China Tobacco Philip Morris International (CTPMI) to launch and
distribute Chinese brands in foreign markets. Based in Switzerland, CTPMI
launched three so-called heritage brands (RGD, Dubliss, and Harmony) in
2008, using PMI's distribution networks in Central and Eastern Europe and
Latin America (Tobacco-Free Kids 2010). In 2012, CTPMI opened an office
in the Democratic Republic of Congo to launch heritage brands (CTI
2014b). Similarly, the CNTC partnered with BAT to form China Tobacco
British American Tobacco (CTBAT) International in 2013, with worldwide
rights to BAT brand State Express 555 and Chinese brand Double Happiness outside of China (BAT 2013). Shanghai Tobacco licensed production of
Zhongnanhai, Golden Deer, and Red Double Happiness to JTI for distribu-
tion in Russia. Joint brands include Win and Xingxin, developed by the
Hongyun Honghe Group and Myanmar's Fu Xing Brothers Group, and
Zhongnanhai (Totem) developed by Shanghai Tobacco and the Chinese-
Mongolian joint venture (CTI 2014c). There have also been negotiations for
a similar joint venture between Yunnan Tobacco Industrial and Imperial
Tobacco (Yu 2015).

It was expected that the CNTC would progress to M&As of small and
medium-sized foreign tobacco companies. For example, there were negotiations between the Hongta Group and Donskoy Tabak in 2012 for Hongta's
purchase of a 0.5 percent share of Russia's largest national tobacco manufacturer. This would permit entry of Hongta brands into the Russian market,
produced and distributed by Donskoy Tabak (Anonymous 2012). While negotiations appear to have been unsuccessful, industry analysts predict that
the CNTC's "massive current account surplus built up over years means
that no company is too large to be purchased for cash" (*EuroMonitor
International* 2008), a sentiment echoed by others (*Economist* 2014b).

By the late 2000s, the Chinese overseas supply chain had also improved.
Foreign operations have been established to secure tobacco leaf from Brazil,
the United States, and Zimbabwe. For example, land in the Zambezi Region
of Namibia has been leased to Namibia Oriental Tobacco to grow tobacco
leaf for China, generating concerns about local food insecurity. Shanghai
Tobacco is opening a distribution centre in Singapore, with initial duty-paid
target markets of Indonesia, Malaysia, the Philippines, and Singapore, and

TABLE 7.2

Tobacco-related foreign-based operations by China, 1989–2015

Company name	Year	Location	Target market
Tianli International Trading Company Ltd.	1989	Hong Kong	
China Tobacco International, Moscow Office	1992 (renamed in 2008)	Russia	Russia
Golden Leaf Macau Group*	1992	Macau	Hong Kong, Macau, Vietnam, Singapore, South Africa, Australia, Panama, Peru
Hongta Hong Kong International*	1992 (restructured in 1998)	Hong Kong	Southeast Asia, Middle East, Africa, South America
Lao Liaozhong Hongta Fortune Tobacco*	1992 (restructured in 2008)	Laos	Laos, Cambodia, Philippines, Malaysia, Hong Kong, Korea, Thailand, Middle East, North Africa
Viniton Group*	1993	Cambodia	Cambodia and Southeast Asia
Myanmar Kokang Factory	1994	Myanmar	Myanmar, India
United Castle International Company Ltd.	1994	Hong Kong	Global
China Tobacco International Europe Company (CTIEC)*	1997 (restructured in 2007)	Romania	Romania, Europe, Africa, Middle East
Dubai Ruishida Trading Company	1997	UAE	Middle East, Africa, West and South Asia
China Tobacco International Hamburg Ltd.	1998 (renamed in 2008)	Germany	Machinery and accessory materials
Taedong River Company Ltd.*	2000	North Korea	
HTS Hongta Switzerland	2000	Switzerland	
China Tobacco Japan	2001	Japan	Japan

Company	Year	Country	Region
Mongolia Tobacco Company Ltd.*	2001	Mongolia	Mongolia, Central Asia, Russia
Raison Company Ltd.	2001	North Korea	North Korea, South Korea, Middle East, Southeast Asia
China Tabaco Internacional do Brasil	2002	Brazil	Leaf procurement
Namibia Oriental Tobacco	2005	Namibia	Sub-Saharan Africa
CTPMI	2005	Switzerland	Global
Tianze Tobacco	2005	Zimbabwe	Africa; leaf procurement
HTS Hongta Services	2007	Romania	Eastern Europe
Hongta Tabaco Latinoamericana SA	2008	Argentina	Latin America, Caribbean
Pyongyang Haikusan Company Ltd.	2008	North Korea	
China Tobacco Argentina Ltd.	2009	Argentina	
United Castle America SA de CV	2009	Mexico	The Americas
China-Brasil Tabacos Exportadora	2012	Brazil	Latin America
CTPMI Democratic Republic of Congo	2012	Democratic Republic of Congo	
China Tobacco Hongyun Honghe (Pty.) Ltd.	2013	Namibia (Walvis Bay)	
Overseas United Inc.*	2012	Panama	Latin America
Shandong Tobacco (Middle East) Trading Company	2012	UAE	Middle East, Africa
Universal Tobacco (Dubai)*	2012	UAE	Middle East, Africa
CTBAT	2013	Hong Kong	Global
US China Tobacco International	2014	USA	Leaf procurement
PT Kolang Citra Abadi	2015	Indonesia	

Note: Company names marked with an asterisk denote those with facilities located in strategically important geographical regions.

Sources: Compiled from BAT 2013; CTI 2014a; CTIEC, n.d.; MOFCOM 2015; STMA 2006, 2009, 2012; Tobacco-Free Kids 2010; United Castle America, n.d.

select duty-free markets within the region (CTI 2014a). There is also rapid growth of Chinese offshore production, with over half of the 50.4 billion sticks of Chinese cigarettes sold internationally (2011) produced overseas (STMA 2012). This increased to 44 billion sticks (two-thirds of global sales) in 2013. Located in strategically important geographical regions, these facilities (marked with asterisk in Table 7.2) reflect expansion plans in Latin America, Asia, Europe, the Middle East, and Africa. For instance, Viniton Group and Lao Liaozhong Hongta Fortune Tobacco have established production and distribution bases in Southeast Asia. The China Tobacco International Europe Company (CTIEC) targets Europe, while United Overseas (Panama) produces Chinese brands for the Americas (CTI 2014c, 2014b).

Table 7.2 lists the CNTC's portfolio of foreign operations, which include distribution offices, manufacturing plants, production and distribution bases, tobacco leaf procurement, and machinery and accessory materials. Led by China Tobacco International, each investment is affiliated with a provincial industrial company (Guangdong Tobacco Industrial and Viniton Group) or municipal subsidiary (Hongyun Honghe Group and Myanmar Kokang Factory). The foreign operation produces brands of the respective parent companies or licensed production of other companies. Importantly, foreign direct investment DI has been coordinated to minimize competition among Chinese companies on the global market (CTI 2014b).

How Global Is the CNTC?

Although the CNTC aspired to "go global," its global business strategy has not followed the pattern of existing global tobacco companies. Most notable has been the domestic restructuring of the industry as a whole and of individual firms. There has been substantial consolidation to transform a highly fragmented and inefficient industry into fewer, larger, and more competitive firms with clearer geographical (national, provincial, and municipal), functional (manufacturing, sales, and administration), and regulatory (central and provincial STMAs) delineation. Supported by favourable government policies and substantial resources, the restructured domestic industry has achieved greater economies of scale. Moreover, while consolidating to compete in the global tobacco market, the Chinese industry has been reconfigured in ways that minimize competition among domestic firms. The resultant structure potentially dwarfs existing global tobacco companies and serves as a springboard for globalization.

Changes to ownership structure do not appear to be part of Chinese global business strategy for the tobacco industry. The industry is likely to remain state-owned and controlled for the foreseeable future. As industry analysts have observed:

> As domestic firms in China mainly dominate the local cigarette industry, the industry's globalization level is relatively low and is expected to remain low in the future ... The industry's globalization level is low due to the low foreign ownership levels of the industry's firms in China. In 2014, the share of revenue contributed by foreign-funded enterprises (including those from Hong Kong, Macau and Taiwan) is expected to be only 0.1 percent of the industry's total. The Chinese Government largely controls China's tobacco sector and limits the investment of foreign manufacturers in China. (IBIS World, n.d.)

While open to adopting foreign technology and expertise since the 1980s, and pursuing joint ventures and other forms of FDI (spanning two SEZs and twenty countries across all continents except Australia by 2015, and leaf growing in Africa), the domestic industry has remained firmly under Chinese ownership.

Another indicator of globalization is product development to promote a small number of Chinese "heritage" brands overseas, as well as premium brands. These are likely to appeal to overseas Chinese rather than serve as global brands, given their close affinity with Chinese cultural tastes and practices. The development of new brands, to appeal to a wider global market beyond Chinese diasporas, is likely to increase via joint ventures with foreign tobacco companies.

Finally, trends in exports suggest an increasingly outward-looking Chinese industry. Exports have grown rapidly by volume (Figure 7.5) following the establishment of five export manufacturing facilities in 2013. A target of 8 million cases by 2020 was declared with the aim of matching the sales volumes of leading tobacco companies internationally (Anonymous 2013a). Export markets have also begun to diversify beyond Asia. While Asia remains a priority region, with the largest number of overseas operations, markets in Latin America, Eastern Europe, and the Middle East are clear targets.

Previous analyses of the global tobacco industry recognize the importance of, but generally exclude, the CNTC because of its strong domestic focus. The findings discussed in this chapter suggest, however, that the Chinese industry has been steadily positioning itself to become a global player since

FIGURE 7.5

CNTC production and export volume, 1980–2013

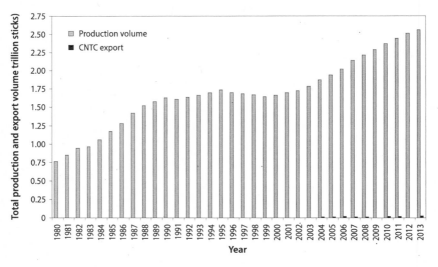

Source: Compiled from STMA 1996–2014.

the late 1990s. While the Chinese tobacco industry is likely to remain, in the medium term, primarily dependent on its huge domestic market of 350 million smokers, indicators suggest the emergence of a new Chinese global tobacco company in the next decade.

Externally, following China's WTO accession in 2001, it was anticipated that market opening would bring greater foreign competition, as in other Asian countries. This, in turn, would lead to a gradual shrinking of domestic market share. To date, however, the Chinese government has retained a firm grip on the industry and market access, limiting joint ventures to technology transfers and leaf development and, more recently, reciprocal production and distribution agreements. More influential has been the broader support, in Chinese economic policy, for the "go global" strategy as key to the country's emergence as a global economic superpower. The sheer size of the Chinese tobacco industry relative to other international tobacco companies, and thus its potential to generate significant foreign earnings, has prompted the government to promote the industry's expansion overseas.

If even partially realized, the global ambitions of the Chinese tobacco industry will have profound impacts for public health. The Chinese industry is advantaged by sheer size, weak domestic regulation, and government support for overseas expansion. If successful, this will lead to increased global competition on price, new products, and intensified marketing, all resulting in greater tobacco consumption. Beyond the WTO, there is much uncertainty over how disputes over tobacco control will be handled within the framework of major new trade and investment agreements, such as the Comprehensive and Progressive Agreement for Trans-Pacific Partnership (CPTPP). As the CNTC increasingly mimics the globalization strategies of other global tobacco companies and engages international markets for the sale of cigarettes, there is a need to now include China in global tobacco control efforts.

Our analysis shows that the "go global" ambitions of the Chinese tobacco industry have been spurred by both internal and external forces. Domestically, the market has neared saturation among adult males, with 53% smoking prevalence rates. Future growth is likely to come from population growth and increasing female smoking rates (currently 2.4% for adult females). However, ratification and implementation of the Framework Convention on Tobacco Control since 2005 has increased support in China for the adoption of stronger tobacco control measures, albeit tempered by weak political will and enforcement. (See Chapter 4.) Although important changes have been made to strengthen tobacco control legislation, "major gaps still exist compared with FCTC requirements" (Li, Ma, and Xi 2016). The SDG agenda requires strengthening of the FCTC in China, but this remains in tension with the business strategy of the CNTC.

ACKNOWLEDGMENT
This chapter originally appeared, open access, in *Global Public Health,* copyright 2016, Fang, Lee, and Sejpan. Published by Informa UK Limited, trading as Taylor & Francis Group. Permission granted via Creative Commons licence.

Fang, Jennifer, Kelley Lee, and Nidhi Sejpal. 2017. "The China National Tobacco Corporation: From domestic to global dragon?," *Global Public Health* 12 (3): 315–34. https://www.tandfonline.com/doi/full/10.1080/17441692.2016.1241293.

NOTE
1 https://sdgs.un.org/goals/goal3.

Exit and Voice Strategies by Patients in Dealing with Incentive Structures in the Chinese Health Care System

NEIL MUNRO and ZIYING HE

In China, inappropriate incentive structures have encouraged health care providers to systematically offer treatment that is not medically indicated, and to take extra money for treatment that has already been paid for. Three practices by Chinese doctors and hospitals have been widely reported: unnecessary diagnostic testing, over-prescription of medicine, and the taking of bribes ("red envelopes" or *hong bao*). Not only are such practices unethical but, as explained in Chapter 1, they also inflate health care costs, pose health risks to patients, and are inconsistent with broader public health goals. Winnie Chi-Man and colleagues (2010) cite the following examples: health care costs have been rising by 16% per year over the past twenty years; 75% of patients with common colds are prescribed antibiotics, compared with a worldwide average of 30%, substantially raising the risks of antibiotic resistance; and all this is occurring against a background of "epidemiological transition," in which the burden of chronic diseases relative to infectious diseases is increasing, placing a premium on effective preventive medicine and primary care.

Agency risks arise whenever the interests of principals (patients) potentially diverge from those of their agents (physicians) and the costs to the principals of ensuring the agents' protection of their interests are prohibitively high (Buchanan 1988; Nguyen 2011; Ryan 1994). For patients and their families, the dilemma is how to ensure that doctors offer the same quality of care as they would provide for themselves or their own family. Different strategies are available to resolve this dilemma, with different implications for the behaviour of health care providers.

This chapter focuses not on provider incentives as most previous studies in this area have done, but on attitudes among the wider public toward unethical practices, particularly on popular strategies aimed at reducing agency risks. It aims to analyze the distribution of preferences for strategies across social boundaries and gradients thought to be characterized by inequality in access to health care. It does this through an examination of data from a survey conducted in thirty-one provinces of mainland China, discussed in more detail below. The strategies are differentiated on a conceptual level as follows. First is the extent to which the strategy proactively engages with or changes the situation. In other words, we can distinguish empowered from passive strategies. Second is the extent to which the basis of the exchange presumed under the strategy is particularistic, that is, it helps the particular patient but not others in a similar situation. The opposite tendency is universalism, which implies a presumption that everyone in a similar situation should be treated the same way. The third dimension distinguishes strategies aimed at changing the providers' behaviour, as opposed to simply changing providers. These distinctions echo Albert Hirschman's contrast between using "voice" to improve the terms of a relationship and "exit," which replaces it with another relationship (Hirschman 1970).[1] Hirschman's third category, "loyalty," corresponds to the behaviour of patients who do what doctors indicate they should do. The different dimensions involved in citizens' choice of strategy are summarized in Figure 8.1.

FIGURE 8.1

Three dimensions of strategies for resolving the agency dilemma

	Universalistic		Particularistic	
	voice	Exit	voice	Exit
Proactive	Make a formal complaint	Change provider	Pay a bribe or ask provider to change decision	Use connections to find another provider
Passive	Accept the treatment without resolving the dilemma "Don't know" Give up treatment			

This chapter argues that citizens' preferences for resolving the agency dilemma have different implications for "diagnosing" the problems of China's health sector as well as for understanding patient behaviour. Passive responses, which involve acceptance of whatever the health care provider offers, may indicate that patients are disempowered. Proactive strategies imply that patients have more influence over the terms of their relationship with providers. If the health care system works like a Weberian bureaucracy, we would expect particularism to be marginal, and the making of formal complaints to be the standard response of patients faced with unsatisfactory service. "Voice" implies that there may be some flexibility in provider behaviour, whereas "exit" implies that only changing providers can resolve the dilemma. This research aligns with the emphasis the United Nations Sustainable Development Goals (SDG) agenda places on reducing corruption and establishing transparent, fair institutions: SDG 16.6 requires countries to "develop effective, accountable and transparent institutions at all levels."[2]

In the remainder of this chapter, we first summarize recent developments in ethics and incentive structures in Chinese hospitals. We then present evidence from the survey concerning the perceived extent of three types of unethical medical practice and the popularity of different strategies for dealing with them. We develop hypotheses about the distribution of preferences between strategies across inequality boundaries and gradients in Chinese society, and examine bivariate relationships as an initial test of the hypotheses. Finally, we speculate on the implications of the analysis for attempts to mitigate patients' agency risks and describe directions for future research.

Medical Ethics and Incentive Structures in China

In the 1980s, the Ministry of Health's response to problems in medical ethics was to introduce the Regulations for Hospital Workers (1981), which emphasized that health care workers should "carry forward the spirit of healing the wounded and rescuing the dying, sympathise with and respect the patients and serve the people wholeheartedly" (Gao, Qiu, and Chen 2002). The next step was to introduce a code of conduct (Ministry of Health 1988). This code exhorted medical personnel to put the interests of patients first in the name of socialist humanitarianism (*shehuizhuyi de rendao zhuyi*); respect patients' rights and treat them equally regardless of nationality, gender, profession, position or financial condition; be courteous and considerate; avoid using medicine for selfish gain; respect patients' confidentiality; be collegial and strive continually to improve their knowledge and skills. It thus provided a broad normative framework.

At around the same time, the Chinese Society of Medical Ethics, affili-ated to the Chinese Medical Association, was also founded. The Chinese debate about medical ethics, conducted in two journals – *Yixue yu zhexue* (*Medicine and Philosophy*), founded in 1980, and *Zhongguo yixue lunlixue* (*Chinese Medical Ethics*), founded in 1988 – largely revolved around the principles of the code of conduct and different methods of institutionaliz-ing it in systems for training medical personnel and assessing their perform-ance, including the establishment of effective incentive structures and mon-itoring systems (such as ethics committees) within hospitals and the health care administration more broadly (Ip 2005; Gao, Qiu, and Chen 2002). In 1993, the Ministry of Health ordered that medical ethics be included in the curricula of higher schools of medicine, at least as an option. In 1998, the National People's Congress passed a law on the licensing of physicians spell-ing out their moral duties, and in 1999, medical ethics became a compulsory subject for licensed physicians' examinations (Gao, Qiu, and Chen 2002). That same year, the ministry issued Regulations for the Morality of Medical Employees (Ke 2002, 61). Chinese medical ethicists recognized that their subject encompassed "the socialistic macro view of health for all," implying shared responsibility of the government, the medical profession, and indi-viduals for public and individual health, as well as recognizing the contribu-tion of medical ethics to social stability (Gao et al. 2005; Ke 2002). In other words, medical ethics was seen to include not only the morality of phys-icians as demonstrated in their professional conduct but also considerations of the implications of medical technology and the ethics of health care poli-cies (Ke 2002). However, medical ethical education in China at this time suffered from deep problems, including lack of training in higher skills such as independent judgment and critical thinking. These shortcomings resulted in graduates who lacked the necessary ethical sensibility. Furthermore, teach-ing typically involved preaching about rules of conduct often in the frame-work of political and ideological education, with little concern for the issues that worry ordinary citizens, especially underprivileged groups (Nie 2002).

In the 1980s and 1990s, lacklustre ethics training coincided with the introduction of market-oriented reforms, leading to changes in the doctor-patient relationship and, it seemed to some, a general weakening of moral responsibility in society (Liu, Han, and Li 2002; Ip 2005). The market was sometimes presented as the source of an unwelcome change in values and in the terms of doctors' relationships with patients. Whereas in the socialist system doctors saw their role as "serving the people," once market reforms were introduced, health care became a commodity like any other. Those with more money "consumed" more and received better care, and doctors focused on serving them, with the result that resources were redistributed in a way that was, from the point of view of the collective interest in better health for all, irrational (Ip 2005).

Focusing on professional conduct, Ruiping Fan (2007) argued that the problem was not market reforms per se but the distorting effects of government policies in a commercialized system of state-owned hospitals: namely, the low salaries of doctors, hospitals' practice of providing bonus payments to doctors for prescribing expensive drugs or procedures, and the ban on direct payments from patients to doctors for higher-quality care. According to Fan (2007), bonus payments were linked to the amount of revenue generated by the physicians' department and hospital, and in big cities these bonuses were thought to have often equalled or exceeded basic salary. For most public hospitals, approximately one-half of total hospital revenue came from drug sales. There were also cases where pharmaceutical companies entered into illegal deals with hospitals or physicians to provide kickbacks in proportion to the amount of drugs prescribed. The underlying problem was a government-prescribed fee schedule that set the prices for some labour-intensive services, such as general consultation, below cost, while allowing hospitals to set prices for technology-intensive services above cost and to charge a 15 percent markup on drug sales (Yip et al. 2010, 2012).

Fan (2007) argued that solutions to the ethics problems could be found in the development of a "Confucian" approach to remuneration of physicians.[3] Claiming that a positive regard for justified remuneration is evident in the *Analects* and Mencius, he suggested that this meant recognizing that higher-quality work deserved higher pay, and that there was no conflict between receiving high pay for high-quality work and the ethical intention of helping patients. Essentially, this involved embracing market principles within a humanitarian framework, and recognizing the utopianism of a socialist morality that presumes that highly skilled physicians should take a low salary for the public good. Aside from liberalizing pay scales, however, this "Confucian" approach did not offer solutions to the problems with incentive structures that Fan identified. As Ole Döring (2002, 76) put it, "a medical system governed by reason and ethics might well allow and encourage commercial profits, but it will at the same time contain them and make them serve the overall welfare of the people." Chinese medical ethicists acknowledged inconsistencies between the aspirational declarations in official codes and the real incentive structures that exacerbated price inflation and unethical practices (Gao, Qiu, and Chen 2002).

The Chinese government conducted a number of experiments to change the incentive structures as part of the nationwide three-year, $850 billion health care reform package announced in April 2009 (Yip et al. 2010, 2012). A particular focus of reform has been the primary care sector (Yip et al. 2010). Experiments carried out at urban community health centres in Shanghai suggested that prospective payment and performance-related pay were able to deliver cost control, although their benefits in the management of chronic diseases were more difficult to assess. In rural Shaanxi, a scheme to pay village doctors a salary and a performance-related bonus, combined with centralized purchasing of drugs, reduced costs and unnecessary prescriptions while increasing utilization of formal health care. Following these successes, in 2009 the government began paying primary health care providers a fixed per capita fee to deliver a defined package of basic public health services to the population in their catchment areas, introduced a zero-profit drug policy for primary health care providers (this policy was extended to county hospitals in 2011), and tied the allocation of their public health budget to an annual performance assessment (Yip et al. 2010). However, local governments in charge of implementing these reforms lacked the capacity and data to assess the performance of providers.

Reforming the governance of public hospitals, which provide 90 percent of in-patient and outpatient services, is proving much more difficult, partly because of the competing priorities of different branches of government (ibid.). The government has designated sixteen cities to experiment with different governance models. Although these models vary considerably, all cities have instituted monitoring measures to control over-prescribing and over-testing, and hospitals in these cities have increased discretionary power to hire, fire, and promote staff, relaxing civil service rules that guarantee doctors job security. Two of the cities, Kunming and Luoyang, prioritized the introduction of market competition between public and private hospitals by privatizing public hospitals. The Ministry of Health began to encourage case-based charging as early as 2004. An experiment involving treatment protocols in Jining appears to have been successful in reducing costs by as much as 33 percent (ibid.). The ministry then started to implement case-based payment with treatment protocols nationwide.

The National Essential Medicine List (NEML) was intended to cap prices for the most-needed drugs and to ensure that all these medicines counted for reimbursement, with competitive bidding between suppliers organized at province level (Docherty, Cao, and Wang 2012). A Ministry of Health report suggests that the use of essential medicines lists has not so far effectively reduced over-prescribing, and stories in the media suggest that the bidding process is still affected by corruption (Yip et al. 2010). Moreover, the extension of the zero-profit drug policy to county-level hospitals has reduced the incomes of these hospitals and their doctors by a significant amount, perhaps by 20–30 percent. To compensate for this, the central government has promised further public investment and has started to experiment with new performance-related pay schemes. In 2014, it issued an "Opinion on Promoting the Comprehensive Reform in County-Level Public Hospitals," which began to raise the prices of diagnosis, surgery, nursing, hospital beds, and traditional Chinese medical services, while encouraging county hospitals to increase their income through quality service (NHFPC 2014). It thus appears that the authorities are attempting to "grasp the nettle" of reforming the system of "supporting medical services using drugs" (*yi yao yang yi*).

At the same time, the government has redoubled its efforts to combat unethical medical practices that have provoked public criticism. In 2012, the Chinese government published the "Guidance on Strengthening the Prevention and Control of the Integrity Risk of Public Medical Institutions," which, among other things, advocated "strengthening the study of medical ethics and professionalism, reinforcing the governance of the under-the-counter payment, improving and perfecting the medical ethics evaluation system and establishing effective incentive and restraint mechanisms" (NHFPC 2012). In 2013, it promulgated the "Nine Prohibitions for Strengthening Ethics Construction for the Healthcare Industry" (NHFPC 2013a). Under-the-counter payments (so-called *hong bao*) are forbidden, as stated in the ninth prohibition. To deal with the *hong bao* problem, the Chinese government published a "Notice Regarding the Agreement between Doctors and Patients on Rejecting the Under-the-Counter Payment" (NHFPC 2013b). According to this notice, public hospitals and doctors are required to sign agreements under which doctors will reject under-the-counter payments, while patients will not offer them to doctors. The agreements will be archived and anyone in violation of them could face punishment, which in mild cases could include criticism, re-education, and delays to promotion, and, in more serious cases, dismissal and even revocation of licences to practise.

It is unclear how effective these various measures have been in reforming unethical practices. We would expect to find that some of the problems have now been ameliorated. However, in nearly all Chinese cities, hospitals still retain their profits and physician bonuses are still linked to profits (Yip et al. 2010; Li, Feng, and Jiang 2018). The government's limited role in financing public hospitals under the current system is thought to have reduced their degree of influence.[4] Moreover, any incentive structure will remain open to abuse through manipulation and misreporting if ethical standards remain lax. There is a Chinese saying, *shang you zhengce, xia you duice* ("above they have policies, below we have countermeasures"). In its battle to reform unethical practices, the government needs allies, not the least of whom are the general public. It is to our data about public attitudes that we now turn.

Data and Research Design

This study is based on analysis of data from a nationwide survey carried out in mainland China from November 1, 2012, to January 17, 2013.[5] The target population comprised mainland citizens aged eighteen to seventy residing for more than thirty days in family dwellings in all thirty-one provinces. The survey used the GPS Assisted Area Sampling Method (Landry and Shen 2005). Stratification took place in stages. At the first stage, the country was divided into three official macro-regions: Eastern, Central, and Western. Each macro-region was divided into urban and rural administrative areas, giving six layers in total; and sixty primary sampling units (PSU) corresponding to county-level administrative divisions were selected at random across the six layers, with probability proportionate to population. Within each PSU, three half-square minutes (HSM) of latitude and longitude were chosen, with probability proportionate to population density; within each of these, again proportionate to population density, a number of spatial square seconds (SSS) corresponding to 90-metre by 90-metre squares were selected at random. Within each SSS, all dwellings were enumerated, and twenty-seven were selected in each HSM by systematic sampling. Within each dwelling, respondents were identified by the Kish method. The result was a sample of 5,424 dwellings in which 3,680 valid interviews were completed, giving a response rate of 67.9%.

To get an estimate of how widespread unethical medical practices are in China, the survey asked respondents how likely it is that in their local city or county hospital medical staff would unnecessarily prescribe medicines not covered by insurance, take bribes or "red envelopes" (*hong bao*) for treatment that has already formally been paid for, and require comprehensive checkups from patients even when the diagnosis is clear (Figure 8.2). The last practice appears to be the most common: 61% consider it very or somewhat likely; 57% consider unnecessary prescription of medicines not covered by insurance to be very or somewhat likely; and only 30% consider bribe taking to be likely. A substantial proportion of respondents said "don't know," but for each question less than 2% refused to answer. Bribe taking is considered unlikely by 57%, and unnecessary comprehensive checkups and prescriptions not covered by insurance by 28% each. The data suggest that medically unethical behaviour is fairly common, at least in the eyes of Chinese citizens.

FIGURE 8.2

Perceived prevalence of unethical medical practices in China

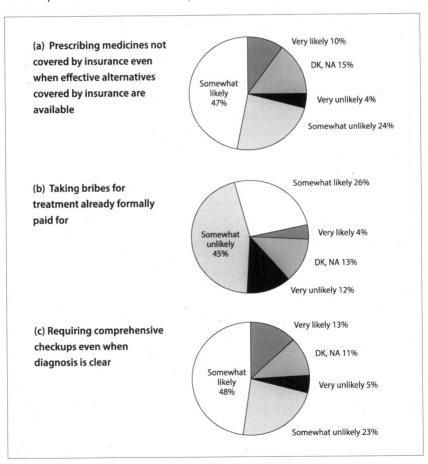

Source: Performance Evaluations, Trust and Utilization of Health Care in China Survey, 2012–13. Fieldwork was carried out from November 1, 2012, to January 17, 2013; *N* = 3,680 (Duckett et al. 2020).

We can combine the three questions into an index to see whether respondents who see unethical behaviour as likely in one situation see it in all situations. This procedure shows that 28% of respondents do not see unethical behaviour as likely in any situation, 20% see it as likely in one situation, 28% see it as likely in two situations, and 24% see it as likely in three situations. The data thus imply that a large majority of respondents see unethical behaviour as likely at least some of the time, and a substantial minority see it as endemic.

Our survey included three items prompting respondents to recommend one course of action to deal with potentially unethical behaviour by doctors. For each, the survey asked respondents to choose from several strategies that differ along the main dimensions discussed above (see Figure 8.1): the extent to which they are proactive or passive, universalistic or particularistic, and whether they involve voice or exit.

The first question concerns dealing with a surgeon who tells the patient that he cannot guarantee the success of a life-saving operation. Although so informing the patient may be a responsible and ethical course of action, we were interested in how many respondents would interpret it as a cue to do something to minimize agency risk. Almost one-third of respondents said that they would recommend just undergoing the operation at one's own risk (Figure 8.3). The second most popular strategy, recommended by just over one-quarter, is to change to another public hospital. Using connections to find another surgeon is the third most popular strategy, chosen by 1 in 10 respondents. Paying a bribe is the recommendation of less than 1 in 20, as is going to a private hospital. Only 3% would recommend making a formal complaint, and the same number gave other replies. Slightly less than 1 in 6 said "don't know," and we combine them with the 1% who gave no answer.

If a doctor prescribes a lot of expensive medicine that is not covered by insurance, even when cheaper alternatives are available, slightly less than a quarter of respondents would just buy the medicine prescribed. The same number would ask the doctor to change it; just over 1 in 8 recommended changing to another public hospital. Around half as many would try a private hospital. Less than 1 in 10 would complain to the hospital administration. Only 1 in 20 would resort to use of connections; less than half that number would pay a bribe; and other strategies are also marginal. Around 1 in 6 said "don't know," and a handful gave no answer.

If a public hospital appears to be requiring unnecessary diagnostic tests, a little less than one-third would recommend doing the tests anyway, just under 1 in 5 think that asking the doctor to keep the tests to a minimum

FIGURE 8.3

Preferred strategies for dealing with unethical medical practices in China

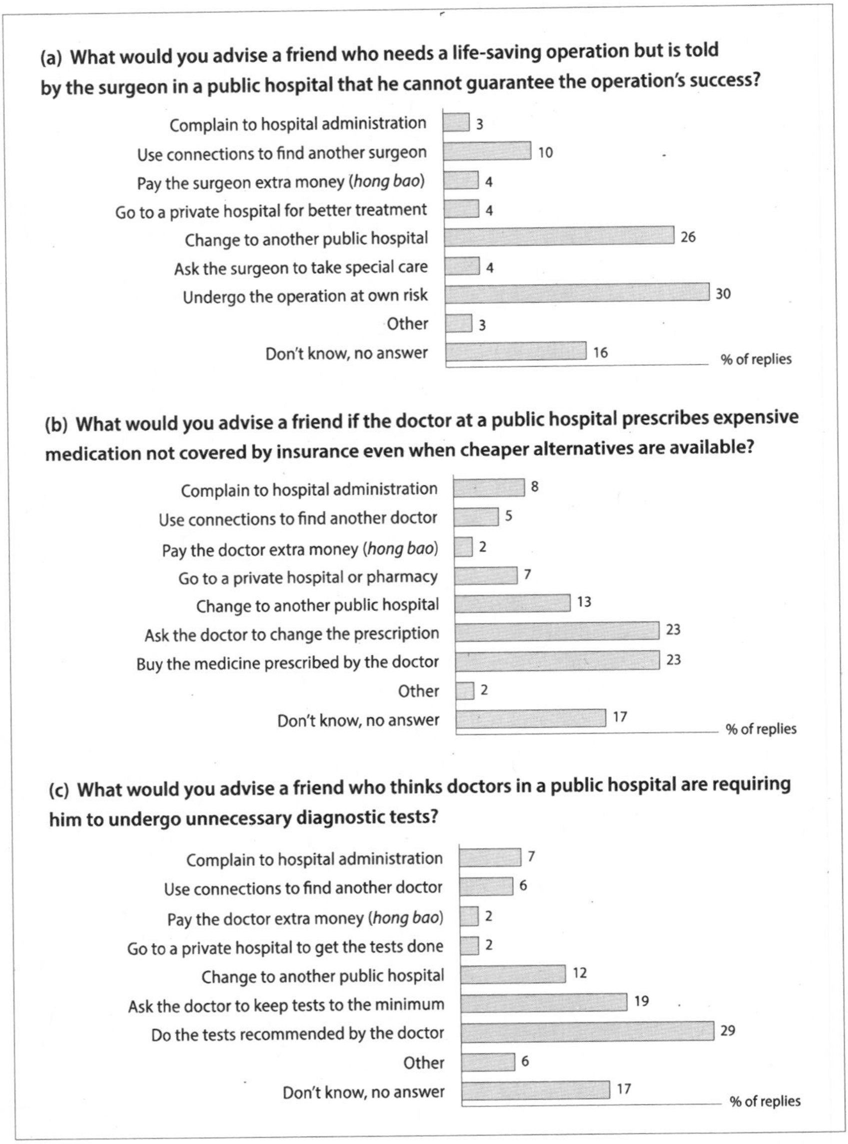

(a) What would you advise a friend who needs a life-saving operation but is told by the surgeon in a public hospital that he cannot guarantee the operation's success?

Strategy	% of replies
Complain to hospital administration	3
Use connections to find another surgeon	10
Pay the surgeon extra money (*hong bao*)	4
Go to a private hospital for better treatment	4
Change to another public hospital	26
Ask the surgeon to take special care	4
Undergo the operation at own risk	30
Other	3
Don't know, no answer	16

(b) What would you advise a friend if the doctor at a public hospital prescribes expensive medication not covered by insurance even when cheaper alternatives are available?

Strategy	% of replies
Complain to hospital administration	8
Use connections to find another doctor	5
Pay the doctor extra money (*hong bao*)	2
Go to a private hospital or pharmacy	7
Change to another public hospital	13
Ask the doctor to change the prescription	23
Buy the medicine prescribed by the doctor	23
Other	2
Don't know, no answer	17

(c) What would you advise a friend who thinks doctors in a public hospital are requiring him to undergo unnecessary diagnostic tests?

Strategy	% of replies
Complain to hospital administration	7
Use connections to find another doctor	6
Pay the doctor extra money (*hong bao*)	2
Go to a private hospital to get the tests done	2
Change to another public hospital	12
Ask the doctor to keep tests to the minimum	19
Do the tests recommended by the doctor	29
Other	6
Don't know, no answer	17

Source: Performance Evaluations, Trust and Utilization of Health Care in China Survey, 2012–13. Fieldwork was carried out from November 1, 2012, to January 17, 2013; *N* = 3,680 (Duckett et al. 2020).

would suffice. Slightly less than 1 in 8 would recommend changing to another public hospital. Less than 1 in 10 would complain to the hospital administration. Just over 1 in 20 would use connections to find another doctor. Just over 1 in 20 volunteered other replies, and when we look at these in more detail, we find that nearly all of them recommended just refusing to do the tests. Only 1 in 50 respondents think bribery would help. Around 1 in 6 are "don't knows," with whom we combine the few who gave no answer.

Again, the combination of replies to different questions gives an overall picture of the popularity of different types of strategies and shows to what extent respondents choose one type of strategy across situations. Three types of strategies are mainstream, although none is consistently endorsed by a majority of respondents. The most popular overall is to simply accept the treatment recommended by the doctor without question: 9% would recommend it in all three situations, 15% in two situations, 25% in one situation, and a bare majority, 51%, would never recommend it. While this "loyalty" strategy allows patients to maintain harmonious relations with the doctor, it is not a way of reducing agency risk. Changing to another public hospital is the second most popular strategy overall: 4% would recommend it in all three situations, 6% in two situations, 26% in one situation, and 64% would never recommend it. Asking the doctor to modify his or her behaviour or the treatment regime is the third most popular strategy: only 1% would recommend it in three situations, 11% in two situations, 22% in one situation, and 66% would never recommend it. Four-fifths of respondents would use one of these mainstream strategies at least once.

Four types of strategies are marginal. The most popular is use of connections (*guanxi*) to find another provider. Only 2% are consistent connections users (*guanxihu*), the same percentage would recommend it in two situations, 11% would recommend it in one situation, and as many as 85% would never recommend *guanxi* as a way of dealing with unethical medical practices. Just over 1% would recommend going to a private hospital in two or three situations, just over 9% would recommend it in one situation, and 89% would never recommend going to a private hospital. Consistent complainers are less than 2%, while 3% would recommend complaining in two situations, 6% in one situation, and 89% would never recommend complaining to the hospital administration. Paying bribes is the most marginal strategy of all: only 1% would recommend it in two or three situations, 4% would recommend it one situation, and just over 94% would never recommend it. Although these are all marginal strategies, more than one-third of respondents chose at least one of them once.

Hypotheses

Since decentralization and marketization have been significant trends in China's provision of social services (Chan, Ngok, and Phillips 2008), both household resources and level of development of the community have been significant factors in determining the availability and quality of health care (Henderson et al. 1995; Liu 2004; Adams and Hannum 2005; Lui, Zwang, Lu, Kwon, and Quan 2007; Eggleston et al. 2008). Urban-rural inequality and inequality between communities have grown against a background of overall improvement in health facilities and outcomes (J. Gao et al. 2002; Akin et al. 2005; Reddy 2008). For poor rural residents, lack of access has often meant doing without desperately needed treatment (Li 2008; Lora-Wainwright 2011). In his research on strategies to obtain a government permit, Neil Munro (2012) found that rural respondents were less likely than urban respondents to use connections, and less likely to write a letter to an official: in other words, they were less proactive, perhaps reflecting their relatively greater social distance from officials. If the same applies in dealing with doctors, we would expect the following hypothesis to be true: *(H1) Urban residents are more proactive than rural residents in dealing with unethical behaviour by health care providers* (ibid.).

Related to urban-rural difference is level of economic development. Doug Guthrie (1999) made the case that economic development encourages the establishment of rational-legal authority. Munro (2012) did not find strong effects from level of development on strategies to obtain a government permit: GDP per capita of the city or county was not a significant influence. An infrastructure measure, based on the utilities available in the area, showed that there was a weak relationship between underdevelopment and passivity, and that people in communities at a medium level of development were slightly more inclined to use universalistic strategies. We propose to test the following hypothesis in relation to strategies for dealing with unethical medical practices: *(H2a) Residents in more developed areas are more proactive than those in less developed areas.* We also need to consider that there is a legitimate market for health care services providing people with choices – in other words, options for exit from a relationship with a particular physician if it proves unsatisfactory. We therefore propose to test whether *(H2b) Residents in more developed areas are more likely to use exit strategies than those in less developed areas.*

We know from prior research that Chinese men more readily take part in non-electoral politics than Chinese women (Tong 2003). This conforms to traditional gender stereotypes. Munro's research (2012, 164–67) on preferred strategies for obtaining a government permit found that men were more likely to use particularistic strategies, but not necessarily more proactive. We can test the following hypotheses with regard to strategies for dealing with unethical health care providers: *(H3a) Men are more proactive than women,* and *(H3b) Men are more likely than women to use particularistic strategies.*

Under Mao Zedong, China's governing ideology was ascetic and egalitarian. Mayfair Yang (1994) suggested that the money fever that began in the 1980s stimulated the rise of particularistic strategies. Generational differences in socialization may generate different normative expectations about the acceptability of, for example, using connections to get what one wants. Munro (2012) found that those born in the 1940s and earlier were less inclined to particularism but also less inclined to universalistic voice, that is, to utilizing bureaucratic channels of appeal, as were those born in the 1950s. In relation to strategies for dealing with unethical health care providers, we can test the following hypotheses: *(H4a) The oldest cohorts are less inclined to particularism,* and *(H4b) The oldest cohorts are less inclined to voice.*

It is well established that education enhances social capital (Lin 2001). We would expect education to provide both the social skills and opportunities to get to know people in positions of authority and learn how to deal with them (Wank 1999). We know that education and income correlate strongly. The richer and better educated people are, the more confidence they are likely to have in dealing with medical professionals. We would therefore expect *(H5a) The more educated and the higher the income of the respondent, the more proactive they are in dealing with unethical practices.* In Munro's multivariate analysis (2012), education was found to be insignificant when income was controlled, but income on its own significantly increased the tendency to use particularistic strategies. Wayne DiFranceisco and Zvi Gitelman's study (1984) of Soviet émigrés in the late 1970s and 1980s suggested that education was a positive influence on use of connections. We can test the following hypothesis: *(H5b) The more educated and the higher the income of the respondent, the greater the tendency to rely on particularism.* Education and income usually confer purchasing power, which gives people additional choices in terms of health care provision. In a commercialized system, we would expect *(H5c) The more educated and the higher the income of the respondent, the greater the tendency to use exit strategies.*

Analysis

In order to identify patterns in bivariate relationships between preferred strategies and independent variables corresponding to our hypotheses, we ran cross-tabulations by social structure and computed mean household income against different strategies. This procedure enables us to identify the statistically significant differences between the categories and shows that some hypotheses fail, in the sense that we cannot reject the null hypothesis, while others pass (Table 8.1). Of course, a bivariate analysis detects gross rather than net effects. Multivariate analyses will be needed to identify net effects of individual variables, but from a policy viewpoint, understanding gross effects is often more important than developing a multivariate model, and it is in any case the prior step.

In China, counties (*xian*) are rural areas, county-level cities are smaller cities, bigger cities are divided into urban districts (*qu*), and these administrative categories correspond to 45%, 17%, and 38% of our sample, respectively. If Hypothesis 1 were correct, we would expect that urban district respondents would be more likely to choose the proactive strategies of making a formal complaint, changing providers, paying a bribe, pleading with the provider, or using connections to find another provider, and less likely to either accept the treatment offered, give up treatment, or say "don't know." Cross-tabulation shows that compared with rural respondents, urban dwellers are indeed consistently more likely to complain or to use connections, and less likely to say "don't know" (see Appendices 1 to 3 for details). For example, in the case of surgery, 14% of urban respondents would use connections, versus 8% of rural respondents, for a difference of 6% ($p < .001$); 5% would complain, versus 3% of rural respondents ($p < .05$); and 11% say "don't know," versus 18% of rural respondents ($p < .001$). Urban respondents are also more likely to change to a private hospital for surgery: 5% versus 3% ($p < .001$). However, urban and rural respondents do not differ significantly in the likelihood of simply accepting what the health care provider offers. In terms of willingness to change to another public hospital, rural respondents are more active in the cases of surgery and over-prescription. On the basis of this evidence, we cannot reject the null hypothesis that urban and rural respondents are equally proactive. Instead, they appear to be proactive in different ways: rural dwellers are more likely to be switchers within the public hospital system, whereas urban dwellers are more likely to try other strategies.

Our survey asked respondents about the availability of four public utilities in the respondent's home: electricity, running water, LPG gas, and an

TABLE 8.1

Summary of findings from bivariate analysis

	Hypothesis	Surgery	Over-prescription	Unnecessary tests
(H1)	Urban residents are more proactive than rural residents in dealing with unethical behaviour by health care providers.	Fail	Fail	Fail
(H2a)	Residents in more developed areas are more proactive than those in less developed areas.	Pass	Fail	Fail
(H2b)	Residents in more developed areas are more likely to use exit strategies than those in less developed areas.	Pass	Pass	Fail
(H3a)	Men are more proactive than women	Fail	Fail	Fail
(H3b)	Men are more likely than women to use particularistic strategies.	Fail	Fail	Fail
(H4a)	The oldest cohorts are less inclined to particularism.	Pass	Pass	Pass
(H4b)	The oldest cohorts are less inclined to voice.	Fail	Pass	Pass
(H5a)	The more educated and the higher the income of the respondent, the more proactive they are in dealing with unethical practices.	Pass	Pass	Pass
(H5b)	The more educated and the higher the income of the respondent, the greater the tendency to rely on particularism.	Fail	Fail	Fail
(H5c)	The more educated and the higher the income of the respondent, the greater the tendency to use exit strategies.	Pass	Fail	Fail

Note: Fail = fail to reject the null hypothesis; Pass = reject the null hypothesis.
Source: Cross-tabulations available from the authors.

Internet connection. More than 99% had electricity but only 84% had running water, 64% had gas, and 44% had an Internet connection. Since these facilities rely on publicly provided infrastructure, we use them to construct an infrastructure index measuring the level of development of the local area. If Hypothesis 2a were correct, we would expect that respondents in areas with maximum utilities would be more likely to choose proactive strategies and less likely to say "don't know" or just accept the treatment offered. Cross-tabulation shows that this is broadly true in the case of surgery but not the other two situations (see Appendices 4 to 6 for details). For example, in dealing with a surgeon, only 27% of those in the most developed areas would undergo the operation at their own risk, compared with 48% in the least developed ($p < .001$), and 9% say "don't know," compared with 16% in the least developed ($p < .001$). In the other two situations, although there are fewer who say "don't know" in the most developed areas, there is no significant difference by level of development in willingness to just accept the treatment offered. In the case of surgery, however, the difference by level of development is massive.

If Hypothesis 2b were correct, those in the most developed areas should be more likely to choose the exit strategies of changing providers and using connections, and less likely to use the voice strategies of making complaints and paying bribes. Cross-tabulation (Appendices 4 and 5) shows that those in the most developed areas are indeed more likely to use connections and to change to another public hospital to deal with a surgeon and with over-prescription. For example, in dealing with a surgeon, 30% in the most developed areas would change to another public hospital, compared with 17% in the least developed, and 16% would use connections, compared with 5% in the least developed (both $p < .001$). In dealing with over-prescription, 14% in the most developed areas would change to another public hospital, versus 10% in the least developed ($p < .05$), and 9% in the most developed areas would use connections, versus 2% in the least developed ($p < .001$). In the case of unnecessary testing (Appendix 6), residents of the most developed areas are also more likely to use connections, 9% versus 2% ($p < .001$), but not to change hospitals. On the basis of this evidence, we can conclude that people in more developed areas are more likely to choose exit strategies in dealing with a surgeon and with over-prescription, but in dealing with unnecessary testing, level of development makes little difference.

If Hypothesis 3a were correct, we would expect to find that men are more likely than women to complain, use connections, plead, pay bribes, or change providers. In fact, however, the genders are equally likely to choose these strategies (see Appendices 7 to 9 for details). Our survey shows that women are significantly more likely to say "don't know" in response to each of the questions: this shows more circumspection but it is not sufficient to support the thesis that women are more passive in the face of potentially unethical medical practices. They are slightly less likely to ask the doctor to keep the diagnostic tests to the minimum in the case of unnecessary testing – 18% versus 21% ($p < .05$) – which suggests that they may be more reticent. But this effect is at the margin of significance, and insufficient to reject the null hypothesis. If Hypothesis 3b were correct, we would expect to find that men are more likely than women to use connections or pay bribes. Again, the cross-tabulations show that this is not the case.

If Hypothesis 4a were correct, age is associated with universalism, and we would expect to find that the oldest cohorts, those born in the 1940s and 1950s in our survey, are less likely to use connections, bribe, or plead with the provider. We find that across all three scenarios, the youngest cohorts are more likely to use connections and to plead with the provider (see Appendices 10 to 12 for details). For example, in dealing with unnecessary testing, 7% of those born in the 1980s and 1990s would use connections, compared with 4% of those born in the 1940s and 1950s ($p < .01$); and 23% of the youngest cohorts would ask the doctor to keep the tests to the minimum, compared with 15% of the oldest cohorts ($p < .001$). We therefore reject the null hypothesis that the generations are equally inclined to universalism.

If Hypothesis 4b were correct, and the elderly are less inclined to voice, the oldest cohorts should be less inclined to complain to the hospital administration. Younger complainers outnumber older complainers by two to one in the cases of over-prescription and unnecessary testing, but not surgery. In sum, age makes little difference in the proclivity to speak up to a surgeon, but the young are more vocal in cases of over-prescription and unnecessary testing.

If Hypothesis 5a were correct, meaning education and income are associated with proactive strategies, then we would expect to find that more educated and richer respondents are more likely to make a formal complaint, pay a bribe, plead, change provider, or use connections to find another provider, and less likely to say "don't know" or simply accept the treatment on the terms suggested by the physician. This is generally the case across all three situations examined (see Appendices 13 to 18 for details). For example, in the case of surgery, we find that 20% of those with university education would use connections, compared with 6% of those with primary education or less; and 6% of the university-educated would go to a private hospital, compared with 2% of those with primary education or less ($p < .001$ for both). Just 6% of those with university education said "don't know," compared with 27% of those with only primary education ($p < .001$); and 30% of those with university education would just undergo the operation at their own risk, compared with 35% of those with only primary education ($p < .05$, Appendix 13). In the case of over-prescription, those who would complain to the hospital administration, use connections, or ask the doctor to change the prescription have annual average household incomes that are, respectively, CNY 20,000, CNY 17,500, and CNY 8,500 higher than those who would simply buy the medicine recommended ($p < .001$ for all three, Appendix 17). We can therefore conclude that poorer or less educated respondents are usually less proactive in dealing with unethical medical practices.

If Hypothesis 5b were correct and privilege is associated with particularism, then more educated and wealthier respondents should be more willing to use connections, pay bribes, or ask the doctor to change his or her behaviour. We find that those with university education are more likely to use connections across all three situations, and in the cases of over-prescription and unnecessary testing, they are more likely to ask the doctor to change behaviour, although there is no difference in propensity to make under-the-counter payments (Appendices 13 to 15). Thus, for example, to deal with unnecessary testing, 11% of the university-educated would use connections, versus only 3% of those with primary education or less ($p < .001$, Appendix 15). In the case of over-prescription, 29% of the university-educated would ask the doctor to change the medicine, versus only 20% of those with primary education or less ($p < .001$). Across all three situations, those who use connections consistently have higher average annual household income than those who simply accept treatment on the terms offered. The same goes for, in the case of surgery, bribe payers and those who plead, and in the case of over-prescription, those who plead. We can therefore conclude that richer or more educated respondents are usually more likely than poorer and less educated respondents to choose particularistic strategies.

We should also note, however, that those who choose the universalistic strategy of making a formal complaint are also richer than those who simply accept treatment. For example, in the case of unnecessary testing, the mean annual household income of complainers is CNY 22,200 higher on average than accepters ($p < .01$). In the case of over-prescription, their income is CNY 20,000 higher ($p < .001$), and in the case of surgery it is CNY 14,500 higher ($p < .01$). There is an association between education and complaining too: in the case of over-prescription, 12% of those with university education would complain, versus only 5% of those with only primary education ($p < .001$); and in the case of unnecessary testing, 10% of those with university education would complain, versus only 5% of those with primary education ($p < .001$). In other words, therefore, it seems possible that the greater propensity of the richer and more educated to engage in particularistic strategies is a function of being more proactive, rather than of being less inclined to universalism.

If Hypothesis 5c were correct, meaning that privilege is associated with exit strategies, then more educated and higher-income respondents should be more willing to go to private hospitals, change to another public hospital, or use connections to find another doctor. What we find is that although the university-educated are 4% more likely than those with primary education to go to a private hospital for surgery ($p < .001$), there are no significant differences in preference for going private or changing hospitals in the other two situations. When we look at income, we find that those who would change to another public hospital for surgery live in households earning on average CNY 9,200 more than those who would undergo the operation at their own risk, but there are no significant income differences for propensity to change public hospitals or go private in the other situations. As mentioned, those with university education are consistently more likely to use connections to find another surgeon, and those who do so have higher incomes than those who just accept the treatment offered. In the case of surgery, we can conclude that higher-status respondents are more likely than the less privileged to choose exit strategies. However, we cannot draw the same conclusion in the other two situations.

Patients, especially well-to-do patients, are part of the problem as well as part of the solution in unethical medical practice. Most analyses focus on the perverse incentive structures within Chinese hospitals that reward unethical practices. It is probably too early to tell what the effects of recent changes to these incentive structures have been. Our survey, conducted more than three years after the start of the latest round of reforms, showed that in the eyes of the public, unethical medical practices were still seen as prevalent. They are part of a culture of health care seeking and medical treatment in which the burden of insuring against agency risk, that is, of ensuring that doctors act in the best interests of patients, is shifted onto the patients themselves. The fact that numerous patients see no alternative but to accept the burden of risk gives little ground for comfort about the nature of the system. Rather, it testifies to the existence of a trap of low expectations on the part of the public with respect to the medical profession. Use of particularistic rather than universalistic strategies to influence doctors is rational in circumstances where codes of conduct and formal regulations are unreliable guides to practice.

To what extent does the market provide solutions to the problem of unethical medical practices? The logic of supply and demand suggests that more and better services should reduce the price of medical care and encourage exit if providers behave unethically. We do not have trend data or cross-regional comparative data that would allow us to judge whether or not this is occurring. However, we do have variations in income and levels of development, which allow us to make a judgment that market forces do, to some extent, encourage both activism and exit strategies in dealing with surgeons. The fact that the well-to-do in China are more inclined to resort to particularistic strategies also cautions against the simplistic assumption that activism and exit necessarily operate in favour of the construction of universalistic institutions.

Empowerment of patients within the public hospital system may offer another way of altering incentive structures and ensuring better enforcement of regulations. The age differences suggest a nuanced conclusion. On the one hand, as older cohorts die off, the demographic trend is toward a more assertive public. On the other hand, except in the case of surgery, such assertiveness is likely among the young to take a particularistic form. It is striking how few respondents believe that complaining to the hospital administration does any good in dealing with unethical medical practices. Since the administration and unethical practitioners are probably in most hospitals embedded in circular relationships of cooperation and mutual guarantees, patients are right to be wary of formal complaints procedures. There is a need for regulatory institutions that command public confidence. It would be desirable, for example, to establish a system of patients' ombudsmen, perhaps chosen from among local people's congress delegates, who stand at arm's length from the hospitals, are empowered to investigate complaints, and have real powers to punish doctors who transgress the code of conduct, and to reward patients who report transgressions. Another possibility is to use the Internet to develop whistle-blowing platforms and to gather intelligence about violations of ethical codes, although of course such platforms would need to be moderated in order to control mischievous reports. Although such reforms could harm the material interests of doctors and hospitals, exacerbate conflicts between doctors and patients, and may not be to the liking of some patients who are accustomed to getting what they want by irregular means, there is an evident need to move beyond exhortation toward enforcement of ethics codes.

In terms of future research, further analysis is needed of the changes in institutional incentive structures emerging from the latest reforms and of the data on patient behaviour and public attitudes. The survey data analyzed here offer the opportunity to develop predictive models concerning which patients prefer which strategies, isolating net effects of significant independent variables, and identifying patterns in their relationships. In addition, we need to systematically examine the wealth of qualitative and anecdotal evidence, including some collected by the authors of this chapter, to try to understand the circumstances in which unethical medical practices are likely to occur. Although this study is no more than an initial pass through the data, we believe it represents one of the first published attempts to analyze the phenomenon of popular response to unethical medical practices based on a large body of survey responses.

APPENDIX TABLE 1

Strategy to deal with a surgeon: tabulation by administrative category (% respondents)

Q. *If your friend needed a life-saving operation but the surgeon in a public hospital told them that he could not guarantee that the operation would be successful, what would you advise the patient to do? (One answer)*

All		County	County-level city	Urban district	Difference: urban-county	Significance
4	Complain to the hospital administration	3	3	5	2	*
10	Use connections to find another surgeon	8	8	14	6	***
4	Pay the surgeon extra money (*hong bao*)	4	3	4	–1	***
4	Go to a private hospital for better treatment	3	3	5	2	***
27	Change to another public hospital	29	25	26	–3	*
4	Ask the surgeon to take special care	4	4	5	1	*
32	Undergo the operation at own risk	32	32	32	0	
16	Don't know	18	22	11	–7	***

Note: Significance of difference: *. 05 level, *** . 001 level.
Source: Performance Evaluations, Trust and Utilization of Health Care in China Survey, 2012–13. Funded by the UK Economic and Social Research Council, Grant No. ES/J011487/1. Fieldwork 1 November 2012–17 January 2013, N=3,680.

APPENDIX TABLE 2

Strategy to deal with over-prescription: tabulation by administrative category (% respondents)

Q. *What would you advise your friend to do if the doctor at a public hospital prescribes a lot of expensive medication which is not covered by insurance even when cheaper alternatives are available? (One answer)*

All		County	County-level city	Urban district	Difference: urban–county	Significance
8	Complain to the hospital administration	5	8	12	7	***
6	Use connections to find another doctor	4	4	7	3	***
2	Pay the doctor extra money (*hong bao*)	3	2	2	–1	*
7	Go to a private hospital or pharmacy for the prescription	7	8	7	0	
13	Change to another public hospital	15	16	10	–5	***
24	Ask the doctor to change the prescription	22	21	27	4	**
24	Buy the medicine prescribed by the doctor	25	20	25	0	
16	Don't know	20	21	11	–8	***

Note: Significance of difference: * .05 level, ** .01 level, *** .001 level.
Source: Performance Evaluations, Trust and Utilization of Health Care in China Survey, 2012–13. Funded by the UK Economic and Social Research Council, Grant No. ES/J011487/1. Fieldwork 1 November 2012–17 January 2013, N=3,680.

Strategy to deal with unnecessary testing: tabulation by administrative category (% respondents)

Q. *What would you advise your friend to do if he thinks doctors in a public hospital are requiring him to do unnecessary diagnostic tests?* (*One answer*)

All		County	County-level city	Urban district	Difference: urban–county	Significance
7	Complain to the hospital administration	4	7	11	7	***
6	Use connections to find another doctor	5	6	7	2	*
2	Pay the doctor extra money (*hong bao*)	2	2	2	0	
2	Go to a private hospital to get the tests done	2	1	3	1	
12	Change to another public hospital	13	12	11	–2	
20	Ask the doctor to keep the tests to the minimum	20	19	19	–1	
30	Do the tests recommended by the doctor	30	26	31	1	
6	Refuse the tests	6	7	5	–2	*
16	Don't know	18	19	11	–7	***

Note: Significance of difference: * .05 level, ** .01 level, *** .001 level.
Source: Performance Evaluations, Trust and Utilization of Health Care in China Survey, 2012–13. Funded by the UK Economic and Social Research Council, Grant No. ES/J011487/1. Fieldwork 1 November 2012–17 January 2013, N=3,680.

APPENDIX TABLE 4

Strategy to deal with a surgeon: tabulation by infrastructure level (% respondents)

Q. *If your friend needed a life-saving operation but the surgeon in a public hospital told them that he could not guarantee that the operation would be successful, what would you advise the patient to do? (One answer)*

All		Infrastructure: number of utilities					
		None	One	Two	Three	Difference: three–none	Significance
4	Complain to the hospital administration	4	4	3	4	0	
10	Use connections to find another surgeon	5	5	9	16	10	***
4	Pay the surgeon extra money (*hong bao*)	2	3	4	4	2	
4	Go to a private hospital for better treatment	2	3	5	4	2	
27	Change to another public hospital	17	23	29	30	13	***
4	Ask the surgeon to take special care	5	4	5	4	–1	
32	Undergo the operation at own risk	48	34	30	27	–20	***
16	Don't know	16	24	16	9	–7	***

Note: Significance of difference: *. 05 level, ***. 001 level.
Source: Performance Evaluations, Trust and Utilization of Health Care in China Survey, 2012–13. Funded by the UK Economic and Social Research Council, Grant No. ES/J011487/1. Fieldwork 1 November 2012–17 January 2013, N=3,680.

APPENDIX TABLE 5

Strategy to deal with over-prescription: tabulation by infrastructure level (% respondents)

Q. *What would you advise your friend to do if the doctor at a public hospital prescribes a lot of expensive medication which is not covered by insurance even when cheaper alternatives are available? (One answer)*

All		None	One	Two	Three	Difference: three–none	Significance
		Infrastructure: number of utilities					
8	Complain to the hospital administration	6	5	8	10	4	**
6	Use connections to find another doctor	2	3	5	9	7	***
2	Pay the doctor extra money (*hong bao*)	3	3	2	2	–1	
7	Go to a private hospital or pharmacy for the prescription	8	5	9	6	–2	
13	Change to another public hospital	10	13	14	14	4	*
24	Ask the doctor to change the prescription	26	22	23	25	–1	
24	Buy the medicine prescribed by the doctor	27	25	22	24	–2	
17	Don't know	19	24	17	10	–10	***

Note: Significance of difference: *. 05 level, ** .01 level, *** .001 level.

Source: Performance Evaluations, Trust and Utilization of Health Care in China Survey, 2012–13. Funded by the UK Economic and Social Research Council, Grant No. ES/J011487/1. Fieldwork 1 November 2012–17 January 2013, N=3,680.

Strategy to deal with unnecessary testing: tabulation by infrastructure level (% respondents)

Q. *What would you advise your friend to do if he thinks doctors in a public hospital are requiring him to do unnecessary diagnostic tests?*
   (One answer)

All		Infrastructure: number of utilities				Difference: three–none	Significance
		None	One	Two	Three		
7	Complain to the hospital administration	6	4	7	9	3	*
6	Use connections to find another doctor	2	3	6	9	6	***
2	Pay the doctor extra money (*hong bao*)	2	2	1	2	0	
2	Go to a private hospital to get the tests done	2	2	3	2	0	
12	Change to another public hospital	13	13	11	13	0	
20	Ask the doctor to keep the tests to the minimum	18	18	22	19	2	
30	Do the tests recommended by the doctor	34	29	25	33	–1	
16	Don't know	19	23	17	8	–11	***
6	Refuse the tests	5	6	7	5	0	

Note: Significance of difference: *. 05 level, ***. 001 level.

Source: Performance Evaluations, Trust and Utilization of Health Care in China Survey, 2012–13. Funded by the UK Economic and Social Research Council, Grant No. ES/J011487/1. Fieldwork 1 November 2012–17 January 2013, N=3,680.

APPENDIX TABLE 7

Strategy to deal with a surgeon: tabulation by gender (% respondents)

Q. *If your friend needed a life-saving operation but the surgeon in a public hospital told them that he could not guarantee that the operation would be successful, what would you advise the patient to do? (One answer)*

All		Female	Male	Difference: male-female	Significance
4	Complain to the hospital administration	3	4	0	
10	Use connections to find another surgeon	10	11	1	
4	Pay the surgeon extra money (*hong bao*)	4	4	0	
4	Go to a private hospital for better treatment	3	4	1	
27	Change to another public hospital	26	28	1	
4	Ask the surgeon to take special care	5	4	0	
32	Undergo the operation at own risk	32	31	−1	
16	Don't know	17	14	−3	***

Note: Significance of difference: *. 05 level, ***. 001 level.
Source: Performance Evaluations, Trust and Utilization of Health Care in China Survey, 2012–13. Funded by the UK Economic and Social Research Council, Grant No. ES/J011487/1. Fieldwork 1 November 2012–17 January 2013, N=3,680.

APPENDIX TABLE 8

Strategy to deal with over-prescription: tabulation by gender (% respondents)

Q. *What would you advise your friend to do if the doctor at a public hospital pre-scribes a lot of expensive medication which is not covered by insurance even when cheaper alternatives are available? (One answer)*

All		Female	Male	Difference: male-female	Significance
8	Complain to the hospital administration	8	8	0	
6	Use connections to find another doctor	6	5	0	
2	Pay the doctor extra money (*hong bao*)	2	2	0	
7	Go to a private hospital or pharmacy for the prescription	7	7	0	
13	Change to another public hospital	13	14	1	
24	Ask the doctor to change the prescription	23	24	1	
24	Buy the medicine prescribed by the doctor	23	25	2	
17	Don't know	18	15	−4	***

Note: Significance of difference: *. 05 level, ***. 001 level.
Source: Performance Evaluations, Trust and Utilization of Health Care in China Survey, 2012–13. Funded by the UK Economic and Social Research Council, Grant No. ES/J011487/1. Fieldwork 1 November 2012–17 January 2013, N=3,680.

APPENDIX TABLE 9

Strategy to deal with unnecessary testing: tabulation by gender (% respondents)

Q. *What would you advise your friend to do if he thinks doctors in a public hospital are requiring him to do unnecessary diagnostic tests? (One answer)*

All		Female	Male	Difference: male-female	Significance
7	Complain to the hospital administration	6	8	1	
6	Use connections to find another doctor	6	5	−1	
2	Pay the doctor extra money (*hong bao*)	2	2	0	
2	Go to a private hospital to get the tests done	2	2	−1	
12	Change to another public hospital	12	13	1	
20	Ask the doctor to keep the tests to the minimum	18	21	3	*
30	Do the tests recommended by the doctor	30	29	0	
6	Refuse the tests	6	6	0	
16	Don't know	17	14	−3	***

Note: Significance of difference: *. 05 level, ***. 001 level.
Source: Performance Evaluations, Trust and Utilization of Health Care in China Survey, 2012–13. Funded by the UK Economic and Social Research Council, Grant No. ES/J011487/1. Fieldwork 1 November 2012–17 January 2013, N=3,680.

APPENDIX TABLE 10

Strategy to deal with a surgeon: tabulation by age cohort (% respondents)

Q. If your friend needed a life-saving operation but the surgeon in a public hospital told them that he could not guarantee that the operation would be successful, what would you advise the patient to do? (One answer)

	All	Born 1940s, 50s	Born 1960s, 70s	Born 1980s, 90s	Difference: young-old	Significance
Complain to the hospital administration	4	3	4	4	1	
Use connections to find another surgeon	10	7	10	12	5	***
Pay the surgeon extra money (hong bao)	4	3	4	4	0	
Go to a private hospital for better treatment	4	3	3	5	2	*
Change to another public hospital	27	21	25	33	11	***
Ask the surgeon to take special care	4	3	5	5	2	*
Undergo the operation at own risk	32	36	33	28	–8	***
Don't know	16	24	16	10	–13	***

Note: Significance of difference: *. 05 level, ***. 001 level.

Source: Performance Evaluations, Trust and Utilization of Health Care in China Survey, 2012–13. Funded by the UK Economic and Social Research Council, Grant No. ES/J011487/1. Fieldwork 1 November 2012–17 January 2013, N=3,680.

Strategy to deal with over-prescription: tabulation by age cohort (% respondents)

Q. *What would you advise your friend to do if the doctor at a public hospital prescribes a lot of expensive medication which is not covered by insurance even when cheaper alternatives are available? (One answer)*

All		Born 1940s, 50s	Born 1960s, 70s	Born 1980s, 90s	Difference: young-old	Significance
8	Complain to the hospital administration	5	8	10	5	***
6	Use connections to find another doctor	5	5	7	2	*
2	Pay the doctor extra money (hong bao)	2	2	2	0	
7	Go to a private hospital or pharmacy for the prescription	7	7	7	0	
13	Change to another public hospital	12	13	15	2	
24	Ask the doctor to change the prescription	19	23	28	9	***
24	Buy the medicine prescribed by the doctor	25	25	22	-3	*
17	Don't know	25	17	10	-15	***

Note: Significance of difference: *. 05 level, ***. 001 level.

Source: Performance Evaluations, Trust and Utilization of Health Care in China Survey, 2012–13. Funded by the UK Economic and Social Research Council, Grant No. ES/J011487/1. Fieldwork 1 November 2012–17 January 2013, N=3,680.

APPENDIX TABLE 12

Strategy to deal with unnecessary testing: tabulation by age cohort (% respondents)

Q. *What would you advise your friend to do if he thinks doctors in a public hospital are requiring him to do unnecessary diagnostic tests? (One answer)*

	All	Born 1940s, 50s	Born 1960s, 70s	Born 1980s, 90s	Difference: young-old	Significance
Complain to the hospital administration	7	5	6	10	5	***
Use connections to find another doctor	6	4	6	7	3	**
Pay the doctor extra money (*hong bao*)	2	2	2	1	−1	
Go to a private hospital to get the tests done	2	2	2	2	0	
Change to another public hospital	12	11	12	13	2	
Ask the doctor to keep the tests to the minimum	20	15	20	23	7	***
Do the tests recommended by the doctor	30	30	31	28	−1	
Don't know	16	25	16	10	−16	***
Refuse the tests	6	5	6	6	1	

Note: Significance of difference: * .05 level, ** .01 level, *** .001 level.

Source: Performance Evaluations, Trust and Utilization of Health Care in China Survey, 2012–13. Funded by the UK Economic and Social Research Council, Grant No. ES/J011487/1. Fieldwork 1 November 2012–17 January 2013, N=3,680.

Strategy to deal with a surgeon: tabulation by education (% respondents)

Q. *If your friend needed a life-saving operation but the surgeon in a public hospital told them that he could not guarantee that the operation would be successful, what would you advise the patient to do? (One answer)*

	All	Primary or less	Junior high	Senior high, technical	University	Difference: university-primary	Significance
Complain to the hospital administration	4	3	3	5	5	2	
Use connections to find another surgeon	10	6	10	11	20	14	***
Pay the surgeon extra money (*hong bao*)	4	3	4	6	4	1	
Go to a private hospital for better treatment	4	2	4	5	6	4	***
Change to another public hospital	27	20	31	31	23	4	
Ask the surgeon to take special care	4	4	5	4	6	1	
Undergo the operation at own risk	32	35	31	29	30	-5	*
Don't know	16	27	14	10	6	-20	***

Note: Significance of difference: * .05 level, *** .001 level.
Source: Performance Evaluations, Trust and Utilization of Health Care in China Survey, 2012–13. Funded by the UK Economic and Social Research Council, Grant No. ES/J011487/1. Fieldwork 1 November 2012–17 January 2013, N=3,680.

Strategy to deal with over-prescription: tabulation by education (% respondents)

Q. *What would you advise your friend to do if the doctor at a public hospital prescribes a lot of expensive medication which is not covered by insurance even when cheaper alternatives are available? (One answer)*

All		Primary or less	Junior high	Senior high, technical	University	Difference: university-primary	Significance
8	Complain to the hospital administration	5	8	9	12	7	***
6	Use connections to find another doctor	3	6	6	11	7	***
2	Pay the doctor extra money (*hong bao*)	2	3	2	2	0	
7	Go to a private hospital or pharmacy for the prescription	6	8	7	6	0	
13	Change to another public hospital	12	14	15	10	–2	
24	Ask the doctor to change the prescription	20	24	26	29	10	***
24	Buy the medicine prescribed by the doctor	25	24	23	21	–4	*
17	Don't know	27	14	11	8	–19	***

Note: Significance of difference: *. 05 level, ***. 001 level.

Source: Performance Evaluations, Trust and Utilization of Health Care in China Survey, 2012–13. Funded by the UK Economic and Social Research Council, Grant No. ES/J011487/1. Fieldwork 1 November 2012–17 January 2013, N=3,680.

Strategy to deal with unnecessary testing: tabulation by education (% respondents)

Q. *What would you advise your friend to do if he thinks doctors in a public hospital are requiring him to do unnecessary diagnostic tests?*
(One answer)

All		Primary or less	Junior high	Senior high, technical	University	Difference: university-primary	Significance
7	Complain to the hospital administration	5	7	9	10	5	***
6	Use connections to find another doctor	3	6	7	11	8	***
2	Pay the doctor extra money (*hong bao*)	1	2	2	2	1	
2	Go to a private hospital to get the tests done	2	3	2	2	0	
12	Change to another public hospital	11	12	14	10	-1	
20	Ask the doctor to keep the tests to the minimum	18	19	21	22	5	***
30	Do the tests recommended by the doctor	29	31	29	32	3	
16	Don't know	26	15	9	6	-20	***
6	Refuse the tests	6	6	7	4	-2	

Note: Significance of difference: *.05 level, **.01 level, ***.001 level.
Source: Performance Evaluations, Trust and Utilization of Health Care in China Survey, 2012–13. Funded by the UK Economic and Social Research Council, Grant No. ES/J01487/1. Fieldwork 1 November 2012–17 January 2013, N=3,680.

APPENDIX TABLE 16

Strategy to deal with a surgeon: mean incomes

Q.   *If your friend needed a life-saving operation but the surgeon in a public hospital told them that he could not guarantee that the operation would be successful, what would you advise the patient to do? (One answer)*

All (%)		Mean household income[1]	Difference from mode (undergo operation)	
		(Yuan 000s)		Significance[2]
4	Complain to the hospital administration	61.3	14.5	**
10	Use connections to find another surgeon	67.7	20.9	***
4	Pay the surgeon extra money (*hong bao*)	63.3	16.5	*
4	Go to a private hospital for better treatment	85.8	39.0	
27	Change to another public hospital	56.0	9.2	***
4	Ask the surgeon to take special care	64.2	17.5	**
32	Undergo the operation at own risk	46.8	0	--
16	Don't know	44.4	-2.3	

Notes:

1   Includes imputed incomes for the 26.3 percent of households not reporting their income. Means are calculated by pooling five imputations based on education of the respondent and the maximum amount of money which the respondent thinks his/her household could access in an emergency.

2   Independent samples t-test comparing the mean income in each category to the modal category of "undergo the operation at own risk": * significant at .05 level, ** .01 level, *** .001 level.

Source: Performance Evaluations, Trust and Utilization of Health Care in China Survey, 2012–13. Funded by the UK Economic and Social Research Council, Grant No. ES/J011487/1. Fieldwork 1 November 2012–17 January 2013, N=3,680.

APPENDIX TABLE 17

Strategy to deal with over-prescription: mean incomes

Q. *What would you advise your friend to do if the doctor at a public hospital prescribes a lot of expensive medication which is not covered by insurance even when cheaper alternatives are available? (One answer)*

All (%)		Mean household income[1]	Difference from mode (buy the medicine)	Significance[2]
		(Yuan 000s)		
8	Complain to the hospital administration	68.6	20.0	***
6	Use connections to find another doctor	66.1	17.5	***
2	Pay the doctor extra money (*hong bao*)	56.1	7.5	
7	Go to a private hospital or pharmacy for the prescription	67.5	19.0	
13	Change to another public hospital	53.9	5.3	
24	Ask the doctor to change the prescription	57.1	8.5	***
24	Buy the medicine prescribed by the doctor	48.6	0	–
17	Don't know	43.7	−4.9	

Notes:
1 Includes imputed incomes for the 26.3 percent of households not reporting their income. Means are calculated by pooling five imputations based on education of the respondent and the maximum amount of money which the respondent thinks his/her household could access in an emergency
2 Independent samples t-test comparing the mean income in each category to the modal category of "buy the medicines prescribed by the doctor": * significant at .05 level, ** .01 level, *** .001 level.
Source: Performance Evaluations, Trust and Utilization of Health Care in China Survey, 2012–13. Funded by the UK Economic and Social Research Council, Grant No. ES/J011487/1. Fieldwork 1 November 2012–17 January 2013, N=3,680.

APPENDIX TABLE 18

Strategy to deal with unnecessary testing: mean incomes

Q. *What would you advise your friend to do if he thinks doctors in a public hospital are requiring him to do unnecessary diagnostic tests? (One answer)*

All (%)		Mean household income[1]	Difference from mode (do the tests)	Significance[2]
		(Yuan 000s)		
7	Complain to the hospital administration	73.9	22.2	**
6	Use connections to find another doctor	67.8	16.0	*
2	Pay the doctor extra money (*hong bao*)	57.7	5.9	
2	Go to a private hospital to get the tests done	59.6	7.9	
12	Change to another public hospital	53.3	1.5	
20	Ask the doctor to keep the tests to the minimum	57.2	5.4	
30	Do the tests recommended by the doctor	51.8	0	–
16	Don't know	43.9	–7.9	
6	Refuse the tests	52.7	0.9	

Notes:

1 Includes imputed incomes for the 26.3 percent of households not reporting their income. Means are calculated by pooling five imputations based on education of the respondent and the maximum amount of money which the respondent thinks his/her household could access in an emergency.

2 Independent samples t-test comparing the mean income in each category to the modal category of "do the tests recommended by the doctor": * significant at .05 level, ** .01 level, *** .001 level.

Source: Performance Evaluations, Trust and Utilization of Health Care in China Survey, 2012–13. Funded by the UK Economic and Social Research Council, Grant No. ES/J011487/1. Fieldwork 1 November 2012–17 January 2013, N=3,680.

NOTES

1　When we refer to "exit," we do not necessarily refer to the use of private health care providers in place of public ones, since publicly owned providers can also be induced to compete in markets. Even changing doctors within one hospital can count as "exit" in this sense.

2　https://sdgs.un.org/goals/goal16.

3　As an example of Confucian reasoning, Fan (2007, 120) paraphrases Mencius as follows: "When a student challenged Mencius concerning whether a gentleman could live a luxurious life, Mencius replied: if there not be a proper ground for taking it, a single bowl of rice may not be received; if there be such a proper ground, receiving all-under-Heaven is not to be considered excessive." See also Lee 2002.

4　Although there are no published statistics, officials typically claim that direct government investment in public hospitals accounts for only around 10 percent of their revenue. See, for example, the interview with a deputy health minister reported in Sina Weibo (2012).

5　Performance Evaluations, Trust and Utilization of Health Care in China Survey, 2012–13, funded by the UK Economic and Social Research Council, Grant No. ES/J011487/1. More information at http://www.gla.ac.uk/petu.

Global Markets in Medicine
Japan's Health Care Service Exports to Singapore and India

HIROYUKI KOJIN

The global medical market has been growing steadily for the past two decades since 2000. The size of the global medical market was about JPY 520 trillion in 2010, with medical services accounting for about JPY 430 trillion (HID 2013). The United Nations Sustainable Development Goals (SDG) agenda, as noted in the Introduction to this book, seeks to "respect each country's policy space and leadership ... domestic public resources, domestic and international private business and finance, international development cooperation, international trade as an engine for development, debt and debt sustainability" (United Nations 2015). Underlying this agenda is the embrace of the belief that the global medical market and trade liberalization can advance global health security. SDG 9 includes the following target: "Develop quality, reliable, sustainable and resilient infrastructure, including regional and transborder infrastructure, to support economic development and human well-being."[1] One of the targets for SDG 3 is to "substantially increase health financing and the recruitment, development, training and retention of the health workforce in developing countries."[2]

Within this context, Japan's Revitalization Strategy, approved by the Cabinet in 2013, identified the health and longevity industry as one of the strategic sectors and an essential pillar for revival of the Japanese economy through the promotion of "inbound" and "outbound" medical and nursing care services, the former referring to the enhancement of systems for medical tourism for the Japanese public and acceptance of medical professionals from abroad, and the latter referring to the export of Japanese-style health care services and medical instruments overseas (Cabinet of Japan 2014). Ideas for global outreach include development of human resources such as doctors and nurses for other countries; promotion of support for establishing public health care insurance systems and use of private insurance; maximum use of Medical Excellence JAPAN (MEJ) to expand medical business, for example, by building hubs for deployment of Japanese medical technologies and services and to promote global public-private clinical research and clinical trials; and programs to simplify the process of approving Japan-approved pharmaceuticals and medical devices in other countries. In addition, support needed for active export of nursing care staff overseas is also being taken up through dialogue with other governments on measures to address the greying of the population (Cabinet of Japan 2014).

In 2013, Japan had the highest life expectancy in the world for women (87 years) and sixth-highest for men (80 years), making it the country with the highest total longevity in the world, at 84 years (WHO 2015). The infant mortality rate was also the lowest in the world. One reason for these record longevity and mortality rates is the excellent access to health care, backed by the universal health insurance system established in 1961, as discussed in Chapter 2. Open access to Japanese medical care is guaranteed under this social health care system, and there are systems in place to ensure the stable receipt of medical services, including state-of-the-art care. (The exception here is Japan's vaccination policy, as discussed in Chapter 5.) The existence of this public insurance system is also a great feature of Japan compared with other countries in terms of costs for medical care services. Specifically, the rise in medical care expenses in Japan in recent years accompanying the aging of its population is being kept from skyrocketing by official prices for health care service compensation, resulting in provision of such services at relatively lower costs than other Organisation for Economic Co-operation and Development (OECD) countries (OECD 2014). In addition, comparing the medical care system of Japan with that of other countries shows that Japan has a smaller number of doctors and nurses per hospital bed, resulting in a relatively less expensive and more effective system. Exporting Japan's health care services and health care system with the above strengths as a package together with Japanese medical instruments and pharmaceuticals is therefore one new growth strategy under Japan's Revitalization Strategy.

In response to these national initiatives, more and more private medical institutions are launching and operating hospitals and clinics in other countries through partnerships with local health care corporations. Meanwhile, medical expenses in the Asia-Pacific (APAC) region have continued to spike and account for one-third of all health care expenditures worldwide (Frost and Sullivan 2014). At the same time, the number of health care professionals per 1,000 population in 2010 was estimated to be only 6.8 in the APAC region, compared with 18.9 in Europe and 24.8 in the United States, indicating a shortage in health care facilities and personnel in that region. There is predicted to be an ongoing rise in global advancement of Japanese health care organizations seeking new growth opportunities in the growing health care needs and greying of populations accompanying the development of economies in the Asia-Pacific region. At the same time, despite strong technological capabilities and economic power, health care organizations in Japan up to now have been limited by language barriers, it being a non-English-speaking country, and few actual cases of global advancement have been seen due to the lack of interchangeable medical licensing systems. Furthermore, opening and running hospitals overseas was not considered in Japan's medical service laws. Specifically, Article 7, paragraph 5 of the Medical Service Act prohibits the establishment of profit-oriented hospitals and clinics, and Article 54 stipulates that health care corporations must not receive dividends of surplus. Operation of hospitals as business corporations is therefore not allowed. The scale of health care organizations in Japan is thus smaller than that of health care groups running international hospitals and clinics, and this, together with the above factors, has resulted in only a very limited number of cases of overseas advancement by Japanese health care organizations. As regulations become more relaxed with the idea of promoting free trade, it is uncertain how the advancement of private Japanese health care organizations will affect trading partner countries and their health care organizations. In particular, the possibility cannot be dismissed that the pursuit of economic interests and expansion of hospitals to take advantage of economies of scale may have adverse effects because of human rights standards.

To determine the current state of global advancement of Japanese private health care institutions into other parts of Asia, we surveyed two medical institutions that agreed to participate in the study. We attempt to use this information to elucidate the globalization trends of Japanese health care services and the problems associated with global advancement and operation, to consider a future course of action and to determine the effects of globalization of Japanese health care services on human rights standards in

Asia. The two study participants were the Sakurajyuji Group, which began running a clinic for Japanese expatriates in Singapore as a joint venture with a local corporation in 2011, and Secom Medical System Company, which opened and began running a general hospital for residents in India as a joint venture with a local financial conglomerate and a Japanese corporation in 2013.

Secom Medical System Company is a part of Secom group, a Japanese company with a major business of security and crime prevention that is embarking on an international expansion in the medical field. Sakurajyuji is a medical business group that runs several hospitals throughout Japan.

For Singapore, we examine the extent of advancement in the local area of clinics for Japanese citizens and investigate the joint venture called Nippon Medical Care, which has been run by the Sakurajyuji Group since 2012. Overseas export of Japanese health care services has helped improve access to medical care and health management of Japanese expatriates. One area that needs to be examined is whether human rights standards, for example, concerning physical safety, freedom of individual movement, and the right to receive social security, are being satisfied. We also consider the effects of lateral support for corporate activity from one's home country in another country on the free trade system.

Next, we examine the situation in India, looking at the Sakra World Hospital, established in 2014 as a joint venture between a corporation that carries out hospital support activities in Japan, a Japanese trading company, and a financial group in India, and examine the advancement of a major hospital group owned by that hospital in Bangalore. An increase in the proportion of middle-income families in India has resulted in a shortage of private hospitals in urban areas, and advancement of the Sakra World hospital may help relieve problems of access to health care services. In addition, areas with hospitals are areas where Japanese companies such as Toyota Motor Corporation are present, and the fact that the presence of Japanese companies has been a foothold for the opening of hospitals applies to Singapore as well. However, the focus in India is on what considerations are being taken with respect to provision of health care services to economically disadvantaged local residents. We also discuss whether these activities can potentially help raise health care standards in India through education for nurses and other health care professionals, and fulfill human rights standards, including protection not only of the right to physical safety and social security but also of the right to receive an education.

Singapore: Nippon Medical Care

Medical Care for Japanese Expatriates in Singapore

Singapore has an area of about 720 square kilometres and about the same amount of land as the twenty-three special wards of Tokyo combined. Despite its small size, it is an economic powerhouse that ranks second on the Global Competitiveness Index, next to Switzerland (Schwab 2011). Singapore has had strong ties with Japan since its foundation, and relations between the two countries have been favourable, without any political concerns. Japan-Singapore exchange is carried out in a wide range of fields, and high-level visits take place. There were 27,525 Japanese expatriates living in Singapore as of November 2012, and 1,069 Japanese companies operating there, indicating a particularly strong potential demand for health care services for Japanese expatriates in Singapore compared with other ASEAN countries (Ministry of Foreign Affairs of Japan 2013).

The Japanese and Singaporean governments signed an Economic Partnership Agreement (EPA) in January 2002 that came into effect in November the same year. Although not regulated in General Agreement on Trade in Services (GATS) cross-border trade Mode 4, an oral agreement was made at the time of the signing to carry out exchange between the two countries, and Singapore agreed to an interchangeable medical licensing system for doctors and nurses with the condition that their services would be limited to Japanese expatriates (Multilateral Trade System Department 2007). The upper limit was raised in 2005, and as of 2022, thirty doctors and fifteen dentists have been approved under this system.

Seven clinics for Japanese expatriates have been established in Singapore as of 2015.[3] They are mostly outpatient clinics, and patients requiring surgical procedures or in-patient care are sent to hospitals of local partner corporations. Treatment is mostly carried out by doctors who have obtained a medical or dental licence based on the interchangeable medical licensing system, and some corporations also hire doctors with a medical licence from Singapore.

Survey on the Global Advancement of Clinics Catering to Japanese Expatriates in Singapore

The Sakurajyuji Group, which runs Nippon Medical Care as a joint venture with a local corporation, agreed to participate in a survey to examine the overseas advancement of clinics catering to Japanese expatriates in

Singapore. The survey involved semi-structured interviews with executives
of the corporation who know the details of overseas advancement. The interview questions were divided into four categories:

• Questions about circumstances leading up to establishment, including
  the catalyst for global advancement, the philosophies and objectives of
  Sakurajyuji toward global advancement, the presence and details of joint
  ventures (including investment ratio), the length of preparation time before advancement, any regulatory problems that arose during advancement, the circumstances during advancement, and the current state of
  the local corporation
• Questions about the local medical corporation, including the establishment, corporation name, relationship with Japanese corporations, management organization, number of patients, types of departments, number of
  staff, types of intended patients, health insurance system and cost of services in the local country, advantages of the established clinics, and the
  use of medical instruments from Japan
• Questions about conditions after establishment in the local country, including progress of initial expectations, changes after establishment, use
  of Japanese-style management, education for local staff, training circumstances, earnings, positive and negative impact on the Japanese corporation with global advancement, problems encountered during global
  advancement, and hardships faced
• Questions about other topics, such as merits and advantages of global
  advancement for the Japanese medical corporation, positive and negative
  impact on local medical corporations and systems, and other relevant
  questions.

Advancement of a Clinic Run as a Joint Venture with a Local
Medical Corporation: Nippon Medical Care

Nippon Medical Care was acquired in 2012 as a joint venture between
Parkway Pantai, which is part of Parkway Shenton, a local corporation in
Singapore, a number of medical corporations in Japan, and the Sakurajyuji
Group, which runs nursing care and other facilities in Japan. Parkway Pantai
is one of the region's largest integrated private health care groups, with a
network of twenty-two hospitals and more than 4,000 beds throughout
Asia, including Singapore, Malaysia, Brunei, India, China, and Vietnam.[4]
In Singapore, Parkway Pantai is the largest private health care provider

and operates Mount Elizabeth Novena Hospital, Mount Elizabeth Hospital, Gleneagles Hospital, and Parkway East Hospital – all accredited by Joint Commission International (JCI). Over 1,400 specialist doctors are credentialed to admit patients to the four hospitals. The Sakurajyuji Group has three hospitals, three clinics, and one health-check centre, and also provides services such as group homes for older adults and home visit medical and nursing care services. Nippon Medical Care is located within Gleneagles Hospital, and is run by three doctors with medical licences from Japan and one doctor with a medical licence from Singapore.

Nippon Medical Care was taken over from a Japanese-affiliated company in 2012 by the Sakurajyuji Group, which began running it as a joint venture. This transfer of management was made possible by the favourable interpersonal relationship between the transferring Japanese-affiliated company and the Sakurajyuji Group. Sakurajyuji put in 30% of the investment and Parkway Pantai 70% to manage Nippon Medical Care. The intended patient base for the clinic comprises employees of Japanese companies carrying out local operations, and the clinic provides general outpatient care and health check ups using the Gleneagles Hospital facilities. Patients requiring surgical procedures or specialist care that cannot be covered at the clinic are referred to Gleneagles Hospital and provided with support for the doctor's visit with a Japanese-language liaison desk.[5]

The clinic receives about thirty outpatient visits a day, including individuals coming for a health check-up based on contracts with companies. Japanese doctors are essential for increasing the scale of the clinic and adding new departments, but there are many competing clinics, and there are more Japanese doctors requesting registration than the upper limit under the interchangeable medical licensing system. Indeed, there is often a waiting list for approval from the Singapore government. Even though there are doctors willing to move to Singapore to work, the clinic is unable to accept them, and this is a great management hurdle. As for nurses, there is no upper limit to the number of staff, but nurses from Japan are not recognized as having a nursing licence in Singapore, and the clinic must hire local staff in addition to Japanese staff. At the time of the survey, the clinic had one Japanese nurse, who also provided interpretation services, and one pharmacist, in addition to the doctor, and had a Japanese administrative employee dispatched from the Sakurajyuji Group to take on managerial work. At the time of the survey, Nippon Medical Care was not providing education or training to local staff.

Advancing into Singapore, which is a member of the Association of Southeast Asian Nations (ASEAN), is the first step to advancing into other growing ASEAN countries, and the corporate image can be expected to improve with global expansion for the Sakurajyuji Group as well. Also, as the older population is expected to grow in ASEAN countries similar to Japan, the experience with Nippon Medical Care may pave the way for global export in the field of long-term care, and there is also potential for expanding the scope of Japanese-style nursing care services to include non-Japanese Singapore residents. There are some challenges, however: Singapore has a different cultural background than Japan (for example, maids are common) and, unlike in Japan, there is no long-term care insurance system.

The clinic may be a potential stepping stone for bringing nurses and professional caregivers to Japan in the future, but Japan's skill training system for foreigners does not currently list health care and long-term care workers among its sixty-nine professions, and foreign nurses and care workers are currently accepted only from Indonesia, the Philippines, and Vietnam under Economic Partnership Agreements (Ministry of Health, Labour and Welfare 2015). Importation of health care staff from Singapore is therefore not likely for the time being, and will likely be considered only once successful advancement of Japanese organizations into ASEAN countries has taken place.

There are nearly 30,000 Japanese citizens living in Singapore, including those who have not submitted a residence report, and health check ups by Japanese doctors may help quell their anxiety. Seamless health management is also possible because of an environment that encourages health check ups, similar to the situation in Japan. On the other hand, the export of Japanese-style health care has only a limited potential at the moment, which remains the case today, as the qualification system is the same as it was then. because of the upper limit of the interchangeable medical licensing system, which makes it difficult to procure a sufficient number of Japanese doctors, and the lack of a mutual licensing system for nurses and other professionals. Moreover, examinations from Japanese doctors at the clinic are limited to Japanese citizens, and provision of health care services to Singaporeans is restricted.

India: Sakra World Hospital

Health Care Situation in India
India has a total land area of 3,287,469 square kilometres, making it the largest country in South Asia. Spread far to the north and south, its climate

and environmental conditions vary greatly by region. It has a population of 1.21057 billion (2011 national census), second in the world only to the People's Republic of China, and has a population growth rate of 17.68%, with a low mean age, with those under twenty-five accounting for over half the population. The population is expected to surpass that of China by around 2030, and it has considerable growth potential.

Japan is India's largest economic aid donor, and historically there has always been a strong affinity toward Japan in India. Economic ties between the two countries continue to strengthen; as of 2013, there were 1,072 Japanese companies across India, with 2,542 offices and factories (Japan External Trade Organization 2021). Of those, about 300, including Toyota Motor Corporation (about 12%), are in Bangalore, the third-largest city in India, located in the south. The area is known as the "Silicon Valley of India" for its thriving information technology industry, and has deep relations with Japanese companies as a result. Because of its location on a plateau, the climate is somewhat cooler than in the rest of India, making it the most desirable place in India for Japanese people to live.

Private general hospitals equipped with the latest medical instruments and clean private rooms have been opening in urban areas of India, including Bangalore, and the standards of medical instruments and outpatient doctors at these urban private general hospitals are generally on par with those of developed countries (Table 9.1). On the other hand, it would be difficult to describe the care provided by nurses, ward assistants, medical technologists, and other medical care staff as being oriented toward general patients as is commonplace in Japan; many hospitals have vertically divided departments, so that patients must complete reception and payment separately for doctor's examinations, blood tests, X-rays, and the pharmacy, for example, and patients may even need a second doctor's visit to receive test results. A number of hospitals have been opened in Bangalore by several major hospital groups, and medical tourism from other countries is readily accepted.

Survey of Global Advancement of Japanese Medical Organizations in Bangalore

In March 2014, Secom Medical System Company and Toyota Tsusho Corporation from Japan and the Kirloskar Group in India jointly formed Takshasila Hospitals Operating Private Limited, which opened the first general hospital in India to be jointly run by Japanese and local companies, in Bangalore, located in the state of Karnataka in the southwestern part of

TABLE 9.1

Major private general hospitals in Bangalore

Group	Hospital	Number of beds
Secom Medical System Company	Sakra World Hospital	294
Columbia Asia	Columbia Asia Hospital, Whitefield	153
	Columbia Asia Referral Hospital, Yeshwanthpur	200
	Columbia Asia Hospital, Hebbal	90
Apollo Hospital	Indraprastha Apollo Hospital	250
Manipal Education and Medical	Manipal Hospital	650
Fortis Healthcare Limited	Fortis Hospital, Bannerghatta Road	400
	Fortis Hospital, Cunningham Road	150
	Fortis Network Hospital, Seshadripuram	75
	Fortis Hospital, Nagarbhavi	70
	Fortis Hospital, Rajajinagar	50

Source: https://www.sakraworldhospital.com/., https://www.mofa.go.jp/mofaj/toko/medi/asia/india.html., https://www.bangalore-nihonjinkai.com/., http://www.fortishealthcare.com/., https://www.columbiaasia.com/.

South India.[6] For this study, Secom agreed to cooperate with a survey about this hospital in order to clarify the details of the advancement of a Japanese medical institution into India. The survey consisted of a semi-structured interview with the Secom CEO, who knew the details behind the opening of this hospital. The interview questions and categories were the same as those of the interview regarding Singapore. The survey was conducted in Tokyo in December 2014.

Advancement of Secom Medical System into India: Sakra World Hospital

The Sakra World Hospital is a general hospital that was opened by a local corporation jointly owned by Secom Medical System Company and Toyota Tsusho Corporation from Japan and the Kirloskar Group in India. It is the first in India to be jointly managed by Japanese and local companies. A medium-sized financial conglomerate, the Kirloskar Group also established a joint venture company with Toyota Motor Corporation in 1997. Its founder, Laxmanrao Kashinath Kirloskar, started out as a farm tool manufacturer in the nineteenth century, producing iron plows, and later established Kirloskar Brothers Limited as a medium-sized company. Today, the company manufactures motors, compressors, pumps, valves, and other parts with core segments of agriculture, water supply, electric power, and air conditioning, and has many export partners in Europe, North America, Asia, and Africa. Toyota Tsusho Corporation is the Toyota Group's general trading company. Under its management vision, titled "Global 2020 Vision," it is focusing on hospital and medical services and nursing care services as one strategic business domain in the "Life and Community" field with the goal of raising living environment conditions. Secom Medical System is a company in the Secom Company group, which was launched in 1962 as Japan's first security company. In addition to its home care and nursing care, outreach nursing care, and preventive care business, the company also provides hospital support to eighteen partner health care organizations in Japan.

These three companies launched Takshasila Hospitals Operating Private Limited in April 2012, which fully opened the Sakra World Hospital with a total of 294 beds in March 2014 in Bangalore. The hospital has six core centres (neurosciences, cardiac science, digestive science, orthopedics, renal and urological science, and woman and child health) and a general hospital with seventeen diagnosis and treatment departments (internal medicine, otorhinolaryngology, radiology, rheumatology, anesthesiology, endocrinology and diabetes, ophthalmology, psychiatry, dermatology, respiratory medicine, plastic and reconstructive surgery, emergency outpatient care, dentistry, rehabilitation, blood transfusion, nutrition, and clinical diagnostics). Unlike in Japan, there is no universal health insurance system in India, and the proportion of those insured by private insurance is low. Medical institutions are divided into two classes – private hospitals with advanced features mostly for upper-income and some middle-income patients, and public hospitals for the rest of the middle-income patients and the lower-income patients that comprise the majority of the population. The economic growth of India in recent years has led to growth of the middle class, and an increasing number of individuals are seeking a higher level of care at private hospitals. Similarly, as the standard of living has risen, there has been an increase in the rate of diabetes and other lifestyle diseases, and there is a demand for health care services developed in Japan in the style of advanced nations, such as health check ups, cancer screening, and diabetes management. In addition, treatment for car accidents, rehabilitation, perinatal care, nosocomial infection control measures, and other fields in which demand is increasing is still lacking in clinical practice in India. The Sakra World Hospital uses the experience of hospital support programs developed in Japan with the aim of providing Japanese-style health care services in India.

As there is no interchangeable medical licensing system for Japan and India, care at the Sakra World Hospital is provided solely by local doctors and nurses. While health care in India is provided by highly skilled doctors trained in Britain and the United States, India has problems similar to those of other Asian regions, such as a shortage of health care facilities, poor education for medical professionals, and low-quality health care service. Secom carries out a hospital support business in Japan and has eighteen partner medical institutions. The company utilizes resources from the group, such as highly specialized doctors and nurses who excel at medical safety, to dispatch medical professionals from Japan to other countries. The company is aiming to create hospitals that provide different services from regular hospitals in India, pursuing advanced hospital management, which includes education for doctors, nurses, and other staff, medical safety, infection control, and multidisciplinary health care services. Specifically, the critical path method for hospital management that has already been established in Japan is not yet commonplace in India. Secom therefore set out to export this system from Japan to standardize the quality of medical care, raise the credentials of nurses and paramedics, and build an environment that is conducive to multidisciplinary cooperation.

Another feature of the Sakra World Hospital is that it is not intended solely for wealthy patients; it aims to fulfill the needs of the local community, symbolized by the comment that they receive many patients who are barefoot. In order to achieve its commitment to providing "medical care that enhances the quality of human life," health care for low-income patients is also given priority.

A specific problem in India is that infrastructure development still lags behind that of other countries. Power outages are common even in urban areas such as Bangalore, and hospitals are not an exception. Cooperation between local medical staff and specialists sent from Japan is another challenge due to differences in cultural backgrounds. Furthermore, at the time of the survey, the hospital was only running at the developing stage with over 100 in-patients. However, Sakra World Hospital has since grown to a 350 in-patient hospital in cooperation with Japanese professional staff.

In this chapter, we discussed the Nippon Medical Care joint venture of the Sakurajyuji Group, and the Sakra World Hospital, which opened and began running a general hospital in 2013 for Indian residents as a joint venture with a local financial conglomerate and a Japanese corporation.

We determined that the joint venture business of Nippon Medical Care in Singapore was an example of overseas development of Japanese health care services aimed at supporting the health care access and health management of Japanese expatriates living abroad. Part III, Article 12, paragraph 1 of the International Covenant on Economic, Social and Cultural Rights (ICESCR) states, "The States Parties to the present Covenant recognize the right of everyone to the enjoyment of the highest attainable standard of physical and mental health."[7] Japan ratified this covenant in 1979. This means that not only citizens living in Japan but also those living abroad are entitled to receive safe and high-quality medical care to the extent attainable in the medical and health care fields when they become ill or injured and, at an earlier stage, to prevent them from becoming ill in the first place. That said, Japanese expatriates are living in countries where Japanese sovereignty does not directly apply, and this right becomes limited under the laws and regulations of the country where they reside. Systemized support from both governments, such as an interchangeable medical licensing system between Japan and the partner country, is therefore essential. In the case of Singapore and Japan, a good relationship has been built to achieve this goal. These points are essential for the advancement of free trade and may be one human rights priority issue that must be considered when Japanese private health care institutions advance into Singapore.

In the case of the Sakra World Hospital joint venture in India, hospital advancement has the potential to fill a niche, i.e., the provision of health care services in India, and the operation of the principles of competition could ensure better-quality health care services. In fact, a feature of the Sakra World Hospital is the provision of Japanese-style services to differentiate themselves from other hospital groups, aiming to spread the excellent aspects of Japanese health care provision systems, such as advanced health care technologies and team-based care, throughout India. In addition, areas with hospitals are areas where Japanese companies such as Toyota are present, and the fact that this has provided a foothold for opening hospitals applies similarly to Singapore. However, the provision of health care services by Sakra World Hospital to economically disadvantaged local residents distinguishes the Indian from the Singaporean case. The Narayana hospital in Bangalore has since 2004 provided poor individuals with primary health-care services, including doctor's visits through its clinic system (Khanna, Rangan, and Manocaran 2005). The Sakra World Hospital will also serve as a test for expanding hospital business to other areas of India. To achieve its commitment to providing "medical care that enhances the quality of human life," it has shown its consideration for human-rights standards, for example, by establishing a Sakra fund to give health care services to the poor and setting up an ethics consultation team. Also, one purpose of the Sakra World Hospital is to help raise health care standards in India through education for nurses and other health care professionals, and its activities may potentially fulfill human rights standards, including protection of not only the right to physical safety and social security but also the right to receive education.

Although the participants for of the survey was extremely limited in this study, we showed that overseas advancement of Japanese medical organizations can potentially improve health care services for Japanese expatriates and local residents yet are associated with critical challenges concerning the protection of social rights and civil liberties. This study focused only on medical organizations that are the providers of services, and a further survey is needed to examine the point of view from the perspective of Japanese expatriates and local residents who are on the receiving end. As global advancement of medical organizations from Japan progresses, such organizations may unintentionally may suffer due to changes in systems and the enforcement of new regulations in the partner country. In addition, any future studies should consider the implications of an outflow of human resources from Japan for the purposes of this global advancement. In addition, future studies should consider the implications of an outflow of human resources from Japan for the purposes of this global advancement.

NOTES

1 https://sdgs.un.org/goals/goal9.
2 https://sdgs.un.org/goals/goal3.
3 The seven clinics are Japan Green Clinic; Japanese Association Clinic, Singapore; Raffles Japanese Clinic; Nichii International Clinic; Nihon Premium Clinic; Healthway Japanese Medical Clinic; and Nippon Medical Care.
4 https://www.gleneaglesglobalhospitals.com/about-parkway-pantai.
5 https://www.nipponmedicalcare.com.sg/.
6 http://www.secom.co.jp/business/medical/international/.
7 https://www.ohchr.org/en/professionalinterest/pages/cescr.aspx.

References

Adams, J., and E. Hannum. 2005. "Children's Social Welfare in China, 1989–1997: Access to Health Insurance and Education." *China Quarterly,* 181: 100–21.

Aga Khan Development Network. 2018. *India: Social Cultural Economic.* https://www.akdn.org/sites/akdn/files/2018_02_akdn_in_india_-_brief_-_web.pdf.

Akin, J.S., W.H. Dow, P.M. Lance, and C.P.A. Loh. 2005. "Changes in Access to Health Care in China, 1989–1997." *Health Policy and Planning* 20 (2): 80–89.

Amon, J. 2010. "The Truth of China's Response to HIV/AIDS." *Los Angeles Times,* July 11. https://www.latimes.com/archives/la-xpm-2010-jul-11-la-oe-amon-china-hiv-20100710-story.html.

Amon, J., R. Pearshouse, J. Cohen, and R. Schleifer. 2013. "Compulsory Drug Detention Centers in China, Cambodia, Vietnam, and Laos: Health and Human Rights Abuses." *Health and Human Rights Journal* 15: 124–37.

Anonymous. 1993. 寻兴华同志在全国烟草工作会议上的总结讲话（摘要）[Summary of Xinghua Xun's speech during the National Tobacco Working Meeting]. April 1. Accessed 31 March 2017. http://www.echinatobacco.com/101588/102220/102455/102459/36131.html.

–. 2003. "Breaking Up Tobacco Monopoly." *Tobacco Journal International,* April 21. http://www.tobaccojournal.com/Breaking_up_tobacco_monopoly.X3113.0.html.

–. 2008. "Merger of Tobacco Giants Approved." *Tobacco Journal International,* November 2. http://www.tobaccojournal.com/Merger_of_tobacco_giants_approved.49303.0.html.

–. 2012. "Hongta Eyes Expansion into Russian Market through Donskoy Tie-up." *Tobacco Campaign,* June 27.

—. 2013a. 年烟草行业拓展国际市场工作会议在北京召开 [2013 tobacco industry working meeting on global market expansion held in Beijing]. Central People's Government of the People's Republic of China, December 23. http://www.gov.cn/gzdt/2013-12/23/content_2552890.htm.

—. 2013b. 从价格标榜到价值标杆: 高端品牌的成长解构与发展预期 [From price to value: the growth and development outlook on luxury brands]. *Tobacco China,* November 23. Accessed 31 March 2017. http://www.tobaccochina.com/news/analysis/wu/201311/20131119154531_595262.shtml.

—. 2014. 中国卷烟品牌市场竞争分析 [Analysis of market competitiveness of Chinese cigarette brands]. *Tobacco Market,* August 6. Accessed 31 March 2017. http://www.etmoc.com/market/looklist.asp?id=31733.

Arcuri, A. 2014. *The Coproduction of the Global Regulatory Regime for Food Safety Standards and the Limits of a Technocratic Ethos.* Robert Schuman Centre for Advanced Studies Working Paper. Florence: European University Institute.

Ashokan, A. 2010. "Self-Reported Morbidity, Inpatient and Outpatient Care and Utilisation of Health Care Services in Rural Kasaragod, Kerala." PhD diss., Pondicherry University, Puduherry, India. http://hdl.handle.net/10603/892.

AT Kearney. 2012. *China's Pharmaceutical Distribution: Poised for Change.* Beijing, CN: AT Kearney Ideas and Insights.

Bai, J. 2014. Jiejue hao yisheng daiyu shi yingzhibiao, 解决好医生待遇是硬指标 [Improve doctors' remuneration is a fixed target], *Renmin wang* [*People.cn*]. http://politics.people.com.cn/n/2014/0409/c1001-24853175.html.

Baldwin, P. 1999. *Contagion and the State in Europe, 1830–1930.* Cambridge: Cambridge University Press.

—. 2021. *Fighting the First Wave: Why the Coronavirus Was Tackled So Differently Across the Globe.* New York, NY: Cambridge University Press.

Baru, R., A. Acharya, S. Acharya, A.K. Kumar, and J.K. Nagaraj. 2010. "Inequities in Access to Health Services in India: Caste, Class and Region." *Economic and Political Weekly* 45 (38): 49–58.

BAT (British American Tobacco). 1999. "Difficulties Encountered in Economic Development of Yunnan Province." May 18. Truth Tobacco Industry Documents, http://legacy.library.ucsf.edu/tid/yjk23a99/pdf.

—. 2013. "CTBAT International Limited Has Officially Commenced Business Operations." August 30. http://www.bat.com/group/sites/UK__9D9KCY.nsf/vwPagesWebLive/DO9B3BUY?opendocument.

Bhagwati, J.N., and A. Panagariya. 2013. *Why Growth Matters: How Economic Growth in India Reduced Poverty and the Lessons for Other Developing Countries.* Illustrated edition. New York: PublicAffairs.

Benedict, C. 2011. *Golden-Silk Smoke: A History of Tobacco in China.* Berkeley: University of California Press.

Bettcher, Douglas. 2010. "China's Global Adult Tobacco Survey and Its Global Context." Beijing, CN: WHO speech in Shenzhen, China, August 17. Accessed 24 January 2018.

Bhanot, D. "Revisiting Ayushman Bharat Scheme: Win-Win or Win-Lose?" *Forbes India.* https://www.forbesindia.com/article/bharatiya-vidya-bhavan039s-spjimr/revisiting-ayushman-bharat-scheme-winwin-or-winlose/68583/1.

Bhat, R., and N. Jain. 2004. "Analysis of Public Expenditure on Health Using State Level Data." Indian Institute of Management Ahmedabad, June 8. http://www. iimahd.ernet.in/publications/data/2004–06–08rbhat.pdf.

Bhat, S., and S. Mitter. 2014. "Budget Landmarks in Post-Liberalisation India." *Forbes India,* July 9. http://forbesindia.com/article/checkin/budget-landmarks-in-post liberalisation-india/38160/1.

Biddulph, S. 2007. *Legal Reform and Administrative Detention Powers in China.* Cambridge: Cambridge University Press.

–. 2015. *The Stability Imperative: Human Rights and Law in China.* Vancouver: UBC Press.

–. 2016. "What to Make of the Abolition of Re-education through Labour?" In *Legal Reforms and the Deprivation of Liberty in China,* edited by Elissa Nesossi, Sarah Biddulph, Flora Sapio, and Susan Trevaskes, 23–42. London: Routledge.

Biddulph, S., and C. Xie. 2011. "Regulating Drug Dependency in China: The 2008 Drug Prohibition Law." *British Journal of Criminology* 51: 978–96.

Bloomberg News. 2012. "China's Tobacco Monopoly Bigger by Profit Than HSBC." March 6. http://www.bloomberg.com/news/2012–03–06/china-s-tobacco -monopoly-bigger-by-profit-than-hsbc.html.

BlueWeave Consulting and Research. "India Health Insurance Market Showing Pro-lific Growth: Forecast to Grow at a CAGR of 10.1% by 2027." https://www. globenewswire.com/news-release/2022/01/25/2372819/0/en/India-Health -Insurance-Market-Showing-Prolific-Growth-Forecast-to-Grow-at-a-CAGR -of-10–1-by-2027-BlueWeave.html.

British Medical Journal. 2020. "Covid-19: India Should Abandon Lockdown and Refocus Its Testing Policy, Say Public Health Specialists." *British Medical Journal* 370: m3422. doi: https://doi.org/10.1136/bmj.m3422.

Brown, A. 2013. "Growth and Success in Kerala." *Yale Review of International Studies,* November. http://yris.yira.org/essays/1150.

Buchanan, A. 1988. "Principal/Agent Theory and Decision-Making in Health Care." *Bioethics* 2 (4): 317–33.

Burkitt, L. 2014. "China Scraps Price Caps on Low-Cost Drugs." *Wall Street Journal,* May 8. http://online.wsj.com/news/articles/SB10001424052702304655304579548933340544044.

Cabinet of Japan. 2014. "Japan's Revitalization Strategy." June 24. In Japanese. http://www.kantei.go.jp/jp/singi/keizaisaisei/pdf/honbun2JP.pdf.

CAC (Codex Alimentarius Commission). 2006. *Understanding the Codex Alimen-tarius.* 3rd ed. Geneva/Rome: World Health Organization/Food and Agriculture Organization.

CCPIT (China Council for the Promotion of International Trade). 2007. 我国"走出去"战略的形成 [Formation of China's "Go Global" strategy]. March 6. Accessed 31 March 2017. http://oldwww.ccpit.org/Contents/Channel_1276/2007/0327/30814/content_30814.htm.

CDC (Centers for Disease Control and Prevention). 2012. "Smoking & Tobacco Use – Fast Facts." http://www.cdc.gov/tobacco/data_statistics/fact_sheets/fast_facts/.

CDC-VFC (Centers for Disease Control and Prevention – Vaccines for Children). 2015. "Archived Vaccine Price List as of February 24, 2015." Atlanta, GA.

CDSCO (Central Drugs Standard Control Organization). 2014. "Functions: Central Drugs Standard Control Organization." Government of India, Ministry of Health and Family Welfare. New Delhi, IN.

Chan, C.K., K.L. Ngok, and D. Phillips. 2008. *Social Policy in China: Development and Wellbeing*. Bristol, UK: Policy Press.

Chao Ma, Z.S., and Q. Zong. 2021. "Urban-Rural Inequality of Opportunity in Health Care: Evidence from China." *International Journal of Environmental Research and Public Health* 18: 7792.

Charnovitz, S. 2007. "Article 1 and Annex A SPS." In *WTO – Technical Barriers and SPS Measures*, vol. 3, edited by R. Wolfrum, P. Stoll, and A. Seibert-Fohr, 75–391. Leiden: Brill.

Chauhan, C. 2014. "'Modicare' to Introduce Free Medicine, Health Insurance for Citizens." *Hindustan Times* (New Delhi), November 5. https://www.hindustan times.com/india/modicare-to-introduce-free-medicine-health-insurance-for -citizens/story-Q3n3iNR8OLiwHIls4gQ7yK.html.

Chen, X., and H. Zhao. 2014. Anhui xian gongli yiyuan gaige, 安徽县公立医院改革 [Reforms at the county-level Public Hospitals in Anhui]. *Fazhi zhoumo [Legal Weekly]*. http://www.legalweekly.cn/index.php/Index/article/id/4952.

China Daily. 2018. "Drug Abuse: How China Is Fighting the Problem." June 26. https://www.chinadaily.com.cn/a/201806/26/WS5b31e428a3103349141 dee03_5.html.

China News. 2013. "Quanguo jiben yaowu jiage pingjun xiajiang 30%" 全国基本药物价格平均下降30% [National essential drug price reduced by 30% average]. March 14. http://www.chinanews.com/gn/2013/03–14/4644642.shtml.

–. 2014. 国家烟草专卖局局长谈 "禁烟令": 高端烟价位下降 [STMA director on smoking ban: declining prices of luxury brands]. *Tobacco Market,* March 6. Accessed 31 March 2017. http://www.etmoc.com/gedi/gedilist.asp?news_id=62289.

China Tobacco. N.d. 中国烟草行业概况 [Profile of the Chinese tobacco industry]. Accessed 31 March 2017. http://www.tobacco.gov.cn/html/10/1004.html.

China Tobacco Industrial Corporation (CTI). 2014a. 境外卷烟产销基地建设季报 (第三期) [Establishing offshore cigarette production bases: quarterly report (third issue)]. Accessed 31 March 2017. http://www.cntiegc.com/src/ewebeditor/ uploadfile/20141023075648497.pdf.

–. 2014b. 境外卷烟产销基地建设季报 (第二期) [Establishing offshore cigarette produc- tion bases: quarterly report (second issue)]. Accessed 31 March 2017. http:// www.cntiegc.com/src/2014–08/10006913.jsp?purview=1,2,3.

–. 2014c. 境外卷烟产销基地建设季报（第四期） [Establishing offshore cigarette produc- tion bases: quarterly report (fourth issue)]. Accessed 31 March 2017. http:// www.cntiegc.com/src/ewebeditor/uploadfile/20150122102319140.pdf.

Covington and Burling LLP. 2014. "Chinese Government Ministries Issue Opinion on Implementing Pharmaceutical Reform." http://www.cov.com/files/Publication/ 9ee0ba08-390b-44e5-8b71-44358d297478/Presentation/Publication Attachment/49f20829-2e53-4510-aa0d-5f90e127e654/Chinese_Government_ Ministries_Issue_Opinion_On_Implementing_Pharmaceutical_Reform.pdf.

Crow, M. 2004. "Smokescreens and State Responsibility: Using Human Rights Strategies to Promote Global Tobacco Control." *Yale Journal of International Law* 29: 209–50.

CTIEC (China Tobacco International Europe Company). N.d. 中烟国际欧洲有限公司 [China Tobacco International Europe Company]. Accessed 31 March 2017. http://www.ctiec.cc/Default-1.aspx.

CUTS (CUTS Centre for Competition, Investment and Economic Regulation). 2006. *Options for Using Competition Law/Policy Tools in Dealing with Anti-Competitive Practices in the Pharmaceutical Industry and the Health Delivery System.* Report prepared for World Health Organization, Office of the WHO Representative to India, and Ministry of Health and Family Welfare, Government of India. New Delhi, IN: World Health Organization.

–. 2013. "Regulatory Framework and Challenges in Indian Pharmaceutical Sector." CUTS Discussion Paper. Accessed 28 January 2018. http://www.cuts-ccier.org/pdf/Regulatory_Framework_and_Challenges_in_Indian_Pharmaceutical_Sector.pdf.

Das Gupta, M., B.R. Desikachari, T.V. Somanathan, and P. Padmanaban. 2009. "How to Improve Public Health Systems: Lessons from Tamil Nadu." World Bank Policy Research Working Paper 5073.

Datta, D. 2018. "Modicare: Will It Work?" *India Today,* February 9. https://www.indiatoday.in/magazine/cover-story/story/20180219-budget-2018-national-healthcare-scheme-modi-care-jaitley-1166257-2018-02-09.

Deloitte. 2011. "The Next Phase: Opportunities in China's Pharmaceutical Market." *National Industry Practice Report.* https://www2.deloitte.com/ch/en/pages/life-sciences-and-healthcare/articles/opportunities-in-chinas-pharmaceutical-markets.html.

–. 2013. Corruption Risk in the Chinese Pharmaceutical Market. *Deloitte Touche Tohmatsu Certified Public Accountants LLP.* https://kipdf.com/deloitte-forensic-china-corruption-risk-in-the-chinese-pharmaceutical-market_5ae3283d7f8b9acb0a8b45f0.html.

Dian Luo, Jing Deng, and Edmund R. Becker. 2021. "Urban-Rural Differences in Healthcare Utilization among Beneficiaries in China's New Cooperative Medical Scheme." *BMC Public Health* 21 (1): 1519–19.

DiFranceisco, W., and Z. Gitelman. 1984. "Soviet Political Culture and Covert Participation in Policy Implementation." *American Political Science Review* 78 (3): 603–21.

Ding, X. 2006. 中国正积极实施"烟草控制框架公约" [China is actively implementing the FCTC]. February 8. http://www.npc.gov.cn/npc/xinwen/fztd/fzsh/2006-02/08/content_344513.htm.

Ding, W., and X. Huang. 2010. Hunan zhili "yaojia xugao," poti jiben yaowu zhidu gaige, 湖南治理 "药价虚高" 破题基本药物制度改革 [Hunan Deals with Inflated Drug Price]. *Xinhua wang [Xinhua net].* http://news.xinhuanet.com/2010-04/12/c_1228512.htm.

Docherty, M., Q. Cao, and H. Wang. 2012. "Social Values and Health Priority Setting in China." *Journal of Health Organization and Management* 26 (3): 351–62.

Döring, O. 2002. "Ethics Education in Medicine and Moral Preaching: Reflections on a Triangular Relationship and Its Human Core." In *Ethics in Medical Education in China: Distinguishing Education of Ethics in Medicine from Moral Preaching*, edited by O. Döring, 75–85. Hamburg: IFA.

Downes, Chris. 2015. "Worth Shopping Around? Defending Regulatory Autonomy under the SPS and the TBT Agreements." *World Trade Review* 14 (4): 1–25.

Drache, D., and L. Jacobs. 2014. *Linking Global Trade and Human Rights: New Policy Space in Hard Economic Times*. New York: Cambridge University Press.

–. 2018. *Grey Zones in International Economic Law and Global Governance*. Vancouver: UBC Press.

Drahos, P. 2008. "'Trust Me': Patent Offices in Developing Countries." *American Journal of Law and Medicine* 34 (2/3): 151–74.

Dresler, Carolyn, and Stephen Marks. 2006. "The Emerging Human Right to Tobacco Control." *Human Rights Quarterly* 28: 599–651.

Drèze, J., and A. Sen. 2013. *An Uncertain Glory: India and Its Contradictions*. Princeton, NJ: Princeton University Press.

Duckett, J., N. Munro, M.A. Sutton, and K. Hunt. 2020. "China National Health Attitudes Survey 2012–13 [Data Collection]." Colchester, Essex: UK Data Archive. 10.5255/UKDA-SN-852091.

Dukes, M.N.G., F.M. Haaijer-Ruskamp, C.P. de Joncheere, and A.H. Rietveld, eds. 2003. *Drugs and Money – Prices, Affordability and Cost Containment*. 7th ed. Amsterdam: IOS Press.

EC – Hormones 1998. Appellate Body Report, European Communities – Measures Concerning Meat and Meat Products, WT/DS26/AB/R, WT/DS48/AB/R, January 16.

Economist. 2014a. "The Cost of Medicine: Physician, Heal Thyself." February 1. http://www.economist.com/news/china/21595431-medicines-are-over-prescribed-and-overpriced-physician-heal-thyself.

–. 2014b. "An Irresistible Urge to Merge." July 19. http://www.economist.com/news/business/21607827-big-american-deal-has-global-implications-irresistible-urge-merge.

–. 2015. "The Gujarat Model: How Modi-Nomics Was Forged in One of India's Most Business-Friendly States." January 8. http://www.economist.com/news/finance-and-economics/21638147-how-modi-nomics-was-forged-one-indias-most-business-friendly-states.

Eggleston, K., L. Li, Q. Meng, M. Lindelow, and A. Wagstaff. 2008. "Health Service Delivery in China: A Literature Review." *Health Economics* 17 (2): 149–65.

EuroMonitor International. 2008. "China Targets Global Expansion via Acquisition and Flagship Brands." November 20. https://www.euromonitor.com/.

–. 2013. "Cigarettes in China." October. https://www.euromonitor.com/.

–. 2015. "Cigarettes in China." August. https://www.euromonitor.com/.

Falcaro, M., A. Castagnon, N. Busani, M. Checchi, K. Soldan, J. Lopez-Bernal, L. Elliss-Brookes, P. Sasieni. 2021. "The Effects of the National HPV Vaccination Programme In England, UK, On Cervical Cancer and Grade 3 Cervical Intraepithelial Neoplasia Incidence: A Register-Based Observational Study." *The Lancet* 398 (10316), 2084–92. https://doi.org/10.1016/S0140-6736(21)02178-4.

Fan, R. 2007. "Corrupt Practices in Chinese Medical Care: The Root in Public Policies and a Call for Confucian-Market Approach." *Kennedy Institute of Ethics Journal* 17 (2): 111–31.

Fang, Y. 2013. *Medicine Prices, Availability and Affordability in Shaanxi Province, Western China*. WHO/HAI Survey Report. Bejing, CN: WHO.

Farmer, Paul. 2005. *Pathologies of Power: Health, Human Rights, and the New War on the Poor*. Berkeley: University of California Press.

–. 2010. *Partner to the Poor*. Berkeley: University of California Press.

Fauci, Anthony S. 2019. "Building Trust in Vaccines." US Department of Health and Human Services, National Institutes of Health, NIH PIO Network. December 4, 2019. https://www.nih.gov/about-nih/what-we-do/science-health-public-trust/perspectives/science-health-public-trust/building-trust-vaccines.

Feldman, E., and R. Bayer. 2011. "The Triumph and Tragedy of Tobacco Control: A Tale of Nine Nations." *Annual Review of Law and Social Sciences* 7: 79–100.

Feng Junxia. 2014. 瞄准重点目标 全力谋求突破－就烟草行业拓展国际市场工作访国家局副局长李克明 [Focusing on key objectives to achieve breakthrough: an interview with State Tobacco Monopoly Administration's deputy-director Li Keming on the industry's global market expansion]. *East Tobacco News*, February 19.

Fidler, D. 1999. *International Law and Infectious Diseases*. Oxford: Oxford University Press.

Fidler, D., and L. Gostin. 2006. "The New International Health Regulations: An Historic Development for International Law and Public Health." *Journal of Law, Medicine and Ethics* 34: 85–94.

FindChinaInfo. 2016. "HIV/AIDS Cases on the Rise in China during 2016." November 29. https://findchina.info/hivaids-cases-rise-china-during-2016.

Fine, P., K. Eames, and D. Heymann. 2011. "Herd Immunity: A Rough Guide." *Clinical Infectious Diseases* 52: 911–16.

Freeman, C.W., and X.U. Boynton, eds. 2011. *Implementing Health Care Reform Policies in China: Challenges and Opportunities*. Washington, DC: Center for Strategic and International Studies.

Freund, P. 2009. "Accomplishing More with Less." *Capitalism, Nature, and Socialism* 20 (2): 126–29. http://www.cnsjournal.org/wp-content/uploads/2014/09/Freund.20.2.Jun_.09.pdf.

Frost, A., and K. Sullivan. 2014. "Global Industrial Trend in Asia." *Nikkei Business*, May 20.

Fu, W., S. Zhao, Y. Zhang, P. Chai, and J. Goss. 2018. "Research in Health Policy Making in China: Out-of-Pocket Payments," *BMJ* 360: k234. https://www.bmj.com/content/bmj/360/bmj.k234.full.pdf.

Gallaher. 2004. "Shanghai Tobacco and Gallaher Launch Brands in China and Russia." News release, May 27. http://www.sec.gov/Archives/edgar/data/1037333/000102123104000366/b752037–6k.htm.

Gao, J., J. Qian, S. Tang, B. Eriksson, and E. Blas. 2002. "Health Equity in Transition from Planned to Market Economy in China." *Health Policy and Planning* 17 (Suppl. 1): 20–29.

Gao, Z., X. Qiu, and R. Chen. 2002. "Education of Medical Ethics in China for the 21st Century." In *Ethics in Medical Education in China: Distinguishing Educa-*

tion of Ethics in Medicine from Moral Preaching, edited by O. Döring, 45–56. Hamburg: IFA.

Garrett, L. 1995. *The Coming Plague: Newly Emerging Diseases in a World Out of Balance.* New York: Penguin Books.

GATT (General Agreement on Tariffs and Trade). 1994. *Marrakesh Agreement Establishing the World Trade Organization,* Annex 1A, 1867 UNTS 187.

General Office of the State Council of the People's Republic of China. January 2019. National Centralized Drug Procurement Pilot Program. http://www.gov.cn/zhengce/content/2019–01/17/content_5358604.htm.

Ghatak, M., and S. Roy. 2014. "Mirror, Mirror on the Wall, Which Is the Most Dynamic State of Them All?" Ideas for India. March 23. Accessed 9 May 2022. https://www.ideasforindia.in/topics/governance/mirror-mirror-on-the-wall-which-is-the-most-dynamic-state-of-them-all.html.

Ghosh, S. 2011. "Catastrophic Payments and Impoverishment due to Out-of-Pocket Health Spending." *Economic and Political Weekly* 46 (47): 63–70. https://www.jstor.org/stable/41720524.

Gitanjali, B. 2010. "National Essential Medicines List of India: Time to Revise and Purge the Mistakes." *Journal of Pharmacology and Pharmacotherapeutics* 1 (2): 73–74.

Global Times. 2014. "Premier Li Urges Deepening Medical Reform." April 5, 2014. http://www.globaltimes.cn/content/852763.shtml.

Gostin, L. 2008. *A Theory and Definition of Public Health Law.* Research Paper No. 8. Washington, DC: O'Neill Institute for National and International Global Health Law Scholarship, Georgetown University.

Gotsadze, G., S. Bennett, K. Ranson, and D. Gzirishvili. 2005. "Health Care-Seeking Behaviour and Out-of-Pocket Payments in Tbilisi, Georgia." *Health Policy and Planning* 20 (4): 232–42.

Gottret, P., and G. Schieber. 2006. *Health Financing Revisited: A Practitioner's Guide.* Washington, DC: World Bank.

Government of China. 2009. "National Human Rights Action Plan of China, 2009–2010." http://www.china.org.cn/archive/2009–04/13/content_17595407_2.htm.

–. 2016. "National Human Rights Action Plan of China, 2016–2020." Accessed 7 May 2022. http://english.www.gov.cn/archive/publications/2016/09/29/content_281475454482622.htm.

Government of India. 2013. "State-Wise Per-Capita Expenditure on Health." Press Information Bureau. https://www.indiastat.com/table/per-capita-availability/state-wise-per-capita-expenditure-health-expenditu/1019702.

Govindarajan, V., and R. Ramamurti. 2013. "Delivering World-Class Health Care, Affordably." *Harvard Business Review* (November): 117–22.

Gruskin, S., M. Grodin, G. Annas, and S. Marks, eds. 2005. *Perspectives on Health and Human Rights.* New York: Routledge.

Guthrie, D. 1999. *Dragon in a Three-Piece Suit: The Emergence of Capitalism in China.* Princeton, NJ: Princeton University Press.

Han, Y. 2013. 烟草税利对国家财政贡献的分析 [An analysis of tobacco industry's contribution to government revenue]. *China Tobacco.* September 1. http://www.echinatobacco.com/zhongguoyancao/2013-09/01/content_416175.htm.

He, A., and J. Qian. 2016. "Explaining Medical Disputes in Chinese Public Hospitals." *Health, Economics, Policy and Law* 11: 359–78.

He, J., M. Tang, Z. Ye, X. Jiang, D. Chen, P. Song, and C. Jin. 2018. "China Issues the National Essential Medicines List (2018 Edition): Background, Differences from Previous Editions, and Potential Issues." *BioScience Trends* 12 (5): 445–49. doi: 10.5582/bst.2018.01265.

Helfer, L.R., and G.W. Austin. 2011. *Human Rights and Intellectual Property: Mapping the Global Interface*. New York: Cambridge University Press.

Henderson, G., S. Jin, J. Akin, X. Li, J. Wang, et al. 1995. "Distribution of Medical Insurance in China." *Social Science and Medicine* 41 (8): 1119–30.

Herdegen, M. 2001. "Biotechnology and Regulatory Risk Assessment." In *Transatlantic Regulatory Cooperation: Legal Problems and Political Prospects*, edited by G. Bermann, M. Herdegen, and P. Lindseth, 301–17. Oxford: Oxford University Press.

HIB (Health Insurance Bureau of the Ministry of Health, Labor, and Welfare). 2020. "Health Care Insurance System." https://www.mhlw.go.jp/english/wp/wp-hw13/dl/02e.pdf.

HID (Healthcare Industries Division, Commerce and Information Policy Bureau, Ministry of Economy, Trade and Industry of Japan). 2013. "Globalization of Japan's Medical Service: Medical Industries Accommodate Increased Demand for Achievement." In Japanese. Accessed 31 January 2019. http://www.meti.go.jp/policy/mono_info_service/healthcare/kokusaika/downloadfiles/about.pdf.

The Hindu. 2018. "TN's Healthcare System Lauded by PM." *The Hindu*, April 21. https://www.thehindu.com/news/national/tamil-nadu/tns-healthcare-system-lauded-by-pm/article23621602.ece.

Hirschman, A.O. 1970. *Exit, Voice and Loyalty: Responses to Decline in Firms, Organizations and States*. Cambridge, MA: Harvard University Press.

Ho, C. 2014. "Health Rights at the Juncture between State and Market: The People's Republic of China." In *The Right to Health at the Public/Private Divide: A Global Comparative Study*, edited by C.M. Flood and A. Gross, 263–87. New York: Cambridge University Press.

Holden, C., K. Lee, A.B. Gilmore, N. Wander, and G. Fooks. 2010. "The Role of Tobacco in China's Accession to the WTO." *International Journal of Health Services* 40 (3): 421–41.

Hu, S., S. Tang, Y. Liu, Y. Zhao, M.-S. Escobar, and D. de Ferranti. 2008. "Reform of How Health Care Is Paid for in China: Challenges and Opportunities." *Lancet* 372 (9652): 1846–53.

Huang, H. 2021. "Deepening the Reform of Medication Review and Approval Scheme, Stimulating Pharmaceutical Companies' Incentive for Innovation." *Globe*. March 2021. http://www.news.cn/globe/2021–03/02/c_139777821.htm.

Huang, X., et al. 2021. "Despite of the Drug Supply Guarantee Mechanisms Shortage, Cheap Lifesaving Drugs are Still in Shortage. Xinhua News." July 2021. http://www.xinhuanet.com/politics/2021–07/07/c_1127632441.htm.

Huang, Y.D. 1993. 适应市场经济发展 实行 "五个转变" [Implementing five changes to adapt to market developments]. *China Tobacco*. http://www.echinatobacco.com/101588/102220/102455/102459/36142.html.

Human Rights Watch. 2003. *Locked Doors: The Human Rights of People Living with HIV/AIDS in China.* New York: Human Rights Watch.

Hyde, S. 2007. *Eating Spring Rice: The Cultural Politics of AIDS in Southwest China.* Berkeley: University of California Press.

IBISWorld. n.d. "Cigarette Manufacturing in China: Competitive Landscape." http://clients1.ibisworld.com.proxy.lib.sfu.ca/reports/cn/industry/competitiveland-scape.aspx?entid=167.

Idegawa, Masahiko. 2013. *Mixed Billing: Destruction of Healthcare by Market Principle* (Tokyo: Iryokeizaisya).

IMA Pharma. 2013. "China's Pharmaceutical Market: A Growing Evolution." Sharing News. http://www.ima-pharma.com/mail/article.aspx?idnwl=159&idart=1421.

India Brand Equity Foundation. 2013. *Pharmaceuticals.* http://www.ibef.org/download/pharmaceuticals-august-2013.pdf.

Indian Express. 2017. "What Is National Health Policy 2017: Everything You Need to Know." *Indian Express,* March 22. https://indianexpress.com/article/what-is/what-is-national-health-policy-2017–4574585/.

Ip, P.-K. 2005. "Developing Medical Ethics in China's Reform Era." *Developing World Bioethics* 5 (2): 176–86.

Jacobs, L. 1993. *Rights and Deprivation.* Oxford: Oxford University Press.

—. 2007. "Rights and Quarantine during the SARS Global Health Crisis: Differentiated Legal Consciousness in Hong Kong, Shanghai, and Toronto." *Law and Society Review* 41 (3): 511–53.

—. 2011. "China's Capacity to Respond to the H1N1 Pandemic Alert and Future Global Public Health Crises." In *Issues in Canada-China Relations,* edited by Pitman Potter and Thomas Adams, 333–43. Toronto: Canadian International Council.

—. 2014. "Global Tobacco Control Law and Trade Liberalization: New Policy Spaces?" In *Linking Global Trade and Human Rights: New Policy Space in Hard Economic Times,* edited by D. Drache and L. Jacobs, 131–50. Cambridge: Cambridge University Press.

—. 2018. "Investor-State Dispute Mechanisms in International Economic Law: The Shifting Ground for Meaningful Access to International Justice from Private Commercial Arbitration to Standing Tribunals and Sectoral Carve-Outs." In *Grey Zones of International Economic Law and Global Governance,* edited by D. Drache and L. Jacobs, 68–90. Vancouver, BC: UBC Press.

—. 2019. "Health and Human Rights Performance in China: Stronger on Entitlements, Weaker on Freedom." In *Handbook on Human Rights in China,* edited by S. Biddulph and J. Rosenweig, 143–60. Cheltenham, UK: Edward Elgar.

Jacobs, L., and P. Potter. 2006. "Selective Adaptation and Health and Human Rights in China." *Health and Human Rights Journal* 9 (2): 142–66.

Jain, K. 2012. "Health Insurance in India: The Rashtriya Swasthya Bima Yojana, Women in Informal Employment Globalizing and Organizing." *WIEGO Policy Brief* #10 (September): 1–6. https://www.wiego.org/sites/default/files/publications/files/Jain-Health-Insurance-Informal-Economy-India-WIEGO-PB10.pdf.

Japan External Trade Organization. 2021. "Japanese Enterprises in India." https://www.jica.go.jp/india/english/office/others/c8h0vm0000f9enll-att/list_02.pdf.

Japan Patients' Association. 2013. "Against the Destructive Lifting of the Ban on Mixed Billing: Health Insurance Should Apply to Required Medical Treatments as a Rule." https://nanbyo.jp/.

Japan Times. 2018. "Japan's Backward Vaccination Policy." June 26. https://www.japantimes.co.jp/opinion/2018/06/26/commentary/japan-commentary/japans-backward-vaccination-policy/#.W8ueWxNKh-U.

Jiating yisheng zaixian. 2013. Zhiliang anquan: guochan yaowu yizhi guobuqu de "kan"? 质量安全: 国产药物一直过不去的 "坎"? [Quality and safety, the insuperable obstacle for domestic drug industry?]. *Jiating yisheng zaixian [Family doctor. com.cn]*. http://m.familydoctor.com.cn/201310/522486.html.

Kalaiyarasan, A. 2014. "A Comparison of Developmental Outcomes in Gujarat and Tamil Nadu." *Economic and Political Weekly* 49 (15): 55–63.

Kalra, A. 2014. "India's Universal Healthcare Rollout to Cost $26 Billion." *Reuters,* October 30. https://www.reuters.com/article/uk-india-health-idINKBN0IJ0VN 20141030.

Kanavos, P., W. Schurer, and S. Vogler. 2011. *The Pharmaceutical Distribution Chain in the European Union: Structure and Impact on Pharmaceutical Prices.* Brussels: European Commission. http://eprints.lse.ac.uk/51051/1/Kanavos_pharmaceutical_distribution_chain_2007.pdf.

Kapczynski, A. 2009. "Harmonization and Its Discontents: A Case Study of TRIPS Implementation in India's Pharmaceutical Sector." *California Law Review* 97: 1,571–1,649.

Kar, S.S., H.S. Pradhan, and G.P. Mohanta. 2010. "Concept of Essential Medicines and Rational Use in Public Health." *Indian Journal of Community Medicine* 35 (1): 10–13. http://www.ncbi.nlm.nih.gov/pmc/articles/PMC2888334/.

Kawabuchi, K., and P. Talcott. 2010. "Getting Vaccine Policy Right: A Global-Standard Comprehensive Policy for Japan." *Shakai Hoken Junpo [Social Insurance News]*, February 1 and 11, 14–20, 20–27. In Japanese.

Kawaguchi, Hiroyuki. 2012. "Research on the Influence of the Payment System for Mixed Billing and Combined Therapies Not Covered by Health Insurance on the Medical System." *Ministry of Finance Policy Research Institute Financial Review* 111 (4): 48–73.

Ke, B. 2002. "Reflections about How to Compile Teaching Materials in Chinese Medical Ethics Education." In *Ethics in Medical Education in China: Distinguishing Education of Ethics in Medicine from Moral Preaching,* edited by O. Döring, 57–62. Hamburg: IFA.

Kerala Medical Services Corporation. 2015. "Welcome to Kerala Medical Services Corporation." http://www.kmscl.kerala.gov.in.

Kesireddy, R.R. 2013. "After Price Cuts, Big Pharma Companies Focusing on Brands Distribution." *Economic Times.* May 30. https://economictimes.indiatimes.com/industry/healthcare/biotech/pharmaceuticals/after-price-cuts-big-pharma-companies-focussing-on-brands-distribution/articleshow/24893441.cms.

Khanna, Tarun, V. Kasturi Rangan, and Merlina Manocaran. 2011. "Narayana Hrudayalaya Heart Hospital: Cardiac Care for the Poor (A)." Harvard Business School Case 505–078, June 2005. (Revised August 2011.) https://store.hbr.org/

product/narayana-hrudayalaya-heart-hospital-cardiac-care-for-the-poor-a/
505078?sku=505078-PDF-ENG.

Knowler, G. 2015. "Investment Floods into China's One Belt, One Road Strategy." *Journal of Commerce*. July 3. http://www.joc.com/international-trade-news/investment
-floodschina%E2%80%99s-one-belt-one-road-strategy_20150703.html.

Kornreich, Y., I. Vertinsky, and P. Potter. 2012. "Consultation and Deliberation in
China: The Making of China's Health-Care Reform." *China Journal* 68: 176–203.

KPMG Advisory (China) Limited. 2011. *China's Pharmaceutical Industry – Poised
for the Giant Leap*. KPMG Advisory (China) Limited. http://www.kpmg.
com/CN/en/IssuesAndInsights/ArticlesPublications/Documents/China-
pharmaceutical-201106–2.pdf.

Lai, C. 2009. 华美:改革开放大潮中的中外合资卷烟企业 [Huamei: A tobacco industry
joint venture during economic reforms]. *China Tobacco*. September 20. http://
www. echinatobacco.com/101588/102041/102524/43525.html.

Landry, P.F., and M.M. Shen. 2005. "Reaching Migrants in Survey Research: The Use
of the Global Positioning System to Reduce Coverage Bias in China." *Political
Analysis* 13 (1): 1–22.

Lanthier, M., Miller, K.L., Nardinelli, C., and Woodcock, J. 2013. "An Improved
Approach to Measuring Drug Innovation Finds Steady Rates of First-In-Class
Pharmaceuticals, 1987–2011." *Health Affairs* 32 (8): 1433–39.

Lee, K., and J. Eckhardt. 2017. "The Globalization Strategies of Five Asian Tobacco
Companies: An Analytical Framework." *Global Public Health* 12 (3): 269–80.

Lee, K., A. Gilmore, and J. Collin. 2004. "Breaking and Re-entering: British American Tobacco in China 1979–2000." *Tobacco Control* 13 (Supp II): 89–95.

Li, C. 2020. "A Brief Analysis of Compulsory License of Drug Patent under Public
Health Crisis." *Theory and Practice of Social Science*. 2 (2): 43–51.

Li, Cheng. 2012. *The Political Mapping of China's Tobacco Industry and Anti-
Smoking Campaign*. Washington, DC: Brookings Institution.

Li, H. 2016. "Lifesaving Cheap Drugs Should Not Die Away." *China Daily*. 4
November.

–. 2013. Tangniao bingren zuiyi fande cuo [Common Mistakes for Diabetics Patients].
Sheng Ming Shi Bao [Life Times]. http://health.sina.com.cn/d/2013-12-06/0918
115871.shtml.

Li, Hongmei. 2017. 公立 医院告别药品加成：病有所医负担减轻 [Pharmaceutical Price
Mark-up Ended in Public Hospitals]. *China Daily*. http://www.gov.cn/xinwen/
2018-01/05/content_5253309.htm.

Li, Hui. 2014. Cong geguo fangzhiyao fazhan xianzhuang jiexi zhongguo fangzhiyao
shichang touzi jihui, 从各国仿制药发展现状解析中国仿制药市场投资机会 [Investment
Opportunities in Chinese Generic Market]. *Geshang licai [Licai.com]*. http://
finance.ifeng.com/a/20140604/12473707_0.shtml.

Li, Hongmei. 2017. 公立医院告别药品加成：病有所医负担减轻 [Pharmaceutical Price
Mark-up Ended in Public Hospitals]. *China Daily*. http://www.gov.cn/xinwen/
2018-01/05/content_5253309.htm.

Li, J. 2008. "Economic Costs of Serious Illness in Rural Southwest China: Household
Coping Strategies and Health Policy Implications." *Human Organization* 67 (2):
151–63.

Li, S., C. Ma, and B. Xi. 2016. "Tobacco Control in China: Still a Long Way to Go." *Lancet* 387 (10026): 1375–76.

Li, Y., T. Feng, and W. Jiang. 2018. "How Competitive Orientation Influences Unethical Decision-making in Clinical Practices?" *Asian Nursing Research* 12 (3):182–89. doi: 10.1016/j.anr.2018.07.001.

Li Yahong. 2014. "Sanwen beijing dabing baoxian" 三问北京大病保险 [Three questions about catastrophic illness insurance policy of Beijing]. *Jiefang ribao* [*Liberation Daily*], January 5. http://finance.sina.com.cn/money/insurance/bxdt/20140105/063917846151.shtml.

Liao Haijin. 2014. "Liuzhu lianjiayao, zhengfu bie quewei" 留住廉价药, 政府别缺位 [Tackle drug shortage, government should not be absent]. *Jingji ribao* [*China Economics*], January 14. http://paper.ce.cn/jjrb/html/2014-01/14/content_185049.htm.

Lin, N. 2001. *Social Capital: A Theory of Social Structure and Action*. Cambridge: Cambridge University Press.

Lin Mingkan. 1984. 引进国外先进技术的"窗口" – 厦门卷烟厂与"雷诺士"合作生产"骆驼牌"香烟的启示 ["Window" of foreign technology transfer – lessons from Xiamen Cigarette Factory's licensed production of Camel cigarettes]. June 13. http://www.cnki.com.cn/Article/CJFDTotal-FLJS198402005.htm.

Liu, M., Q. Zhang, M. Lu, C.S. Kwon, and H. Quan 2007. "Rural and Urban Disparity in Health Services Utilization in China." *Medical Care,* 45 (8): 767–74.

Liu, X.S., W. Han, and S.B. Li. 2002. "Ideas on Reforming Medical Ethics Education of China." In *Ethics in Medical Education in China: Distinguishing Education of Ethics in Medicine from Moral Preaching,* edited by O. Döring, 120–23. Hamburg: IFA.

Liu, Y. 2004. "Development of the Rural Health Insurance System in China." *Health Policy and Planning* 19 (3): 159–65.

Liu, Y., K. Rao, J. Wu, and E. Gakidou. 2008. "China's Health System Performance." *Lancet* 372 (9653): 1914–23. http://www.ncbi.nlm.nih.gov/pubmed/18930536.

Lobo, R. 2011. "Has ESIC Outlived Its Utility?" *Financial Express,* May 7. http://www.financialexpress.com/news/has-esic-outlived-its-utility-/786970.

Lora-Wainwright, A. 2011. "'If You Can Eat and Walk You Do Not Go to Hospital': The Quest for Healthcare in Rural Sichuan." In *China's Changing Welfare Mix: Local Perspectives,* edited by B. Carrillo and J. Duckett, 104–25. London: Routledge.

Lovell White Durrant. 1996. "The China National Tobacco Corporation and BAT Far East Holdings Limited." June 29. Truth Tobacco Industry Documents, http://legacy.library.ucsf.edu/tid/nqo04a99/pdf.

Luhmann, N. 1996. *Soziologie des Risikos.* Berlin: Walter de Gruyter.

Lui, J. 2012. "Healthcare Expenditure Booms in China: Report." *China Daily,* August 29. http://www.chinadaily.com.cn/bizchina/2012-08/29/content_15717138.htm.

Lux Research. 2013. "China Investing Billions in Bid to Catch Up with Western Pharma." Global R&D Funding Forecast. R&D World, August. http://www.rdmag.com/news/2013/08/china-investing-billions-bid-catch-western-pharma.

Maidana-Eletti de Amstalden, M. 2014. "Food Quality, Food Labelling and Market Access: Some Comments on the WTO's TBT Applicable Rules." *New Zealand Yearbook of International Law* 2: 1–17.

–. 2015. "Public Health and Nutrition: The Next Frontier at the SPS Agreement." In *Mobility: Recht der mobilen Gesellschaft,* edited by S. Bernet, G. Gertsch, R. Harasgama, and R. Schister, 229–43. St. Gallen, Switzerland: Dike Verlag.

Manikandan, S., and B. Gitanjali. 2012. "National List of Essential Medicines of India: The Way Forward." *Journal of Postgraduate Medicine* 58 (1): 68–72.

Mann, J. 1998. "AIDS and Human Rights: Where Do We Go from Here?" *Health and Human Rights Journal* 3: 143–49.

Marmot, M., and R. Wilkinson, eds. 1999. *Social Determinants of Health.* Oxford: Oxford University Press.

Masabayashi, Tadaaki. 2021. "Vaccine Unit Price, Recent Trends in Immunization Administration. Director, Tuberculosis Infectious Disease Division, Health Bureau, Ministry of Health, Labour and Welfare." Accessed 30 January 2021. https://www.niid.go.jp/niid/images/idsc/kikikanri/H24/20121017–02.pdf.

Mavalankar, D.V., K.S. Vora, K.V. Ramani, P. Raman, B. Sharma, and M. Upadhyaya. 2009. "Maternal Health in Gujarat, India: A Case Study." *Journal of Health, Population and Nutrition* 27 (2): 235–48. http://www.ncbi.nlm.nih.gov/pmc/articles/PMC2761782/.

McKinlay, J.B., F. Trachtenberg, L.D. Marceau, J.N. Katz, and M.A. Fischer. 2014. "Effects of Patient Medication Requests on Physician Prescribing Behavior." *Medical Care* 52 (4): 294–99.

Meng, Q., and S. Tang. 2010. *Universal Coverage of Health Care in China: Challenges and Opportunities.* World Health Report. Geneva: World Health Organization.

Meng, Q., L. Xu, Y. Zhang, J. Qian, M. Cai, Y. Xin, and S. Barber. 2012. "Trends in Access to Health Services and Financial Protection in China between 2003 and 2011: A Cross-Sectional Study." *Lancet* 379 (9818): 805–14. http://linkinghub.elsevier.com/retrieve/pii/S0140673612602785.

Miao, Z., and Y. Wu. 2014. Fangzhiyao youhuo, 仿制药诱惑 [Temptation of Generic Drugs]. Zhongguo jingji he xinxihua [China Economy and Informatization]. http://finance.sina.com.cn/chanjing/cyxw/20140519/181819155511.shtml.

Ministry of Chemicals and Fertilizers [of India]. 2012. "National Pharmaceuticals Pricing Policy, 2012 (NPPP-2012)." *Gazette of India* (Hindi and English version), December 7. http://apps.who.int/medicinedocs/documents/s20106en/s20106en.pdf.

–. 2013. "Drug Price Control Order." Department of Pharmaceuticals, Ministry of Chemicals and Fertilizers. http://www.idma-assn.org/pdf/drug-price-control-order-2013.pdf.

Ministry of Finance. 2018. 关于2017年全国社会保险基金决算的说明 [Explanation of the Balance of the National Social Insurance Funds in 2017]. *China Government.* http://www.gov.cn/xinwen/2018-10/31/content_5336284.htm.

Ministry of Foreign Affairs of Japan. 2013. "Republic of Singapore: Basic Data." http://www.mofa.go.jp/mofaj/area/singapore/data.html.

Ministry of Health [of the People's Republic of China]. 1988. *Yiwu renyua yide guifan ji shishi banfa* [Ethical codes for medical personnel]. Beijing: Ministry of Health.

–. 2006. "China National Health Economics Institute China National Health Accounts Report 2006" [in Chinese]. Beijing: Ministry of Health.

Ministry of Health, Labour and Welfare [of Japan]. 2014. "Basic Plan on Immunization," Norihisa Tamura, March 28. https://www.mhlw.go.jp/bunya/kenkou/kekkaku-kansenshou20/dl/yobou140529–1.pdf.

–. 2015. "Employment Policy for Foreign Workers." http://www.mhlw.go.jp/stf/seisakunitsuite/bunya/koyou_roudou/koyou/gaikokujin/other22/index.html.

–. 2021a. "Availability of Vaccines." Accessed 30 January 2021. https://www.mhlw.go.jp/stf/seisakunitsuite/bunya/kenkou_iryou/kenkou/kekkaku-kansenshou03/index_00002.html.

–. 2021b. "Vaccine Unit Price, Recent Trends in Immunization Administration." Accessed 30 January 2021. https://www.niid.go.jp/niid/images/idsc/kikikanri/H24/20121017–02.pdf.

Ministry of Health and Family Welfare [of India]. 2013. "National Health Mission." https://nhm.gov.in/.

–. 2021. "Future Action on Routine Vaccination for Human Papillomavirus Infection, Director-General of the Health Bureau, Ministry of Health, Labor and Welfare," *Kensho* 1126 (1), November 26, 2021, https://www.mhlw.go.jp/content/000875155.pdf.

Ministry of Human Resources and Social Security. 2013. gongfei yiliao fanwei suojian zhi gebie shengfen," 公费医疗范围缩减至个别省份 [reducing the range of free medical service]. Jingji Cankao Bao [经济参考报]. http://news.xinhuanet.com/fortune/2013-11/18/c_125716794.htm.

Ministry of Labour and Employment [of India]. N.d. "Employees' State Insurance Corporation." Accessed 9 May 2022. https://www.esic.nic.in/.

Ministry of Law and Justice [of India]. 2007. "Constitution of India." Accessed 7 May 2022. https://legislative.gov.in/constitution-of-india.

Miyauchi, Yoshihiko. 2002. Interview in *Shūkan Tōyō Keizai* (magazine), January 26.

MOFCOM (Ministry of Commerce of the People's Republic of China). 2015. 王卫华代表考察湖南中烟公司巴拿马工厂 [Wang Weihua visits Hunan Tobacco Industrial's Panama factory]. August 21. http://panama.mofcom.gov.cn/article/swfalv/201508/20150801087520.shtml.

Mordor Intelligence. 2020. "India Health and Medical Insurance Market: Growth, Trends, Covid-19 Impact, and Forecast (2022–2027)." https://www.mordorintelligence.com/industry-reports/india-health-and-medical-insurance-market.

Morgan, S., and C. Cunningham. 2011. Population Aging and the Determinants of Healthcare Expenditures: The Case of Hospital, Medical, and Pharmaceutical Care in British Columbia, 1996 to 2006. *Healthcare Policy* 7 (1): 68–79.

Morrow, M., and S. Barraclough. 2001. "Tobacco Control and Gender: A Need for New Approaches for the Asia-Pacific Region." *Development Bulletin* 54: 23–26.

Mukherjee, R. 2015. "NDA Fund Cuts Put Healthcare on the Sickbed." *Economic Times*, April 15. http://economictimes.indiatimes.com/news/politics-and-nation/NDA-fund-cuts-put-healthcare-on-the-sickbed/articleshow/46929476.cms.

Multilateral Trade System Department [of Japan]. 2007. *The 2007 Report on Compliance by Major Trading Partners with Trade Agreements – WTO, FTA/EPA, BIT. Part III FTA/EPA and BIT.* Accessed 10 May 2022. https://www.meti.go.jp/english/report/data/gCT07_1coe.html.

Munro, N. 2012. "Connections, Paperwork and Passivity: Strategies of Popular Engagement with the Chinese Bureaucracy." *China Journal* 68: 147–75.

Nagarajan, R. 2015. "Central Scheme of Free Drugs Gets a Quiet Burial." *Economic Times,* April 5. http://economictimes.indiatimes.com/articleshow/46811632. cms?utm_source=contentofinterest&utm_medium=text&utm_campaign= cppsteconomictimes.indiatimes.com/industry/healthcare/biotech/healthcare/Central-scheme-of-free-drugs-gets-a-quiet-burial/articleshow/46811632. cms.

Nanfang ribao [*Nanfang Daily*]. 2014. Weijiwei "nengyong fangzhiyao buyong yuanyanyao" zhishuo re zhengyi, 卫计委 "能用仿制药不用原研药" 之说惹争议 [Controversy over Health and Family Planning Commission's policy of preferentially prescribing generic drugs]. *Nanfang ribao* [*Nanfang Daily*]. http://www. xinyaohui.com/news/201405/13/2169.html.

National Bureau of Statistics of China. 2021. "Communiqué of the Seventh National Population Census, No. 2–Basic Information of the National Population." *Office of the Leading Group of the State Council for the Seventh National Population Census May 11, 2021.* http://www.stats.gov.cn/english/PressRelease/202105/t20210510_1817187.html.

National Cancer Center Japan. 2014. "Medical Expenses in the Case of Using Non-Approved Drugs." http://www.ncc.go.jp/jp/about/senshiniryo/senshiniryo_01_01.html.

National Development and Reform Commission. 2016. Opinion on Promoting Drug Pricing Reform. May 2016. https://www.ndrc.gov.cn/xxgk/zcfb/tz/201505/t20150505_963815.html.

—. 2012. Guanyu kaizhan chengxiang jumin dabing baoxian gongzuo de zhidao yijian, 关于开展城乡居民大病保险工作的指导意见 [Guiding Opinions on the Supplementary Insurance of Major Diseases for Urban and Rural Residents]. Xinhua net. http://news.xinhuanet.com/politics/2012-08/30/c_112908096.htm.

National Health Commission of the People's Republic of China. 2021. Statistical Communiqué of the People's Republic of China on National Health Care Development in 2020. http://www.nhc.gov.cn/guihuaxxs/s10743/202107/af8a9c98453c4d9593e07895ae0493c8.shtml.

National Health and Family Planning Commission. 2012. Zhongguo de Xinxing Nongcun Hezuo Yiliao Zhidu Fzhan, 中国的新型农村合作医疗制度发展 [Development of China's New Rural Cooperative Healthcare System]. http://www.moh. gov.cn/mohbgt/s3582/201209/55893.shtml.

National Health Security Administration. 2019. Opinion on Expanding the Implementation of the National Centralized Drug Procurement Pilot Program. September 2019. http://www.nhsa.gov.cn/art/2019/9/30/art_37_1817.html.

—. 2022. State Council's Briefing on the Development of the Centralized Drug Bulk-Buying Reform. http://www.nhsa.gov.cn/art/2022/2/11/art_14_7835.html.

National Healthcare Security Administration. 2022. Brief Report on Healthcare Development in 2021. http://www.nhsa.gov.cn/art/2022/3/4/art_7_7927.html.

New York Times. 2020. "India COVID Map and Case Count." November 15. https://www.nytimes.com/interactive/2020/world/asia/india-coronavirus-cases.html#states.

Ngorsuraches, S., W. Meng, B-Y. Kim, and V. Kulsomboon. 2012. "Drug Reimbursement Decision-Making in Thailand, China, and South Korea." *Value in Health* 15 (1): S120–S125.

Nguyen, Ha. 2011. "Principal-Agent Problems in Health Care: Evidence from Prescribing Patterns of Private Providers in Vietnam." *Health Policy and Planning* 26 (Suppl. 1): i53–i62.

NHFPC (National Health and Family Planning Commission of the People's Republic of China). 2012. "Guidance on Strengthening the Prevention and Control of the Integrity Risk of Public Medical Institutions." Accessed 31 July 2014. http://wsb.moh.gov.cn/mohjcg/s3577/201209/55937.shtml.

–. 2013a. "Nine Prohibitions for Strengthening the Ethics Construction for the Healthcare Industry." Accessed 31 January 2018. http://www.nhfpc.gov.cn/jcj/s7692/201312/09bd7a8be8f8420d91997a0041aa868e.shtml.

–. 2013b. "Notice Regarding the Agreement between Doctors and Patients on Rejecting the Under-the-Counter Payment." Accessed 31 January 2018. http://www.moh.gov.cn/yzygj/s3577/201402/b7f939aeaeee41c28ba80023b74c4187.shtml.

–. 2014. "Opinion on Promoting the Comprehensive Reform in County-Level Public Hospitals." http://www.gov.cn/xinwen/2014–04/08/content_2654774.htm.

Nicol, A.F., C.V. Andrade, F.B. Russomano, L.L. Rodrigues, N.S. Oliveira, and D.W. Provance Jr. 2016. "HPV Vaccines: A Controversial Issue?" *Braz J Med Biol Res* 49 (5): (2016): e5060. doi: 10.1590/1414–431X20155060.

Nie, J. 2002. "Bringing Ethics to Life: A Personal Statement on Teaching Medical Ethics." In *Ethics in Medical Education in China: Distinguishing Education of Ethics in Medicine from Moral Preaching,* edited by O. Döring, 63–74. Hamburg: IFA.

OECD (Organisation for Economic Co-operation and Development). 2009. *OECD Economic Surveys: Japan 2009.* Paris: OECD Publishing. doi: 10.1787/eco_surveys-jpn-2009-en.

–. 2014. "Health Status." OECD.Stat. http://stats.oecd.org/index.aspx?DataSetCode=HEALTH_STAT.

Office of Registrar General [of India]. 2011. "Maternal and Child Mortality and Total Fertility Rates: Sample Registration System (SRS)." July 7. http://censusindia.gov.in/vital_statistics/SRS_Bulletins/MMR_release_070711.pdf.

Parthasarathi, R. and S.P. Sinha. 2016. "Towards a Better Healthcare Delivery System: The Tamil Nadu Model," *Indian Journal of Community Medicine* 41, 4 (2016): 302–4. http://www.ijcm.org.in/article.asp?issn=0970–0218;year=2016;volume=41;issue=4;spage=302;epage=304;aulast=Parthasarathi.

Pauwelyn, Joost. 1999. "The WTO Agreement on Sanitary and Phytosanitary (SPS) Measures as Applied in the First Three SPS Disputes: EC-Hormones, Australia-Salmon and Japan Varietals." *Journal of International Economic Law* 2: 641–64.

Pawar, T. 2014. "Employees' State Insurance Corporation to Take Action against 25 Defaulting Companies." *Times of India,* April 15. http://timesofindia.indiatimes.com/city/nashik/Employees-State-Insurance-Corporation-to-take-action-against-25-defaulting-companies/articleshow/33755319.cms.

Peel, Jacqueline. 2007. "A GMO by Any Other Name ... Might Be an SPS Risk! Implications of Expanding the Scope of the WTO Sanitary and Phytosanitary Measures Agreement." *European Journal of International Law* 17 (5): 1009–31.

Pharmaceutical and Medical Device Regulatory Science Society of Japan. 2012. *Instructive Lessons about Drug-Induced Incidents We Need to Know.* Tokyo: Yakuji Nippo Press.

–. 2013. *Drug-Induced Suffering in Japan.* Tokyo: Yakuji Nippo Press.

Planning Commission [of India]. 2012. "Drugs and Pharmaceuticals: Report Working Groups/Steering Committees for the Twelfth Five Year Plan (2012–2017)." New Delhi, IN: Government of India.

–. 2013. *Twelfth Five Year Plan (2012–2017) Social Sectors Volume III.* New Delhi: SAGE Publications India. https://nhm.gov.in/images/pdf/publication/Planning_Commission/12th_Five_year_plan-Vol-3.pdf.

PMI (Philip Morris International). 1993. "1993 Board Presentation – Opening." Truth Tobacco Industry Documents, http://legacy.library.ucsf.edu/tid/zwd42e00/pdf.

–. 2002. "China-Vision 2000+." February 1. Truth Tobacco Industry Documents, http://legacy.library.ucsf.edu/tid/zoq19e00/pdf.

Polanyi, K. (1994) 2001. *The Great Transformation: The Political and Economic Origins of Our Time.* Boston: Beacon Press.

Prachitha, J., Dhume, A., and Subramanian, S. "India in Pursuit of Millennium Development Goals: Were the Targets Really Feasible?" *Journal of Developing Societies* 35 (1): 105–33. https://doi.org/10.1177/0169796X19826737.

PricewaterhouseCoopers. 2009. *Investing in China's Pharmaceutical Industry,* 2nd ed., London: PricewaterhouseCoopers.

Qiu, S., and G. MacNaughton. 2017. "Mechanisms of Accountability for the Realization of the Right to Health in China." *Health and Human Rights Journal* 19: 279–92.

Raghavan, P. 2018. "Modicare: The World's Largest National Health Protection Scheme." *Economic Times,* February 2. https://economictimes.indiatimes.com/news/economy/policy/modicare-the-worlds-largest-national-health-protection-scheme/articleshow/62748128.cms.

Reddy, S.G. 2008. "Death in China: Market Reforms and Health." *International Journal of Health Services* 38 (1): 125–41.

Reuters. 2018. "India Allocates $1.5 Billion for 'Modicare' Health Insurance." *Reuters,* March 22. https://www.reuters.com/article/us-india-health/india-allocates-1-5-billion-for-modicare-health-insurance-idUSKBN1GY1GK.

Revikumar K., R. Veena, S. Lekshmi, P.K. Manna, and G.P. Mohantha. 2013. "Tamil Nadu Medical Services Corporation – A Critical Study on Its Functioning during the Period 1995–2012." *International Journal of Pharmaceutical and Chemical Sciences* 4 (3): 966–84.

RJ Reynolds. 2000. "Memorandum of Understanding. Party A: China National Tobacco Corporation (CNTC). Party B: RJ Reynolds Tobacco Company (RJRT)." Truth Tobacco Industry Documents, http://legacy.library.ucsf.edu/tid/kmf20d00/pdf.

Rochan, M. 2015. "India: Prime Minister Modi Applies Brakes on Universal Healthcare Rollout." *International Business Times,* March 27. https://www.ibtimes.co.

uk/india-prime-minister-modi-applies-brakes-universal-healthcare-rollout
-1493785.

Ryan, M. 1994. "Agency in Health-Care: Lessons for Economists from Sociologists." *American Journal of Economics and Sociology* 53 (2): 207–17.

Sachs, J., C. Kroll, G. Lafortune, G. Fuller, and F. Woelm. 2021. *Sustainable Development Report 2021: The Decade of Action for the Sustainable Development Goals.* Cambridge: Cambridge University Press.

Sampat, B.N. 2010. "Institutional Innovation or Institutional Imitation? The Impacts of TRIPS on India's Patent Law and Practice." World Intellectual Property Organization, July 5. http://www.wipo.int/meetings/en/doc_details.jsp?doc_id= 149671.

Sanneving, L., A. Kulane, A. Iyer, and B. Ahgren. 2013. "Health System Capacity: Maternal Health Policy Implementation in the State of Gujarat, India." *Global Health Action* 6. http://www.ncbi.nlm.nih.gov/pmc/articles/PMC3606923/.

Schwab, Klaus. 2011. *The Global Competitiveness Report 2011–2012.* Geneva: World Economic Forum. http://www3.weforum.org/docs/WEF_GCR_Report_2011–12. pdf.

Science and Environmental Health Network. 2013. "Wingspread Conference on the Precautionary Principle, August 5th, 2013." https://www.sehn.org/sehn/wing spread-conference-on-the-precautionary-principle.

Sengupta, A., R.K. Joseph, S. Modi, and N. Syam. 2008. Economic Constraints to Access to Essential Medicines in India. New Delhi, IN: Amit Sen Gupta/ Progressive Printers.

Shan Juan, and Wang Qingyun. 2012. "Cost of Medicine Falls as Health Reform Starts." *China Daily*, July 3. http://usa.chinadaily.com.cn/china/2012–07/03/ content_15543764.htm.

Shepherd-Smith, A. 2012. "Free Drugs for India's Poor." *Lancet* 380: 874. https:// www.thelancet.com/action/showPdf?pii=S0140-6736%2812%2961489-5.

Shimazaza, R., and M. Ikeda. 2012. "The Vaccination Gap between Japan and the UK." *Health Policy* 107: 312–17.

Shimizu, K., G. Wharton, H. Sakamoto, and E. Mossialos. 2020. "Resurgence of COVID-19 in Japan." *British Medical Journal* 370: 1–2.

Sina. 2012. "Yaoyong jiaonangchang yong pige feiliao suoshengchan mingjiao zuo yuanliao" 药用胶囊厂用皮革废料所生产明胶作原料 [Drug capsules made of industrial gelatin]. Yangshi meizhou zhiliang baogao [CCTV Weekly Quality Report], April 15. http://news.sina.com.cn/c/sd/p/2012–04–15/135324275218.shtml.

Sohu. 2017. "List Of Average Doctor Salaries by Specialty in China in 2016." *Sohu.* https://www.sohu.com/a/138068412_642249.

Srinivasan, S., T. Srikrishna, and A. Phadke. 2013. "Drug Price Control Order: As Good as a Leaky Bucket." *Economic and Political Weekly* 48 (2): 27–29.

State Administration for Market Regulation. 2020. Measures for the Administration of Drug Registration. January. https://gkml.samr.gov.cn/nsjg/fgs/202003/ t20200330_313670.html.

State Council Information Office of the People's Republic of China. 2017. "Development of China's Public Health as an Essential Element of Human Rights." http://www.scio.gov.cn/32618/Document/1565200/1565200.htm.

State Council of the People's Republic of China. 1981. 国务院批转轻工业部关于实行烟草专营的报告的通知 [State Council approves the Ministry of Light Technology's tobacco monopoly.] May 18. http://www.chinalawedu.com/falvfagui/fg22016/12453.shtml.

—. 1983. 烟草专卖条例 [Tobacco Monopoly Regulations]. September 23. http://www.chinalawedu.com/falvfagui/fg22016/12441.shtml.

—. 2011. "The 12th Five-Year Plan for the Health Sector Development (2011–2015)." Beijing: State Council. http://www.wpro.who.int/health_services/china_nationalhealthplan.pdf.

—. 2016. "Thirteenth Five-Year Plan for Economic and Social Development of the People's Republic of China (2016–2020)" https://en.ndrc.gov.cn/policies/202105/P020210527785800103339.pdf.

—. 2017. "White Paper: Development of China's Public Health as an Essential Element of Human Rights." http://english.gov.cn/archive/white_paper/2017/09/29/content_281475894089810.htm.

State Food and Drug Administration. N.d. "Yaopin zhuce guanli banfa (xiugai caoan)" 药品注册管理办法 (修改草案) [Drug Registration Regulation (draft)]. Accessed 28 January 2018. http://www.sda.gov.cn/directory/web/WS01/images/0qnGt9eisuG53MDtsOy3qKOo0N64xLLdsLijqS5kb2M=.doc.

STMA (State Tobacco Monopoly Administration). 1996. 中国烟草年鉴1991–1995 [China tobacco almanac 1991–95]. Beijing: China Economics Publishing House.

—. 1997. 中国烟草年鉴1981–1990 [China tobacco almanac 1981–90]. Beijing: China Economics Publishing House.

—. 1998. 中国烟草年鉴1996–1997 [China tobacco almanac 1996–97]. Beijing: China Economics Publishing House.

—. 2000. 中国烟草年鉴1998–1999 [China tobacco almanac 1998–99]. Beijing: China Economics Publishing House.

—. 2002. 中国烟草年鉴2001 [China tobacco almanac 2001]. Beijing: China Economics Publishing House.

—. 2003. 中国烟草年鉴2002 [China tobacco almanac 2000]. Beijing: China Economics Publishing House.

—. 2004. 国家烟草专卖局关于印发《卷烟产品百牌号目录》的通知 [STMA's notice on the announcement of "one hundred brands list"]. August 19. http://www.chinalawedu.com/.

—. 2005. 中国烟草年鉴2004 [China tobacco almanac 2004]. Beijing: China Economics Publishing House.

—. 2006. 中国烟草年鉴2005 [China tobacco almanac 2005]. Beijing: China Economics Publishing House.

—. 2009. 中国烟草年鉴2008 [China tobacco almanac 2008]. Beijing: China Economics Publishing House.

—. 2012. 中国烟草年鉴2011–2012 [China tobacco almanac 2011–12]. Beijing: Science and Technology Press of China.

—. 2014. 中国烟草年鉴2013 [China tobacco almanac 2013]. Beijing: Science and Technology Press of China.

Sun, M, J. Shen, C. Li, C. Cochran, Y. Wang, F. Chen, P. Li, J. Lu, F. Chang, X. Li, and M. Hao, 2016. "Effects of China's New Rural Cooperative Medical Scheme on

Reducing Medical Impoverishment in Rural Yanbian: An Alternative Approach." *BMC Health Services Research* 16 (1): 422. https://www.ncbi.nlm.nih.gov/pmc/articles/PMC4994392/.

Sun, Q., M.A. Santoro, Q. Meng, C. Liu, and K. Eggleston. 2008. "Pharmaceutical Policy in China: Health Affairs." *Lancet* 27: 1042–50.

Süssmuth-Dyckerhoff, C., and J. Wang. 2010. "China's Health Care Reforms." *Health International* 10: 54–67.

Takada, K. 2013. "Bribery Serves as Life-Support for Chinese Hospitals." Reuters. http://www.reuters.com/article/2013/07/23/us-china-hospitals-bribery-idUSBRE96M12Y20130723.

Tezuka, Y. 2010. *Structure and Dilemmas of Postwar Government.* Kishiwada, Osaka, Japan: Fujiwara Shoten. In Japanese.

Times of India. 2012. "Cracking the Kerala Myth." January 2. http://timesofindia.indiatimes.com/edit-page/Cracking-the-kerala-myth/articleshow/11329131.cms.

Tobacco-Free Kids. 2010. "China National Tobacco Corporation and Philip Morris International's partnership." April. http://global.tobaccofreekids.org/files/pdfs/en/IW_cntc_pmi_bg.pdf.

Toebes, B. 1999. *The Right to Health as a Human Right in International Law.* Oxford: Hart.

Tokyo Midtown Clinic. 2021. "Influenza Vaccine Shot at Tokyo Midtown Clinic." January. https://www.tokyomidtown-mc.jp/en/news/2012/01/influenza-vaccine-shot-at-tokyo-midtown-clinic.html.

Tong, E., M. Tao, Q. Xue, and T. Hu. 2008. "China's Tobacco Industry and the World Trade Organization." In *Tobacco Control Policy Analysis in China,* edited by T. Hu, 211–58. River Edge, NJ: World Scientific.

Tong, J. 2003. "The Gender Gap in Political Culture and Participation in China." *Communist and Post-Communist Studies* 36: 131–50.

Trade Map. 2015. "China Tobacco Imports" (data file). http://www.trademap.org/Product_SelCountry_TS.aspx.

Tribal Health Initiative. 2015. "Brief History." http://www.tribalhealth.org/?page_id=30.

UN Committee on Economic, Social and Cultural Rights. 2014. *Concluding Observations on the Second Periodic Review of China.* June 13. Geneva: United Nations.

UN Comtrade Database. 2015. "China Tobacco Exports" (data file). http://comtrade.un.org/data/.

UNCESCR (United Nations Committee on Economic, Social and Cultural Rights). 2000a. CESCR General Comment No. 14: The Right to the Highest Attainable Standard of Health (Art. 12). http://www.refworld.org/pdfid/4538838d0.pdf.

UNGA (United Nations General Assembly). 1948. Universal Declaration of Human Rights. Resolution 217A (III), A/810, 71, Article 25. http://www.un.org/en/documents/udhr/.

–. 1966. International Covenant on Economic, Social and Cultural Rights. Resolution 2200 (XXI), Article 12. http://www.un-documents.net/icescr.htm.

United Castle America. n.d. About us. http://unitedcastle.com.mx/aboutus.html.

United Nations Human Rights Council. 2011. *Report of the Special Rapporteur on the Right of Everyone to Enjoyment of the Highest Attainable Physical and Mental*

Health: Expert on Access to Medicines as Fundamental Component of the Right to Health. 57th session, A/HRC/171.

University College of London School of Pharmacy. 2013. "Health and Health Care in India: National Opportunities, Global Impacts." Accessed 31 August 2020. http://www.efpia.eu/uploads/UCL_india.pdf.

Varatharajan, D. 2003. "Public Sector and Efficiency: Are they Mutually Exclusive? An Alternative Policy Framework to Improve the Efficiency of Public Health Care System in Tamil Nadu, India," *Journal of Health & Population in Developing Countries* (July 14), https://www.longwoods.com/product/download/code/17622.

Varatharajan, D., R. Thankappan, and S. Jayapalan. 2004. "Assessing the Performance of Primary Health Centres under Decentralized Government in Kerala, India." *Health Policy and Planning* 19 (1): 41–51. http://www.who.int/health_financing/documents/phc_performance.pdf?ua=1.

Veggeland, F., and S. Borgen. 2002. *Changing the Codex: The Role of International Institutions.* Oslo: Norwegian Agricultural Economics Research Institute.

–. 2005. "Negotiating International Food Standards: The World Trade Organisation's Impact on the Codex Alimentarius Commission." *Governance* 18 (4): 675–708.

Velásquez, G., Y. Madrid, and J. Quick. 1998. *Health Reform and Drug Financing Selected Topics.* Geneva: World Health Organization.

Vidhi, D. 2018. "India Just Announced a Vast New Health Insurance Program. But Can It Afford It? *The Washington Post,* February 2018. https://www.washingtonpost.com/world/asia_pacific/india-just-announced-a-vast-new-health-insurance-program-but-can-it-afford-it/2018/02/01/805efb46-0757-11e8-ae28-e370b74ea9a7_story.html.

Waldmeir, P. 2013. "China's Doctors Not Part of Society's Elite." *Financial Times,* October 6. http://www.ft.com/cms/s/0/35a081ae-2653-11e3-8ef6-00144feab7de.html#ixzz35b8hmFRR.

Wang, L. 2005. *Comprehensive Report: Chinese Nutrition and Health Survey in 2002.* Beijing: People's Medical Publishing House.

Wang, N., Ying Yang, Luxinyi Xu, Zongfu Mao, and Dan Cui. 2021. "Influence of Chinese National Centralized Drug Procurement on the Price of Policy-Related Drugs: An Interrupted Time Series Analysis." *BMC Public Health* 21, 1883 (2021). https://doi.org/10.1186/s12889-021-11882-7.

Wang, Jianmin. 2014. Woguo yiyao shichang 98% de fen'e bei fangzhiyao zhanju, 我国医药市场98%的份额被仿制药占据 [Generics make up 98% of the China's pharmaceutical market]. *Wenhui bao* [*Wei Wei Po*]. http://www.ce.cn/cysc/sp/info/201404/30/t20140430_2746594.shtml.

Wang Jie. 2013. "Pianyiyao jueji yuanyin yin Zhengyi" 便宜药绝迹原因引争议 [Disappearance of cheap drugs sparked controversy]. *Henan shangbao* [*Henan Business*], December 28. http://henan.qq.com/a/20131228/001602.htm.

Wang Qingyun. 2014. "More Medical Reimbursement for Unemployed." *China Daily,* January 2. http://www.chinadaily.com.cn/china/2014-01/02/content_17212690.htm.

Wangyi caijing 网易财经. 2012. "Chenzhu: zhongguo de weisheng feiyong zhan GDP bizhong jin 5.1%, zhanbi taidi" 陈竺: 中国的卫生费用占GDP比重仅5.1%占比太低 [Chen

Zhu: China's ratio of health care spending to GDP is too low]. September 12. http://money.163.com/12/0912/14/8B77I2RI00254S8R.html.

Wank, D.L. 1999. *Commodifying Communism: Business, Trust, and Politics in a Chinese City.* Cambridge: Cambridge University Press.

Wasem, J., S. Greß, and K.G.H. Okma. 2004. "The Role of Private Health Insurance in Social Health Insurance Countries." In *Social Health Insurance Systems in Western Europe,* edited by R.B. Saltman, R. Busse, and J. Figueras, 227–47. Berkshire, UK: Open University Press.

Wee, Sui-Lee. 2018. "China's Health Care Crisis: Lines before Dawn, Violence and 'No Trust.'" *New York Times,* September 30. https://www.nytimes.com/2018/09/30/business/china-health-care-doctors.html.

Wei Qing. 2013. "Kefou jianli lianyao chubei zhi" 可否建立廉药储备制 [Is drug reservation a possibility?]. *Hualong wang.* http://opinion.china.com.cn/opinion_84_74684.html.

Wen Xuping. 2014. "Dijiayao jiang quxiao zuigao xianjia" 低价药将取消最高限价 [Possible removal of price ceilings for cheap drugs]. *Jingji guancha wang* [*Economics Observation*], April 16. http://www.eeo.com.cn/2014/0416/259243.shtml.

WHO (World Health Organization). N.d. "Regulation and Prequalification: What Is Pharmacovigilance?" https://www.who.int/teams/regulation-prequalification/pharmacovigilance.

–. 1946. "Constitution of the World Health Organization." http://apps.who.int/gb/bd/PDF/bd47/EN/constitution-en.pdf.

–. 2003. *WHO Framework Convention on Tobacco Control.* Geneva: WHO Document Production Services. http://apps.who.int/iris/bitstream/handle/10665/42811/9241591013.pdf?sequence=1.

–. 2007a. "International Health Regulations." http://www.who.int/topics/international_health_regulations/en/.

–. 2007b. *International Health Regulations (2005): Areas of Work for Implementation.* Lyon: WHO Publications. http://www.who.int/ihr/finalversion9Nov07.pdf.

–. 2008. *International Health Regulations (2005).* 2nd ed. Geneva: WHO Publications. http://whqlibdoc.who.int/publications/2008/9789241580410_eng.pdf.

–. 2015. *World Health Statistics 2015.* Geneva: World Health Organization. http://apps.who.int/iris/bitstream/10665/170250/1/9789240694439_eng.pdf?ua=1&ua=1.

–. 2017a. "2017 Health SDG Profile: India." https://country-profiles.unstatshub.org/ind.

–. 2017b. *Global Tuberculosis Report 2017.* Geneva: World Health Organization. http://www.who.int/tb/publications/global_report/en/.

–. 2017c. *National List of Essential Medicines (NLEM) 2015 India.* https://digicollections.net/medicinedocs/#d/s23088en.

–. 2019. "WHO Global Report on Trends in Prevalence of Tobacco Use, 2000–2025, Third Edition." https://www.who.int/publications/i/item/who-global-report-on-trends-in-prevalence-of-tobacco-use-2000–2025-third-edition.

–. 2020. "COVID-19: Q&A with Dr Galea." May 6. https://www.who.int/china/news/detail/06–05–2020-covid-19-q-a-with-dr-galea.

WHO China (World Health Organization Representative Office in China). 2010. "Protect Women from Tobacco Marketing and Smoke." (Fact Sheet) Accessed 20 July 2018. https://www.who.int/china.

WHO and FAO (World Health Organization and the Food and Agriculture Organization of the United Nations). 2010. *Codex Alimentarius Commission: Procedural Manual.* 19th ed. Rome: Joint FAO/WHO Food Standards Programme.

WHO-UNODC (World Health Organization and the United Nations Office on Drugs and Crime). 2016. *International Standards for the Treatment of Drug Use Disorders – Draft for Field Testing.* Geneva: World Health Organization/United Nations Office on Drugs and Crime. https://www.unodc.org/documents/commissions/CND/CND_Sessions/CND_59/ECN72016_CRP4_V1601463.pdf.

Wilkinson, L. 2013. "Universal Rural Health Care in China? Not So Fast." *Atlantic* (September 6). https://www.theatlantic.com/china/archive/2013/09/universal-rural-health-care-in-china-not-so-fast/279429/.

Wilkinson, R. 1996. *Unhealthy Societies.* London: Routledge.

World Bank. 2015. "Maternal Mortality Ratio (Modeled Estimate, per 100,000 Live Births)." http://data.worldbank.org/indicator/SH.STA.MMRT.

–. 2016. "India's Poverty Profile." May 27. http://www.worldbank.org/en/news/infographic/2016/05/27/india-s-poverty-profile.

–. 2018. "World Bank Open Data." https://data.worldbank.org/.

–. 2020. *Learning Forward: COVID-19 and China's Reform Agenda.* Washington, DC: World Bank Publications.

–. 2021. "Poverty & Equity Brief East Asia & Pacific China." https://databank.worldbank.org/data/download/poverty/987B9C90-CB9F-4D93-AE8C-750588BF00QA/AM2021/Global_POVEQ_CHN.pdf.

–. 2022. "World Development Indicators." https://databank.worldbank.org/source/world-development-indicators#.

World Health Organization and World Bank. 2021. *Global Monitoring Report on Financial Protection in Health 2021.* https://www.who.int/publications/i/item/9789240040953.

World Medical Association. 2018. "WMA Declaration of Lisbon on the Rights of the Patient." August 7. https://www.wma.net/policies-post/wma-declaration-of-lisbon-on-the-rights-of-the-patient/.

WTO (World Trade Organization). 1997. *Canada – Certain Measures Concerning Periodicals.* WTO Appellate Body Report, June 30. WT/DS31/AB/R.

–. 1998. *Australia – Measures Affecting the Importation of Salmon.* WTO Appellate Body Report, October 20. WT/DS18/AB/R.

–. 1999a. *Japan – Measures Affecting Agricultural Products.* WTO Appellate Body Report, February 22. WT/DS76/AB/R.

–. 1999b. *Korea – Taxes on Alcoholic Beverages.* WTO Appellate Body Report, January 18. WT/DS84/AB/R.

–. 2000. *Argentina – Measures Affecting the Export of Bovine Hides and the Import of Finished Leather.* WTO Panel Report, December 19. WT/DS155/R.

–. 2006. *European Communities – Measures Affecting the Approval and Marketing of Biotech Products.* WTO Panel Report, June 29. WT/DS291/R, WT/DS292/R, WT/DS293/R.

–. 2014. *India – Measures Concerning the Importation of Certain Agricultural Products.* WTO Appellate Body Report, June 4. WT/DS430/AB/R.

Wu, J. 2006. Shequ yiyuan jiang shitui "shouzhenzhi." xiaobing buchu shequ 社区医院将试推"首诊制,"小病不出社区 [Small Illnesses will be Treated in Community Hospitals]. *Renmin wang* [*People.cn*]. http://politics.people.com.cn/GB/1026/4095514.html.

Wu, R., and L. Li. 2013. Jiben yaowu shao, yisheng qianshao buyuan zhi, ba bingren "bi"qu dayiyuan? 基本药物少,医生钱少不愿治,把病人"逼"去大医院? [Essential drug Shortage pushes patients to large hospitals], *Guangzhou Ribao* [*Guangzhou Daily*]. http://gzdaily.dayoo.com/html/2013-01/28/content_2139756.htm.

Xie, J. 2003. 对工商分离改革的认识和思考 [Thoughts on the separation of commerce and manufacture]. *Tobacco China.* September 30. http://www.tobaccochina.com/management/Industry/management/20039/2003930000_193484.shtml.

Xinhua. 2019. "Chinese Public Hospitals Receive Increasing Government Funds." http://www.chinadaily.com.cn/a/201906/14/WS5d03bfd8a3103dbf1432853d.html.

–. 2021. "China to Advance Reform of Centralized Drug Bulk-Buying to Ease Patients' Financial Burden." http://www.xinhuanet.com/english/2021–01/16/c_139671414.htm.

Xinhua ribao [*Xinhua Daily*]. 2014. Jinkou kangaiyao neng zhibing que chibuqi, 进口抗癌药能治病却吃不起 [Unaffordable imported anti-cancer drugs drugs]. *Xinhua ribao* [*Xinhua Daily*]. http://js.people.com.cn/html/2014/04/09/301072.html.

Xinhua wang [*Xinhua Net*]. 2011. Weishengbu buzhang chenzhu huiying "kanbing nan, kanbing gui" liuda wenti, 卫生部部长陈竺回应"看病难、看病贵"6大问题 [Health Minister Chen Zhu responds to 6 major questions on "Kan bing nan. Kan bing gui"]. *Xinhua wang* [*Xinhua Net*]. http://www.gov.cn/jrzg/2011-02/19/content_1806198.htm.

Xu, C., and Y. Liu. 2014. Shanghai de shequ weisheng fuwu zhongxin meiyou yiliao shajia, 上海的社区卫生服务中心没有医疗差价 [No Markup at Community Clinics in Shanghai]. *Dongfang wang* [*Eastday*]. http://sh.eastday.com/m/20140417/u1a8036740.html.

Xu Wei. 2017. "China to Expand Reform in Public Hospitals." State Council of the People's Republic of China. http://english.gov.cn/premier/news/2017/10/09/content_281475902231546.htm.

Yagi, A., Y. Ueda, M. Kakuda, S. Nakagawa, K. Hiramatsu, A. Miyoshi, E. Kobayashi, T. Kimura, M. Kurosawa, M. Yamaguchi, S. Adachi, R. Kudo, M. Sekine, Y. Suzuki, A. Sukegawa, S. Ikeda, E. Miyagi, T. Enomoto, and T. Kimura. 2021. "Cervical Cancer Protection in Japan: Where Are We?" *Vaccines* 9 (11): 1263–75. https://doi.org/10.3390/vaccines9111263.

Yan, G. 2013. Zhongguo fangzhiyao de ganga, 中国仿制药的尴尬 [China's generic industry in a dilemma]. *Fazhi zhou mo* [*Legal Weekly*]. http://finance.china.com.cn/industry/medicine/yygc/20131009/1856571.shtml.

Yang, C., and L. Li. 2010. "Drug Procurement Bidding." *China Business Review,* January 1. http://www.chinabusinessreview.com/drug-procurement-bidding/.

Yang, G., Y. Wang, Y. Zeng, G.F. Gao, X. Liang, M. Zhou, and C.J.L. Murray. 2013. "Rapid Health Transition in China, 1990–2010: Findings from the Global

Burden of Disease Study 2010." *Lancet* 381 (9882): 1987–2015. http://www. thelancet.com/journals/lancet/article/PIIS0140–6736(13)61097–1/abstract.

Yang, M.M.-h. 1994. *Gifts, Favors, and Banquets: The Art of Social Relationships in China.* Ithaca, NY: Cornell University Press.

Yip, W.C., W. Hsiao, Q. Meng, W. Chen, and X. Sun. 2010. "Realignment of Incentives for Health-Care Providers in China." *Lancet* 375: 1120–30.

Yu, Y.D. 2015. 把握新常态 立足新起点 努力打造国际市场新的增长点——云南中烟2015 年全国会议经验交流材料 [Experience from Yunnan Tobacco Industrial]. http:// www.cntiegc.com/src/2015-04/10007804.html.

Yu, Z. 2016. "Multiple Pharmaceutical Companies Halted Production of Pyridostigmine Bromide." *Jinling Evening News,* October 8.

ZaubaCorp. 2013. "Gujarat Medical Services Corporation Limited." https://www. zaubacorp.com/company/GUJARAT-MEDICAL-SERVICES-CORPORATION-LIMITED/U85110GJ2012SGC071667.

Zeng, L. 2014. Babuwei litui fangzhiyao jiang zhongcuo waizi yaoqi, 八部委力推仿 制药将重挫外资药企 [Eight ministries and commissions promote generic drugs]. *Jingji cankao bao* [*Economic Information Daily*]. http://www.jjckb.cn/2014-04/16/content_500282.htm.

Zeng, Y. 2010. 重点骨干品牌谋求"规模与效益"双突破 [Breakthrough in size and efficiency of key brands]. *Tobacco China.* May 19. http://www.tobaccochina.com/ news/analysis/wu/20105/20105198552_410313.shtml.

Zhang, H. 2010. "China's Irrational Medical Pricing Scheme." *Lancet* 375 (9716): 726.

Zhang, Y. 2013. "China Begins to Lose Edge as World's Factory Floor." *Wall Street Journal,* January 17. http://www.wsj.com/articles/.

Zhejiang Provincial Bureau of Statistics. 2014. Wosheng di shouru nonghu Yiiao Zhichu Zhan Shenghuo Xiaofei Zhichu de Bizhong Gaoda 18.8%, 我省低收入农户 医疗支出占生活消费支出的比重高达 18.8% [Medical Spending of Low-income Rural Households Accounts for 18.8% of Living Expenditure]. *Zhejiang Provincial Bureau of Statistics.* http://www.zj.stats.gov.cn/tjxx/tjkx/201404/t20140416_127642.html.

Zhou, Y. 2004.中国烟草的工商分离及其困境与根本出路 [Industrial and commercial separation of the Chinese tobacco industry, its challenges and the way forward]. *Tobacco China,* August 10. *https://www.tobaccochina.com/.*

Zhou Tian. 2014. "Xinyigai touru chao 3wanyi, yisheng gongzi reng piandi" 新医改 投入超3万亿, 医生工资仍偏低 [3 trillion yuan over five years has hardly raised medical worker pay]. *Caixin Online,* April 8. http://china.caixin.com/2014–04 –08/100662376.html.

Zhu, H. 2019. "Four Decades of Development of Health Care Services and Health Care Insurance Systems." *China Economic Transition* 2 (2): 110–17.

Zhu, P. 2019. "New Measures of the State Council to Tackle Drug Shortage and Unreasonable Pricing," *21st Century Business Herald* August 2019. http://www. gov.cn/zhengce/2019–08/17/content_5421943.htm.

Zi, Y. 1998. "Medical Insurance System Gets a Makeover." *China Daily.* http://www. chinadaily.com.cn/epaper/html/cd/1998/199812/19981212/19981212004_1. html.

Contributors

Tiffany Chua is a consultant for Asian policy with a focus on trade, investment, and innovation. She is a former research fellow at the Asia Pacific Foundation of Canada and a former faculty member at Ateneo de Manila University and De La Salle University. She has also worked for Taiwan's representative office in Manila – the Taipei Economic and Cultural Office – and collaborated with the Asian Development Bank, Philippine Department of Energy, and Ramon Magsaysay Awards Foundation (often known as the Asian Nobel Prize) on short-term projects. Tiffany holds an MBA from the Smith School of Business at Queen's University and an MA in Asia Pacific Policy Studies from the University of British Columbia.

Jennifer Fang is a senior project coordinator/research fellow at the Faculty of Health Sciences at Simon Fraser University in Vancouver, British Columbia.

Ziying He is an associate professor in Comparative Social Policy at the School of Public Affairs, Zhejiang University, China. He completed his PhD on comparative welfare states in 2008 at Sun Yat-sen University, China. He has more than twenty publications on Chinese social policy development, focusing especially on Chinese public hospital reform.

Lesley Jacobs is Vice-President, Research and Innovation at Ontario Tech University as well the holder of the Tier 1 York Research Chair in Human Rights and Access to Justice at York University in Toronto. He has held a range of distinguished visiting appointments at other universities, including Harvard Law School, Oxford Centre for Socio-Legal Studies, Law Commission of Canada, University of California at Berkley, University of Toronto, University of British Columbia, Waseda University,

Woodrow Wilson International Center for Scholars (Fulbright Visiting Research Chair in Canada-US Relations), Institute for International Economic Law at Georgetown University, and Department of Law at the European University Institute. His research interests include international economic law, especially investor state dispute settlement and new trade platforms; comparative public policy (especially health equity issues, health law and policy, and human rights); empirical social-legal research; courts and social policy; health and human rights; intersections between international human rights and trade law; and theoretical work on social justice. His recent books include *Balancing Competing Human Rights in a Diverse Society* (Irwin Law Books, 2012); *Linking Global Trade and Human Rights: New Policy Space in Hard Economic Times* (Cambridge University Press, 2014); *Privacy Rights in the Global Digital Economy: Legal Problems and Canadian Paths to Justice* (Irwin Law Books, 2014); *Grey Zones of International Economic Law and Global Governance* (UBC Press, 2018); and *The Justice Crisis* (UBC Press, 2020). He was elected a fellow of the Royal Society of Canada for his contributions to international scholarship on equal opportunity, human rights, and access to justice.

Hiroyuki Kojin, MD, JD, is an assistant professor in Preventive Medicine and Public Health, Faculty of Medicine at the Tokyo Medical University, and a visiting lecturer in Environmental Medicine and Public Health, Faculty of Medicine at the Shimane University, Japan. He completed his Juris Doctor degree program at Waseda Law School in 2008. Dr. Kojin is engaged in medical conflict management as an in-house mediator. He has also practised as an orthopedic doctor for over fifteen years. In addition, he serves as an expert adviser for Tokyo District Court in medical malpractice cases.

Kelley Lee is a professor of Health Sciences and Canada Research Chair at the Faculty of Health Sciences at Simon Fraser University. She is trained in International Relations and Public Administration with a focus on international political economy. She spent over twenty years at the London School of Hygiene and Tropical Medicine, where she remains Honorary Professor of Global Health Policy, initially analyzing the role of the United Nations in health. She was a core member of two major donor-led studies on World Health Organization (WHO) reform during the 1990s. She co-established the WHO Collaborating Centre on Global Change and Health, and chaired the WHO Resource Group on Globalization, Trade and Health. Dr. Lee also co-led a major international initiative to secure public access to tobacco industry documents, as well as analyze their contents in relation to the globalization of the tobacco industry. She has authored around ninety scholarly papers, fifty book chapters, and ten books including *Globalization and Health, An Introduction* (Palgrave Macmillan, 2003), *The World Health Organization* (Routledge, 2008), *Global Health and International Relations* (with Colin McInnes, Polity Press, 2012), and *Asia's Role in Governing Global Health* (co-edited with Tikki Pang and Yeling Tan, Routledge, 2012). She joined the Faculty of Health Sciences at Simon Fraser University in 2011 as Associate Dean, Research and Director of Global Health. She is an Associate Fellow of the Centre on Global Health Security, Chatham House, London; Fellow of the Faculty of Public Health, Royal College of Physicians; and Fellow of the Canadian Academy of Health Sciences.

Wenqin Liang received her PhD in law from the Peter A. Allard School of Law, University of British Columbia. Her doctoral thesis focused on the regulatory and oversight framework of China's domestic cap-and-trade pilot markets. Her research interests lie in international dispute resolution, market-based environmental policy, climate change law and policy, and intellectual property. From 2009 to 2010, she served as an executive member of the UBC Graduate Law Students' Society. In 2012, she worked as a research intern at the Development Research Centre of the State Council of People's Republic of China in Beijing, conducting research on China's newly introduced market-based initiatives for greenhouse gas mitigation. From 2013 to 2014, she worked as a project assistant at the Sauder School of Business at UBC, focusing on the issue of providing affordable medicines in China. Prior to her doctoral studies, she graduated with honours from Wuhan University, with a master's degree in international law and a bachelor's degree in law.

Mariela de Amstalden is a Swiss-trained lawyer who is a lecturer in the Birmingham Law School in the United Kingdom. She also holds an appointment as a visiting scholar at the Institute of International Economic Law at the Georgetown University Law Center in Washington, DC. She graduated with a PhD in Legal Sciences from the University of Lucerne, an LLM in International Business Law from the Free University in Amsterdam, and a Master in Law from the Universidad Nacional de Educación a Distancia (UNED) in Madrid. She is admitted to the Spanish bar and has practised international and domestic commercial law in Switzerland. Her research interests primarily focus on international economic law at the intersection with food and public health regulation.

Marc McCrum has an MA degree from the University of British Columbia's Asia Pacific Policy Studies Program. He has held research and policy analyst positions with UBC's Sauder School of Business, the China Council, and the Centre for Chinese Research, as well as at the Asia Pacific Foundation of Canada. He currently serves as a trade commissioner in the Northeast Asia and Oceania Division of Global Affairs Canada headquarters in Ottawa, where he focuses on the promotion of Canada's commercial relations with Japan and Australia.

Neil Munro is Senior Lecturer in Chinese politics at the University of Glasgow. Previously he has been Senior Research Fellow in the Centre for the Study of Public Policy, University of Strathclyde (and during 2005–11, University of Aberdeen) and Visiting Lecturer in Chinese Politics at the University of Edinburgh. He is the lead author of articles published in *The China Journal, Journal of Contemporary China, Health Expectations,* and *Europe-Asia Studies.* He is the co-author of four monographs on the politics of post-communist transformation.

Toshimi (Momo) Nakanashi is an associate professor at Yamagata University Medical School and a member of the Medical Conflict Management Committee of the Japan Council for Quality Health Care (JCQHC). Her original fields of study were obstetrics and gynecology, medical conflict resolution, and patient safety. She is an established medical mediator according to the Japanese model with law professor Yoshitaka Wada. She is currently engaged in research and education on the integration of patient safety and patient advocacy into the medical dispute resolution process. She also works as a mediator for court-annexed mediation at Yamagata District Court in Japan. As a program manager for medical and hospital associations in the JCQHC, she organizes and teaches health care mediation theory and skills.

Dr. Nidhi Sejpal Pouranik is a medical doctor with post-graduate work in public health. She has around ten years of progressive work experience in healthcare programs management, program implementation and coordination, and capacity-building. She is presently working with The International Union Against Tuberculosis and Lung Disease, New Delhi, as Senior Technical Advisor – Tobacco Control (TC). In her present capacity, she works on strengthening enforcement of TAPS ban with a focus on point-of-sale through tobacco vendor-licensing in India. Prior to her work at the union, Dr. Nidhi was with the Ministry of Health and Family Welfare (MoHFW), supported by WHO – India, providing technical assistance on non-communicable diseases (NCDs). She also has experience in the non-governmental sector across multi-disciplinary areas such as NCDs, TC, public health nutrition, acute flaccid paralysis (AFP), and routine immunization.

Ilan Vertinsky is a Vinod Sood Professor of International Business Studies, Strategy and Business Economics at the Sauder School of Business at the University of British Columbia, and a professor at UBC's Institute of Asian Research. He is also an associate of the Peter Wall Institute of Advanced Studies and a former Distinguished Scholar in Residence of the institute. He is currently an honorary professor at the Business School of the University of International Business and Economics (UIBE, Beijing). He received his PhD from the University of California at Berkeley. Before joining UBC, he served on the faculty of Northwestern University. He has published more than 250 refereed journal articles, book chapters, and books. His publications have appeared in journals including *Management Science, Operation Research, Administrative Science Quarterly, Journal of Public Health Policy,* and *Medical Care and Health Services Research.* His research awards include UBC's Killam Research Prize, the Sauder School Faculty's Professional Research Excellence Prize, and the Seagram Senior Faculty Award. He is a former editor of the *Journal of Business Administration* and co-editor of the journal *Information Systems and Operational Research (INFOR).* Currently he serves as an area editor for the *Journal of International Business Studies (JIBS)* and on the editorial boards of several international journals.

Yoshitaka Wada is a professor at Waseda University Law School. He teaches Theory of Law, Legal Counseling and Negotiation, Alternative Dispute Resolution (ADR),

Mediation, and Japanese Legal Culture. His research interests include law and society theory, ADR, medical malpractice, and legal profession. He has published many books, including *Healthcare Conflict Management, Deconstruction of Law and Society Studies, Skills for Legal Counseling,* and *Negotiation and Dispute Resolution.* He also serves as a vice president of the Japan Healthcare Mediator Association and as chair of the Center for Dispute and Negotiation Research at Waseda University.

Index

Agreement on the Application of
Sanitary and Phytosanitary
Measures (SPS Agreement), 11,
154, 157–58
double science standard of review,
155–66
*Australia – Measures Affecting the
Importation of Salmon*, 159,
161–62
Ayushman Bharat-National Health
Protection Mission (Modicare), 84,
97, 99

Bangalore, India
hospitals, 232, 236–40, 241–42
Bolar exemption, 34
Britain
billing of innovative services, 47
British American Tobacco (BAT), 170,
180, 181

CAC. *See* Codex Alimentarius Commission (CAC)
Canada
billing of innovative services, 46–47

Central Drugs Standard Control Organization (India), 79
Cetuximab, 67–68
Chan, Margaret, 110
China
civil rights, 103–4, 117–23; administrative detention, 118–20
costly health care, 19–21, 42–43,
45n11, 188; medicines, 19, 20, 21–
22, 23, 24, 27–30, 35, 36–37, 43,
45n9, 197–98; over-prescription,
188, 192, 193–94, 195–96; perverse
incentives for medical treatment,
23, 29, 43, 122, 188, 192–95,
197–98
COVID-19, 111, 113
demographics, 22–23, 106; tobacco
use, 115, 116, 169, 187
disease control, 122; tobacco control,
114, 115–17, 187
drug dependencies, 117–20
expenditure on health care, 20
H1N1, 110
health insurance, 24–27, 30–31, 43,
45n7; inefficient fund management,

37–38; rural-urban divide, 25, 31–32, 44n5

HIV/AIDS, 105, 109–10

hospitals: drug sales as source of revenue, 23, 29–30, 122, 188, 192–98; inadequate funding, 38–39; medical care disputes, 121–22, 188–96, 197, 207–9

human rights to health, 103–7, 123n1; entitlements, 107–17; freedoms, 10, 117–23; judicial and social accountability, 120–22, 123n8

as market society, 12, 13–14

Millennium Development Goals, 106

patent protection, 32–35, 40–41, 44

patients: empowerment, 190, 208–9; responses in medical disputes, 13–14, 121–22, 123n8, 188–228

primary health care issues, 35, 39–40; public health scandals, 121

rural-urban divide: health insurance, 25, 31–32, 44n5; patient responses to unethical medical behaviour, 202

SARS, 110

tobacco industry: brand development, 176–78, 185; exports, 178–79, 185, 186; history, 170–71; imports, 173–74; international operations, 180–84, 186–87; structure, 170–71, 174–76, 179–85

traditional medicine, 44n6

unethical medical behaviour: bribes (*hong bao*), 37, 188195–196; measures to counteract, 190–95, 207–9; unnecessary check ups, 195–96, 197

China National Tobacco Corporation business strategies, 13, 114, 169–70, 172–84, 185–87

Fang, Lee and Pouranik research: findings, 172–84; methodology, 171–72

history, 170–71

China Tobacco Industrial Corporation, 170

Codex Alimentarius Commission (CAC), 158–59

Comprehensive and Progressive Agreement for Trans-Pacific Partnership (CPTPP), 5–6, 59, 187

COVID-19, 111–13
India, 112–13
Japan, 111–12

CPTPP. *See* Comprehensive and Progressive Agreement for Trans-Pacific Partnership (CPTPP)

diseases
COVID-19, 111–13, 121, 148
drug dependencies, 117–20
H1N1, 110
HIV/AIDS, 105, 109–10
SARS, 109, 110

doctors
China: inadequate salaries, 38–39, 43, 192; patient responses in medical disputes, 13–14, 121–22, 123n8, 188–228; poor prescription practices, 23, 29, 42, 188, 192, 193–94, 195–96
India, 77, 237
Japan: hospital and clinic doctors, 60–61, 230; licensing in Singapore, 233, 235, 236; research doctors, 61–62

Doha Declaration, 32, 33

double science standard of review, 155–66

drugs
drug dependencies, 117–20
See also medicines; vaccination policies

economic interests. *See* China National Tobacco Corporation; international trade; patent protection; private health care

FCTC. *See* Framework Convention on Tobacco Control (FCTC)

food additives, 158–59
food security
    public health measures: as barriers to
        trade, 11, 154–66
Framework Convention on Tobacco
    Control (FCTC), 113–15
    China, 114, 115–17, 169, 187

GATT. *See* General Agreement on
    Tariffs and Trade (GATT)
General Agreement on Tariffs and
    Trade (GATT), 160–61
    Chinese tobacco industry and,
        172–73
GlaxoSmithKline (GSK plc), 37
global health security
    definition, 3
    economic interests and, 5–6, 11–13,
        229
    emerging infectious diseases and,
        107–9, 113
    Sustainable Development Goals and,
        5–6, 15, 104
    See also food security; patent protec-
        tion; private health care; rights to
        health; Sustainable Development
        Goals; vaccination policies; World
        Health Organization (WHO)
Gujarat (India), 86–98

H1N1, 110
health care professionals
    China, 38–39
    India, 77, 84, 98, 237, 240, 242
    Japan, 230, 236
    See also doctors
health insurance
    China, 24–27, 30–31, 43, 45*n*7; in-
        efficient fund management, 37–38;
        rural-urban divide, 25, 31–32, 44*n*5
    India, 82–84; inequalities within, 83;
        Modicare, 83–84, 97, 99; private,
        78
    Japan, 48–49, 230; effects of expand-
        ing coverage of new medicines,

69–72; excessive consumption of
    resources, 57, 70, 72; limitations of,
    47; private plans, 54, 60
HIV/AIDS, 105, 109–10
hospitals
    Bangalore, India, 232, 236–40, 241–42
    China: drug sales as source of rev-
        enue, 23, 29–30, 43, 122, 188, 192–
        98; inadequate funding, 38–39;
        medical care disputes, 121–22, 188–
        96, 197, 207–9
    Japan: overseas, 231, 232–42
human rights. *See* rights to health

ICCPR. *See* International Covenant on
    Civil and Political Rights (ICCPR)
IHR. *See* International Health Regula-
    tions (IHR)
India
    Avian influenza and import restric-
        tions, 11, 155–56
    central government: policies, 75, 76–
        84; responsibilities, 75, 85
    COVID-19, 112–13
    demographics, 76–77, 78; children's
        health, 88, 91; economic develop-
        ment, 86, 87, 91; Gujarat, 86, 87;
        infant mortality rates, 76, 88;
        Kerala, 86–87; life expectancy, 76,
        87, 90–91; maternal health, 89–90,
        91; Tamil Nadu, 86, 87
    health care partnership with Japan,
        14–15, 232, 233–36, 241
    health care services, 236–37, 238; for
        the economically disadvantaged,
        239, 240, 241–42; limited access
        to, 77, 82–83, 85, 97–99; limited
        access to medicines, 78, 79–81,
        97, 98
    health insurance plans, 82–84; in-
        equalities within, 83; Modicare,
        83–84, 97, 99; private, 78
    inadequate government funding,
        77–78, 84, 85, 92–93, 99
    as market society, 12

Modi administration, 83–84
National Health Mission, 78–79
National Rural Health Mission, 79
patent protection, 11, 81–82, 98
patient private expenditures, 77–78,
    92, 95
private hospitals: Japanese medical
    organizations, 14–15, 232, 236–40,
    241–42
rural-urban divide, 78, 79
state governments, 86–98; policy
    choices, 93–95, 98–99; responsibil-
    ities, 85
*India – Measures Concerning the
    Importation of Certain Agricul-
    tural Products*, 155–56, 159–60,
    162–64
insurance. *See* health insurance
intellectual property rights. *See* patent
    protection
International Bill of Human Rights,
    104–5, 123n1
International Covenant on Civil and
    Political Rights (ICCPR), 103
International Covenant on Economic,
    Social and Cultural Rights
    (ICESCR), 75, 103
International Health Regulations (IHR),
    108–9
International Sanitary Conferences, 107
international trade, 5, 11–12
    Comprehensive and Progressive
        Agreement for Trans-Pacific
        Partnership (CPTPP), 5–6, 59, 187
    General Agreement on Tariffs and
        Trade (GATT), 160–61, 172–73
    public health measures as barriers to,
        11, 154–66
    See also World Trade Organization
        (WTO)

Japan
    Abe administration, 55–59, 63, 64, 65
    access to new therapies, 53, 54, 63,
        72n8, 72n9, 72n10, 72n11
    billing of innovative services, 47–48
    COVID-19, 111–12, 148
    demographics, 57, 230
    efficiency of health services, 230
    globalization of health services, 229–
        31, 242; India, 14–15, 232, 236–40,
        241–42; Singapore, 14–15, 232,
        233–36, 241
    health insurance plans, 48–49, 230;
        effects of expanding coverage of
        new medicines, 69–72; excessive
        consumption of resources, 57,
        70, 72; limitations of, 47; private,
        54, 60
    Koizumi administration, 53–54, 56–
        59, 63, 64–65, 69
    as market society, 12
    mixed billing, 47–48; attitudes of
        drug and medical equipment
        manufacturers to, 59; attitudes of
        insurance industry to, 60; attitudes
        of medical professionals to, 60–62;
        attitudes of patient groups to, 62–
        64; effects on affordability of health
        care, 66–72; litigation concerning,
        49–53; OECD report on, 65–66;
        policy debate concerning, 53–59
    overseas Japanese expatriates: health
        care, 232, 233–36, 241
    pharmaceutical and medical equip-
        ment industries: attitudes to mixed
        billing, 59
    relationship with India, 237
    vaccinations: approval processes,
        22, 125, 150; costs, 129, 130; hist-
        ory of disasters table, 140–41;
        HPV, 124, 130, 133–34, 136, 138–
        39, 147–48, 150; insufficiencies
        (vaccination gap), 124–25, 132,
        137–42, 149–52; malpractice
        avoidance dilemma, 125–26,
        133–35, 138–48; policy revision
        recommended, 150–52; public
        understandings of product safety,
        10, 148–52

Japan Medical Association
  resistance to mixed billing, 54, 55,
  56, 61
Japan Patients' Association, 55, 63–64
Japan Revitalization Strategy, 229–30

Kerala (India), 86–98

LAK cell treatment, 49–53

Mann, Jonathan, 105
Marmot, Michael, 105–6
medical ethics
  Munro and He research: data, 195–
    99, 210–27; findings, 202–9; meth-
    odology, 195, 197
medicines
  China: attitudes to branded drugs,
    22, 42, 43–44; costs, 19, 20, 21–
    22, 23, 24, 27–30, 35, 36–37, 43,
    45n9, 197–98; generic, 21–22,
    34–35, 40–41; National Essential
    Medicine List, 27–28, 193–94;
    over-prescription, 188, 192, 193–
    94, 195–96; sales as source of hos-
    pital revenue, 23, 29–30, 122, 188,
    192–98; shortages, 36, 39, 45n9
  India: inadequate access, 78, 79–81,
    97, 98; National List of Essential
    Medicines, 79–82
  Japan: approval processes, 22, 125,
    150; exclusion of new medicines
    from health insurance coverage,
    47–72; mixed billing, 46–73
  See also patent protection; pharma-
    ceutical production and distribu-
    tion; vaccination policies
Millenium Development Goals, 87–88,
  106
mixed billing. See Japan: mixed billing
Miyauchi, Yoshihiko, 54, 69
Modi, Narendra, 86

National Essential Medicine List (China),
  27–28, 193–94

National Health Assurance Mission
  (India), 83–84
National List of Essential Medicines
  (India), 79–82
New Rural Cooperative Medical Scheme
  (China), 20
Nippon Medical Care
  clinic in Singapore, 232, 233–36, 241
nurses
  Japan, 230; licensing in Singapore, 14–
    15, 233, 235

Olaparib, 68
Organisation for Economic Co-operation
  and Development
  report on mixed billing ban in Japan,
    65–66

patent protection
  China, 32–35, 40–41, 44
  India, 11, 81–82, 98
patients
  China: empowerment, 190, 208–9;
    responses in medical disputes, 13–
    14, 121–22, 123n8, 188–228
  India: private expenditures, 77–78,
    92, 95
  Japan: attitudes to mixed billing,
    62–64
patient rights to self-determination,
  127, 129
pharmaceutical production and
  distribution
  China, 24, 28–30, 45n10; drug short-
    ages, quality and corruption issues,
    14, 36–37, 39, 45n9; lack of prod-
    uct innovation, 41–42; National
    Essential Medicine List, 27–28, 193–
    94; patent protection, 32–35, 40–
    41, 44
  India: National List of Essential Medi-
    cines, 79–82; patent protection, 11,
    81–82, 98; Tamil Nadu model, 96
  Japan: slow drug approval protocols,
    66

pharmacovigilance, 136
United States: Tylenol, 135–36
See also medicines
pharmacogenomics, 150, 153n5
physicians. *See* doctors
private health care
China, 13–14; perverse incentives for medical treatment, 23, 29, 43, 122, 188, 192–95, 197–98
India: Japanese companies, 14–15, 232, 236–40, 241–42; patient expenditures, 77–78, 92, 95
Japan: mixed billing, 46–73; services in India, 14–15, 232, 236–40, 241–42; services in Singapore, 14–15, 232, 233–36, 241
Singapore: Japanese companies, 14–15, 232, 233–36, 241

rights to health, 4–5, 74–75
China, 104–7; entitlements versus freedoms, 9–10, 103–23
India, 75–99
Japan: overseas hospitals, 231–42
social determinants of health, 105–6
See also Sustainable Development Goals

Sakurajyuji Group
clinic in Singapore, 232, 233–36, 241
SARS, 109, 110
Secom Medical System Company hospital in India, 232, 236–40, 241–42
Singapore
Japanese health services, 14–15, 232, 233–36, 241
smoking, 115–16, 169, 187
SPS Agreement. *See* Agreement on the Application of Sanitary and Phytosanitary Measures (SPS Agreement)
State Tobacco Monopoly Administration (China) (STMA), 170–71
STMA. *See* State Tobacco Monopoly Administration (China) (STMA)

Sustainable Development Goals, 5–6, 104
SDG 2.1, 9, 155
SDG 3, 6, 9, 10, 14–15, 19, 46, 75, 106–7, 113, 117, 124, 229
SDG 8, 12
SDG 9, 12, 229
SDG 10, 12–13
SDG 16.6, 14, 120

Tamil Nadu (India), 86–98
tobacco companies. *See* China National Tobacco Corporation
tobacco use
China: demographics, 115, 116, 169, 187; tobacco control, 114, 115–17, 187
trade agreements. *See* international trade

United Nations
International Bill of Human Rights, 104–5, 123n1
International Covenant on Civil and Political Rights, 103
International Covenant on Economic, Social and Cultural Rights, 75, 103
Office on Drugs and Crime, 117–18
Universal Declaration of Human Rights, 74
See also Sustainable Development Goals
United States
India – Measures Concerning the Importation of Certain Agricultural Products, 155–56, 159–60, 162–64
Universal Declaration of Human Rights, 74
Urban Employee Basic Medical Insurance (China), 24–25, 30
Urban and Rural Residents' Basic Medical Insurance Scheme (China), 25, 30

vaccination policies
  herd immunity, 126–27, 128
  international norms, 10, 124–25, 126
  patient rights to self-determination,
    127, 129
  risk assessment, 133–35, 136–37
  vaccine costs, 129, 130–31
  vaccine safety, 129, 132
  See also Japan: vaccinations

WHO. *See* World Health Organization
  (WHO)
Wilkinson, Richard, 105–6
Wingspread Statement on the Pre-
  cautionary Principle, 136–37
World Health Organization (WHO)
  constitution (1946), 4, 74
  Framework Convention on Tobacco
    Control, 113–15; China, 13, 114,
    115–17, 169, 187
  International Health Regulations,
    108–9

International Sanitation Regulations,
  107, 108
national public health capacities,
  109
treatment of drug dependencies,
  117–18
World Trade Organization (WTO)
  Agreement on the Application of
    Sanitary and Phytosanitary Meas-
    ures, 154, 157–58; double science
    standard of review, 155–66
  Agreement on Trade-Related Aspects
    of Intellectual Property Rights
    (TRIPS), 32; Doha Declaration,
    32, 33
  *European Communities – Measures
    Affecting the Approval and Market-
    ing of Biotech Products* (report),
    158–59
WTO. *See* World Trade Organization
  (WTO)